Modern European History

A Garland Series of Outstanding Dissertations

General Editor
William H. McNeill
University of Chicago

Associate Editors

Eastern Europe
Charles Jelavich
Indiana University

France
David H. Pinkney
University of Washington

Germany
Enno E. Kraehe
University of Virginia

Great Britain
Peter Stansky
Stanford University

Russia
Barbara Jelavich
Indiana University

MODERN EUROPEAN HISTORY

The Central Workers' Circle of St. Petersburg, 1889–1894:

A Case Study of the
"Workers' Intelligentsia"

Michael Share

Garland Publishing, Inc.
New York and London 1987

Copyright © 1987 Michael Share
All rights reserved

Library of Congress Cataloging-in-Publication Data

Share, Michael.
　The Central Workers' Circle of St. Petersburg, 1889–1894.

　　(Modern European history)
　　Thesis (Ph.D.)—University of Wisconsin—Madison, 1984.
　　Bibliography: p.
　　1. TSentral'nyĭ rabochiĭ kruzhok (Saint Petersburg, Russia) 2. Labor and laboring classes—Russian S.F.S.R.—Leningrad—History. 3. Leningrad (R.S.F.S.R.)—Social conditions. 4. Leningrad (R.S.F.S.R.)—Economic conditions. I. Title. II. Series.
HD8522.T753S53 1987   305.5'62'0947453
87-374
ISBN 0-8240-8063-7 (alk. paper)

All volumes in this series are printed on acid-free, 250-year-life paper.

Printed in the United States of America

THE CENTRAL WORKERS' CIRCLE OF ST. PETERSBURG,
1889-1894:
A CASE STUDY OF THE WORKERS' INTELLIGENTSIA

Michael Share

Under the Supervision of
Professor Michael B. Petrovich

During the latter part of the nineteenth century, Russia underwent a rapid period of industrialization. To work in the new, often technologically modern factories, thousands of peasants moved to the cities, especially St. Petersburg and Moscow. A few of these peasant-workers became highly skilled and educated, and formed a "workers' elite." To expand their knowledge, some of them formed discussion groups or circles. During the 1880's, the number of circles in St. Petersburg expanded rapidly. To better coordinate their political, social and cultural activities, leaders from these circles in St. Petersburg met and formed a supervisory board, the Central Workers' Circle. Despite a few interruptions and police repression, the board survived until spring 1894 when arrests destroyed the organization.

The Central Circle oversaw about twenty circles with a total of 100 to 150 members. Students assisted them in educational work. They formed a Central Treasury to coordinate the disbursement of their limited funds to purchase books, to aid strikers, and to cover other expenses. They organized a lending library of nearly 1,000 volumes to prepare lectures and discussions. During 1890-91 the Central Circle organized several political activities. They aided strikers at two major St. Petersburg factories with money and leaflets. They joined a large funeral procession for the writer N.V. Shelgunov. The height of their activities came in May 1891 when the Central Circle put on a May Day celebration, the first in Russia.

    The eight or ten workers in the Central Circle formed the leadership of a workers' intelligentsia, who, in turn, were the chief activists among the workers' elite. They were generally young, from rural peasant backgrounds, unmarried, often isolated from other workers and from their student teachers. While they opposed the current tsarist government, they never clearly enunciated a program for a futre Russian government. While they formed a nucleus for any future legal trade union movement, their isolation prevented their becoming the leaders of a broad based labor movement. Workers' memoirs, speeches, booklists and leaflets reveal, nevertheless, the remarkably broad intellectual interests of this early workers' movement.

THE CENTRAL WORKERS' CIRCLE OF ST. PETERSBURG, 1889-94: A CASE STUDY OF THE "WORKERS' INTELLIGENTSIA"

by

MICHAEL SHARE

A thesis submitted in partial fulfillment of the requirements for the degree of

Doctor of Philosophy
(History)

at the

UNIVERSITY OF WISCONSIN-MADISON

1984

TABLE OF CONTENTS

		Page
PREFACE		iv
MAPS		xii
CHAPTER I.	INTRODUCTION: THE RUSSIAN LABOR MOVEMENT IN ST. PETERSBURG AND THE DEVELOPMENT OF THE WORKERS' ELITE AS OF 1889	1
	A General Description of Industrial St. Petersburg by 1890	1
	The Formation of the Labor Movement in Russia	18
	A Description of the Workers' Elite	32
	Educational Opportunities for the Workers	41
CHAPTER II.	INTELLECTUAL AND WORKERS' GROUPS IN ST. PETERSBURG BY 1890	50
	Survey of Student Intellectual Groups in St. Petersburg	50
	Formation of the Central Workers' Circle	90
PHOTOGRAPHS		118
CHAPTER III.	THE MEMBERSHIP OF THE CENTRAL WORKERS' CIRCLE	126
	The Background of the Membership of the Central Workers' Circle	126
	The Attitudes and Values of the Membership	143
CHAPTER IV.	THE ORGANIZATION AND THE SOCIAL AND CULTURAL ACTIVITIES OF THE CENTRAL WORKERS' CIRCLE	172

TABLE OF CONTENTS (Con't)

		Page
	The Organization of the Central Workers' Circle	172
	The Social and Cultural Activities of the Central Workers' Circle	194
CHAPTER V.	THE POLITICAL ACTIVITIES OF THE CENTRAL WORKERS' CIRCLE	221
	The Strikes at the Thornton Factory and the Port	223
	The Shelgunov Funeral Procession, April 1891	231
	The May Day Holiday, 1891; the Background and the Events	247
	Expansion of the Central Workers' Circle to Other Cities	271
	May Day, 1892	291
CHAPTER VI.	THE RISE AND FALL OF THE REVIVED CENTRAL WORKERS' CIRCLE, 1892-1894	302
	The Rebirth of the Central Workers' Circle	302
	The Activities of the Revived Central Workers' Circle	316
CHAPTER VII.	CONCLUSIONS: THE ROLE OF THE CENTRAL WORKERS' CIRCLE IN THE RUSSIAN LABOR MOVEMENT	345
APPENDIX		358
BIBLIOGRAPHY		372

PREFACE

About ten years ago at the London School of Economics and Political Science when the author was a member of Professor Leonard Schapiro's seminar on the Russian revolutionary movement, he suggested that I investigate some aspect of Russia during Alexander III's reign. He correctly believed that the 1880's and early 1890's were a much neglected area in Russian history. A few years later my major professor at the University of Wisconsin, Michael B. Petrovich, advised me to investigate the labor movement in Russia during the late nineteenth century. For several months the author read the available works in English and Russian on the subject. Throughout those readings, a little known subject fascinated me. A tiny but growing number of skilled and somewhat educated urban workers developed in Russia, especially in its cities, during the late nineteenth century. From that group of workers, the section, which was most highly skilled and best educated, formed a workers' elite, and sought further education for themselves. To fulfill those needs some of the workers established small groups or circles where they discussed the books or journal articles they had recently read. Because of their often intense desire for more knowledge and a curiosity about the outside world, those members of the workers' elite have often been called the "workers' intelligentsia." During the mid-1880's, the number of workers' circles greatly increased. By 1889, representatives from many of those circles met in St. Petersburg, and decided to organize a Central Workers' Circle to coordinate the activities of the various groups.

Neither the narrower subject of the Central Workers' Circle in St. Petersburg nor the wider question of a "workers' intelligentsia" has been described from the perspective of the worker by either Soviet or Western historians. Soviet historians have treated the workers' movement either as a series of confrontational strikes; or as workers'-intellectuals' social democratic organizations becoming unified eventually in one centrally directed Social Democratic Party. Ties between workers' and intellectuals' groups were stressed with the "leading-role" given to the latter. The workers' movement in all its facets has been treated as an adjunct in the early development of the Russian Social Democratic Party. Most American scholars, such as Richard Pipes in <u>Social Democracy and the St. Petersburg Labor Movement, 1885-1897</u> (Cambridge, 1963), have also treated the workers' movement within the context of the origins of the Social Democratic Party. Reginald Zelnik's book, <u>Labor and Society in Tsarist Russia, the Factory Workers of St. Petersburg, 1855-70</u> (Stanford, 1971), has a much broader aim by taking many different aspects of the city's workers, and relates them to their place in Russian society. But he deals with a much earlier period than this author does, the years up to 1870.

Thus, while political perspectives have differed, both American and Soviet authors, except for Zelnik, Richard Stites, and Robert Johnson, have examined Russian workers' activities from the narrow context of their relationship with revolutionary Marxist intellectual and political groups. A major reason for this study is to fulfill a real need to look at the labor movement in the late nineteenth century from the perspective of the politicized workers themselves. This work examines not only their attitudes toward the student intellectuals but also toward the rank and file workers, as well as themselves. These attitudes are essential to understand the extent and the focus of the "workers' intelligentsia's" political and cultural activities. While the political activities of the Central Workers' Circle such as the first May Day rally in Russia in 1891 have been better known to scholars, very little has been written concerning their various social and cultural activities. For example, the Central Workers' Circle established libraries, reading rooms, clubs, cooperatives, and canteens for interested workers in St. Petersburg. Reading and subsequent group discussions were considered a positive alternative form of entertainment for workers to counter the prevailing sordid drinking culture in taverns and beer bars. These cultural activities were crucial because they usually involved the greatest interaction of members of the "workers' intelligentsia" with their fellow though unskilled workers, often called the "grey masses" by the "workers' intelligentsia." Thus, this study is an examination of the membership, the activities, and the attitudes of at least some of the newly emerged "workers' intelligentsia."

The author chose this period, the mid-80's to the mid-90's, because it was a period of relative labor calm at the same time that it was a period of rapid industrial development. For the first time, some workers extensively organized cohesive groups and circles. Specifically, in 1889 several workers formed a Central Workers' Circle. Yet in 1894 that organization collapsed as a result of sudden police repression. St. Petersburg became the focus of this study because not only was it a national capital and the largest city; but it was also the locale of Russia's most technologically advanced industries: metallurgy, shipbuilding, printing, and engineering. St. Petersburg had the largest number of highly skilled and semi-skilled workers concentrated in one place.

At the University of Wisconsin Memorial Library during 1975-77, the author read numerous Soviet and American secondary sources along with the library's rich Russian underground revolutionary collection. The staff of the library's interlibrary loan department was very helpful in providing me photocopies of primary source material from libraries all over the United States. The author owes them a deep debt of appreciation for their assistance. During the summer of 1978 the author went first to Great Britain to conduct research in the British Museum Reading Room Library in London, and then to Finland to work in the Slavic Library of the University of Helsinki. For over one hundred years until the Revolutions in 1917, Finland was a part of the Russian Empire. The Helsinki Library received, by law, copies of works--books, journals, and newspapers--published in Russia, as a library of deposit. In 1979, the author returned to Helsinki to spend six more months researching at the Slavic Library.

Both trips were made possible due to a grant received from the Department of History at the University of Wisconsin.

The sources at both London and Helsinki were published ones. Memoir accounts by students, workers, and teachers involved with members of the Central Workers' Circle were especially rich. Many articles written in "thick journals" of the time such as <u>Mir Bozhii</u>, <u>Russkaia Shkola</u>, and <u>Severnyi Vestnik</u> discussed education and other opportunities of advancement for workers, as well as observations of the new phenomenon, as they called it, of a "workers' intelligentsia." The author is very appreciative to the entire staff at the Slavic Library in Helsinki for their hospitality and assistance in obtaining and photocopying works from their collection, as well as from Moscow's Lenin Library through interlibrary loan. As a result of my stays in both London and Helsinki, along with the use of interlibrary loan in this country, the author has consulted the obtainable published materials located outside the USSR concerning the "workers' intelligentsia" and the Central Workers' Circle. The main drawback is that the author was unable to utilize archival collections in the Soviet Union, a highly recommended task for anyone who wishes to pursue this topic further. Nevertheless, the author believes that further archival research, while quite interesting and useful, would most likely not change this study's conclusions.

The system of transliteration employed in this work is the one used by the Library of Congress. The only exceptions are the names of emperors and such familiar places as Moscow and St. Petersburg (not Moskva and Sankt Peterburg). Where the Gregorian calendar was used, I indicated that with the abbreviation NS for New Style. Otherwise all dates are given according to the Julian calendar, in use in Russia until 1918, rather than the Gregorian calendar used in the West. By 1890 the former was twelve days behind the latter. All translations, unless otherwise indicated, are my own.

This dissertation would not have been possible without the assistance of several individuals and staffs. First, I owe my appreciation to Leonard Schapiro, Professor Emeritus at the London School of Economics, who first suggested the general topic of the 1880's to me. In Helsinki, my work was enriched by consultations with Professor Richard Stites of Georgetown University who advised me to widen my topic to a more general view of the "workers' intelligentsia" and their role in Russian history. It is a great pleasure to acknowledge my debt to the staffs at the British Museum Reading Room in London as well as the Slavic Library in Helsinki for their assistance and hospitality far beyond was was required of them. I am especially grateful to my major professor, Michael B. Petrovich, who initially aided me to focus on the Central Workers' Circle in St. Petersburg, and saw the need for a study in that area, for his gracious and more than generous patience, and for his extremely useful comments on the dissertation throughout all its stages. Professors Robert Koehl and Gary Rosenshield at UW-Madison and Anne Robb Taylor and Egal Feldman at UW-Superior have all given me the benefit of their valuable comments. I have tried to incorporate all of the above-named individuals' suggestions into this work. However, all shortcomings are my sole responsibility. Most of all I want to thank my parents, Harold and Beatrice Share, who gave me needed moral and financial support at critical moments throughout the long years which took for the completion of this study. To them I dedicate this work.

MAP SECTION

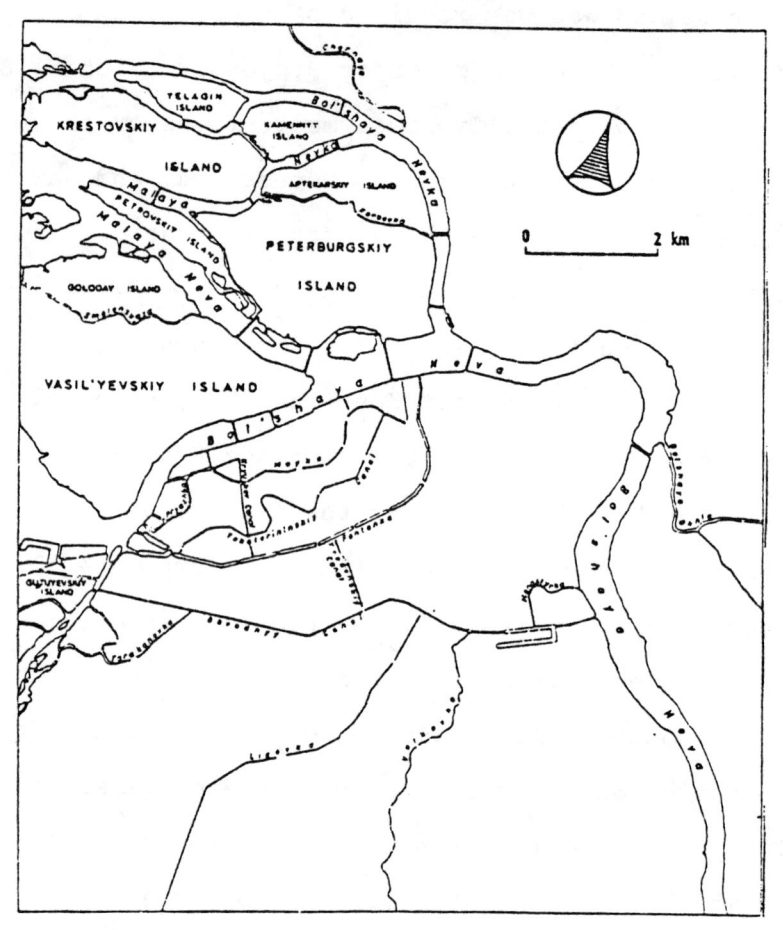

MAP 72. Topographic features.

James H. Bater, St. Petersburg, Industrialization and Change (Montreal, 1976), p. 474.

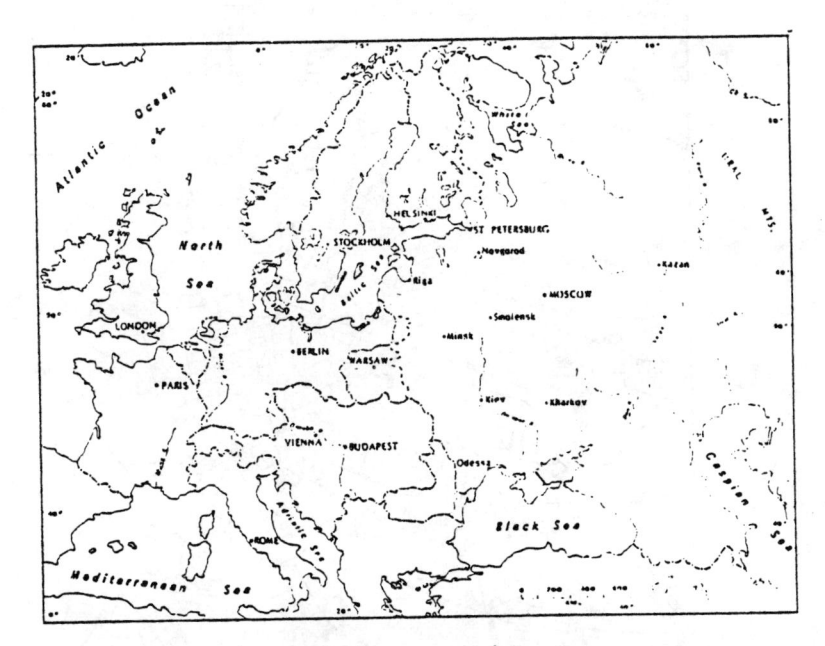

MAP 1. *St Petersburg in the European setting*

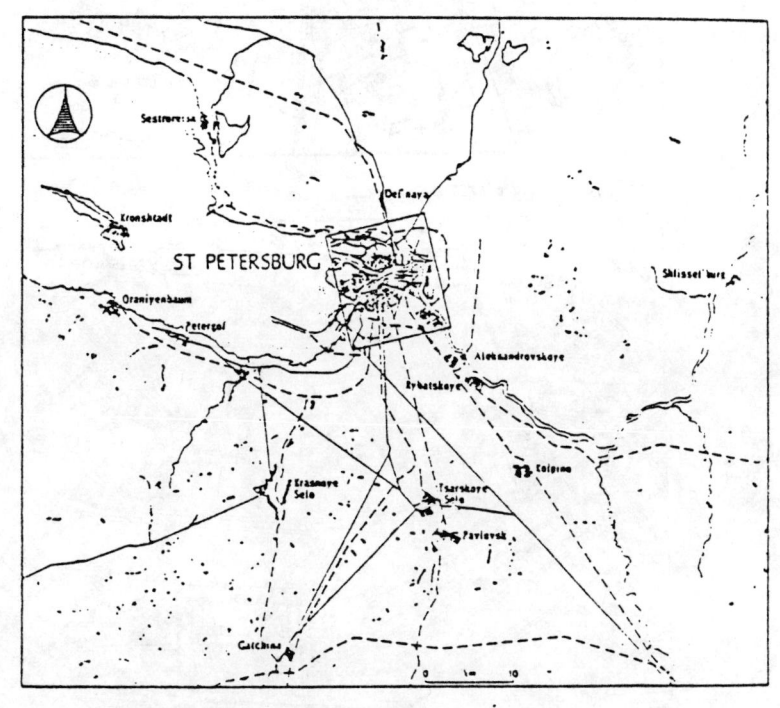

MAP 54. *Populated places in the St Petersburg region*

Bater, St. Petersburg, p. 3 and p. 302.

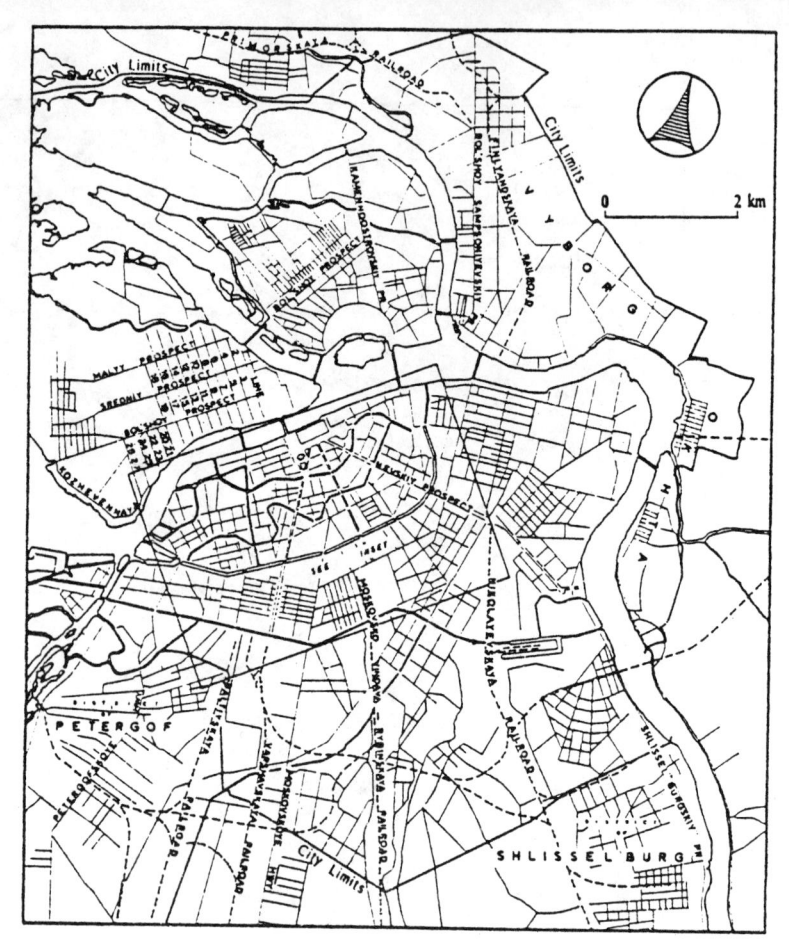

MAP 70. *St. Petersburg, 1914.*

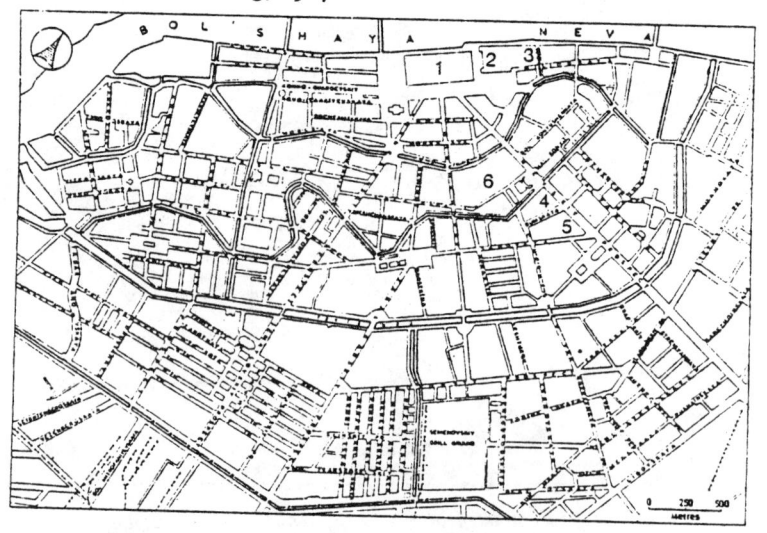

MAP 71. Inset (see map 70) of central city, 1914. 1: Admiralty; 2: Winter Palace; 3: Hermitage; 4: City Hall; 5: Gostinyy Dvor; 7: Foundling Home.

Bater, St. Petersburg, p. 472 and p. 473.

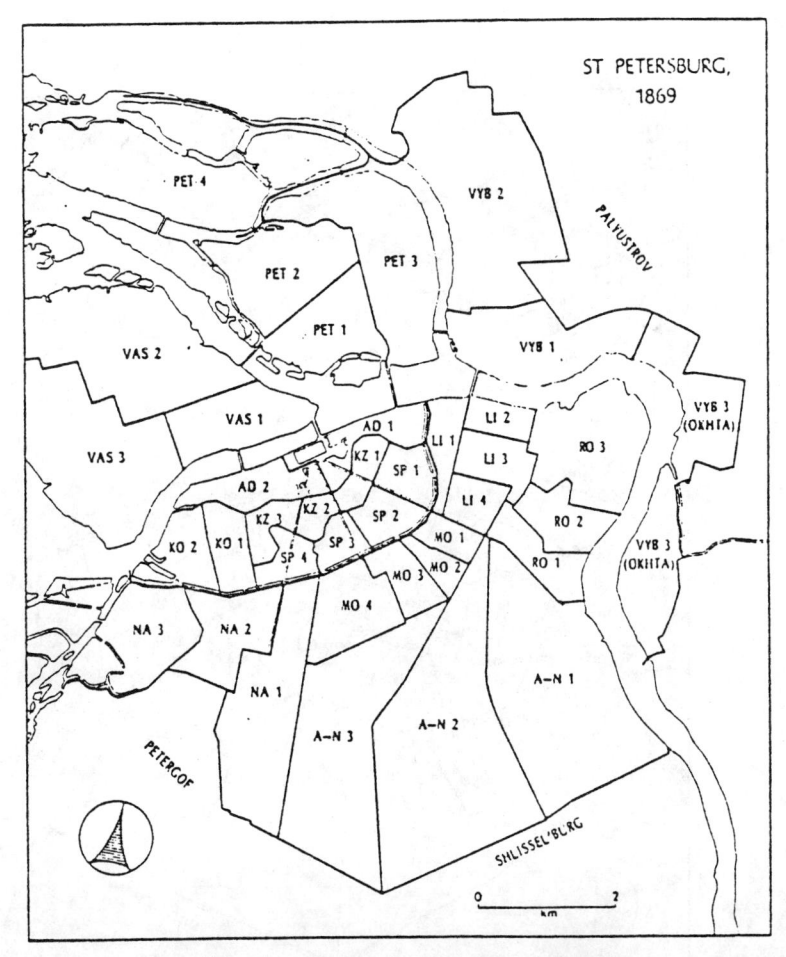

MAP 68. *St. Petersburgh, 1869. Boroughs:* AD: Admiralteyskaya; KY: Kazanskaya SP: Spasskaya; KO: Kolomenskaya; NA: Narvskaya; MO: Moskovskaya; A-N: Aleksandro-Nevskaya; RO: Rozhdestvenskaya; LI: Liteynaya; VAS: Vasil'-yevskaya; PET: Peterburgskaya; VYB: Vyborgskaya; N-D: Novo-Derevnya; Okhta. Numerals refer to Wards within the Boroughs.

Bater, St. Petersburg, p. 470.

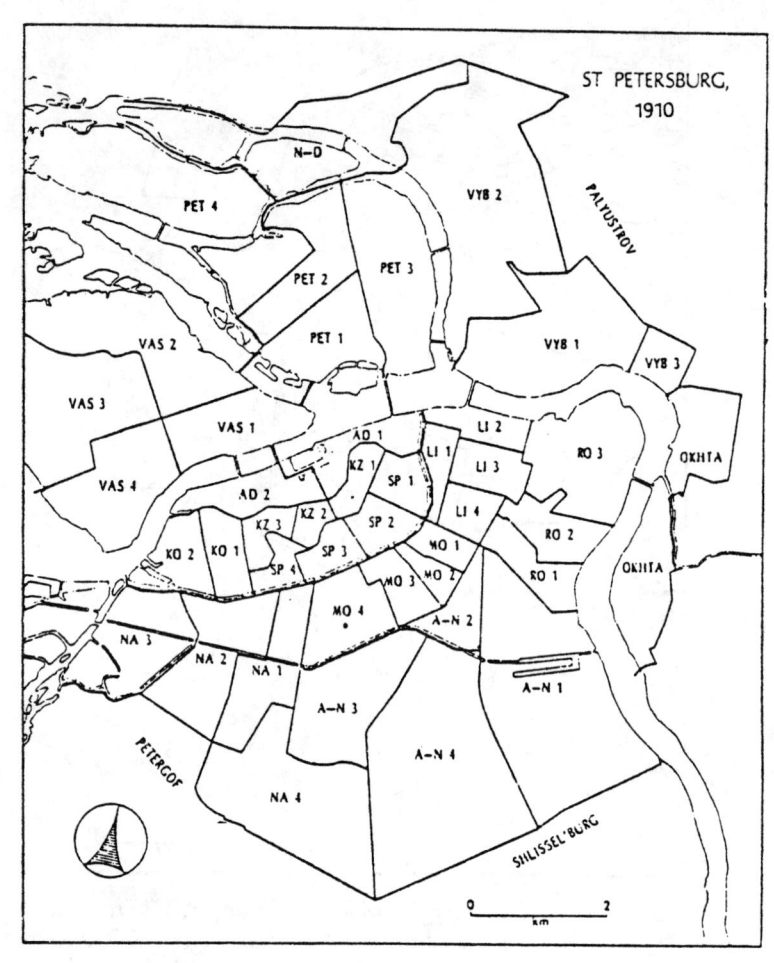

MAP 69. *St. Petersburg, 1910.* See map for key.
(on previous page)

Bater, St. Petersburg, p. 471.

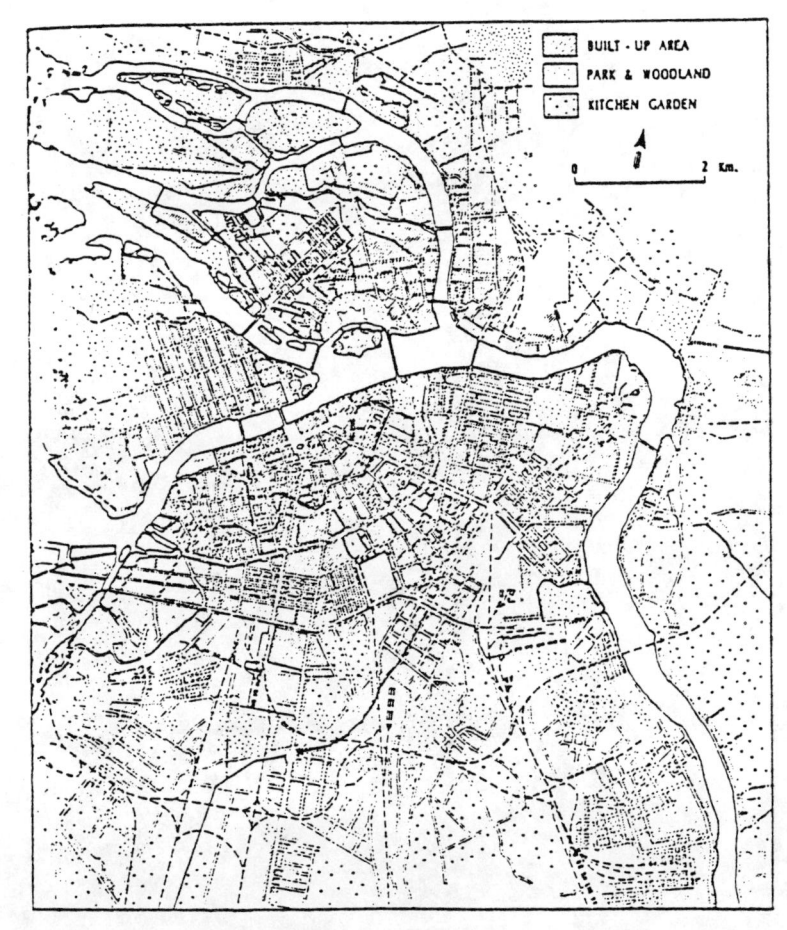

MAP 59. *St Petersburg, 1914*

Bater, St. Petersburg, p. 323.

CHAPTER 1

THE RUSSIAN LABOR MOVEMENT IN ST. PETERSBURG AND
THE DEVELOPMENT OF THE WORKERS' ELITE AS OF 1889

A General Description of Industrial St. Petersburg by 1890

Until its collapse in 1917, the Russian Empire remained primarily a rural society with an agrarian economy. Nevertheless, in its last fifty years the country seethed with change.[1] One highly visible and major change was the beginning and the acceleration of Russia's Industrial Revolution. Throughout the first half of the nineteenth century, there had been little industrial growth. Russia's loss to Great Britain and France on its own soil during the Crimean War in 1853-56 convinced the government of Tsar Alexander II that Russia had to modernize its industry and transportation network. Government measures encouraged the development of large industrial plants, a railroad system with accompanying extensive foreign investment. During the

_____

[1] An excellent and very recent book describing the changes in the Russian Empire for the period 1891 through 1914 is W. Bruce Lincoln, In War's Dark Shadow, the Russians before the Great War (New York, 1983).

two decades of the 1880's and 1890's, Russia's industrial development culminated in the most rapid rate for all of Europe, averaging 5% a year. During the 1880's railroad construction produced over 8,000 kilometers of track. That construction foreshadowed a larger boom in which over 40,000 kilometers were built between 1891 and 1914. In the last two decades of the nineteenth century, coal production rose by 50%, iron and steel production doubled and oil production trebled. In fact by 1900 Russia was the world's largest producer of oil.[2] Yet this development was both uneven industrially and geographically. Areas such as St. Petersburg, Moscow, Poland, the Baltic States, sections of the Ukraine, along with areas in the Caucasus and the Volga regions utilized the most modern methods and equipment Western Europe could offer as models. However, virtually all the rest of the country had little industry except handicrafts which used the same methods for centuries in peasant huts or _izbas_. Nevertheless, within Russia a formerly semi-feudal and agrarian society was rapidly

---

[2] These figures were taken from P.A. Khomov, _Ekonomicheskoe razvitie Rossii v XIX-XX vekakh_ (Moscow, 1950), pp. 456-462. Two very good books in English describing Russia's Industrial Revolution are: Theodore van Laue, _Sergei Witte and the Industrialization of Russia_ (New York and London, 1963) and John P. McKay, _Pioneers for Profit: Foreign Entrepreneurship and Russian Industrialization, 1885-1913_ (Chicago, 1970).

changing. Those changes created dislocations which culminated in the Revolutions of 1905 and 1917.

One of the largest centers for Russia's Industrial Revolution was its capital, St. Petersburg. In 1890, St. Petersburg, the largest city in the Russian Empire and the fourth largest in Europe, had a population of 954,400 and had an area of 53.4 square kilometers (over 25 square miles).[3] The city was divided into twelve sections or boroughs: Admiralteiskaia, Kazanskaia, Spasskaia, Kolomenskaia, Narvskaia, Moskovskaia, Aleksandro-Nevskaia, Rozhdestvenskaia, Liteinaia, Vasilyevskaia, Peterburgskaia, and Vyborgskaia. Each borough was divided into two, three, or four wards. The first four boroughs, the area between the Bol'shaia Neva River and the Fontanka Canal, was described as the Central City. This section contained many of the large government and public buildings such as the Admiralty, the Winter Palace, the Hermitage, and the City Hall, along with the large shops on and near the Nevskii Prospekt, St. Petersburg's major street, and the Gostinyi Dvor, the large shopping bazaar. While generally considered a prestigious area in which to reside, especially along the river embankment, and along the broad avenues which

---

[3] V. Pokrovskii, <u>Statisticheskii ocherk St. Petersburga</u> (St. Petersburg, 1895), p. 5.

radiated from the Admiralty, the region was quite socially mixed. The second and third wards of Spasskaia, and the second ward of Kolomenskaia boroughs all were generally overcrowded, unhealthy, poor and populated by workers. For example, the Spasskaia and Kazanskaia boroughs had a population density of over 50,000 people per square verst.[4] Even in the upper class Admiralty borough, cellars, attics, and other undesirable housing units were rented to those who could afford nothing better, namely the peasantry and the workers. Across the Bol'shaia Neva River, the northern half of Vasilyevskii Island was predominantly working class. The southern half of the island was more affluent because it housed a large foreign population and was a very desirable location as it was very near to the Central City. It also had its share of poor people who lived in cellars and attics.

While less densely populated than the Central City districts, the outlying districts experienced a major population increase after 1860, and this increase was predominantly working class or peasant.[5] The two

---

[4] Pokrovskii, Statisticheskii, p. 5. One verst equaled .66 mile.

[5] S. Peterburg po perepisi 15 dekabria 1890 goda (St. Petersburg, 1892), part 2, p. 74.

southern boroughs, Narvskaia and Aleksandro-Nevskaia, contained the railway stations where most of the migrant population disembarked. The population of Narvskaia also increased when the navigation season opened because the principal dockyards were located there. The second ward of the borough of Kolomenskaia, located just to the north of Narvskaia, also had a large number of factory and dock workers. The remaining boroughs, those to the north of the Central City, had always been considered the most isolated sections of the city particularly as there were few bridges to link them with the rest of the city. This isolation generally kept out the more affluent population because these regions of St. Petersburg were the most susceptible to frequent flooding and were the farthest from their businesses.[6] Even so, many affluent residents of St. Petersburg had their summer dachas along the river front section of the Peterburgskaia borough. The Vyborgskaia borough with its Okhta section to the southeast was the population center for the construc-

---

[6] K.A. Pazhitnov, Polozhenie rabochego klassa v Rossii, Vol. II (Leningrad, 1924), p. 56.

tion workers, a characteristic dating back to the eighteenth century.[7]

The social distribution of the population was fairly heterogeneous throughout the city. There were sections which were predominantly affluent and sections which were predominantly working class, but no borough and few wards were exclusively so. Surprisingly, factory owners, usually quite wealthy, often lived right inside their factory yards next to barracks housing the factory workers. Poor people lived in cellars and attics in the best sections of the city. This feature of heterogeneity was in dramatic contrast to American and Western European cities which had already become stratified.

Most workers went to work on foot, which limited their selection of housing to places in or near their factories. First, the public transport system in St. Petersburg of horse-drawn street cars was too inadequate, particularly in the outlying districts, to accommodate more than a tiny portion of the working class. The city, unlike any other major European capital, had no system of suburban or urban railway.

---

[7] S. Bernshtein-Kogan, *Chislennost', sostav i polozhenie Peterburgskikh rabochikh* (St. Petersburg, 1910), p. 23.

Even if a street car line was conveniently located for a worker, that worker probably could not afford the fare regularly because of his low salary. Secondly, most people did not want to spend much time walking to work because the long work day ranged from ten to fourteen hours. While certain districts were predominantly industrial, all districts including those in the Central City had a fair proportion of industry.[8]

Most of the industrial activity in the St. Petersburg guberniia (province) was concentrated in the capital city itself, except for a few major factories such as the Okhtenskii gunpowder works east of the capital, the Sestroretsk armaments plant northwest of the city, the Admiralty metal works located due south of the city in Kolpino, and the shipyards in Kronstadt west of St. Petersburg. In 1890 there were over 400 factories in St. Petersburg. That number of large factories had doubled over the past thirty years.[9] The principal industrial activites were textiles (cotton and wool), metal works (railway construction and armaments), food

---

[8] S.N. Valk, Istoriia rabochikh Leningrada, Vol. I (Leningrad, 1972), pp. 126-130.

[9] B.M. Kochakov, Ocherki istorii Leningrada, Vol. II (Leningrad, 1957), p. 124.

processing and tobacco, and paper products and printing. Textiles encompassed roughly a quarter of all industrial production. Most textile plants were large in comparison to other factories and employed usually ninety or more workers.[10] There were even several factories which employed over a thousand workers. Industries became more mechanized. The complexity of certain machinery required a skilled labor force. The largest single sector was the metal works which employed nearly forty percent of the work force in St. Petersburg. That particular industry was generally mechanized, which required that most employees were at least semi-skilled.

Not only was there a rapid growth in industry and in industrial production during the period of 1860 to 1890, but there was also an accompanying growth in the number of workers and in the proportion of workers in the total population. In 1869 out of a total population of 750,000 in St. Petersburg, there were 35,000 industrial workers. By 1890 the population had grown by a third to one million while the number of industrial

---

[10] V.K. Iatsunskii, "Rol' Peterburga v promyshlennom razvitii dorevoliutsionnoi Rossii," Voprosy istorii, 1954, no. 9, pp. 98-99.

workers doubled to 70,000.[11] The industrial workers were the fastest growing group of factory workers in St. Petersburg. At the same time individual factories increased their work force dramatically. For example, the Putilov factory in 1857 had about 500 workers; in 1885 it had 1,933 workers; in 1890 it had 3,250; and by 1900 the work force jumped to 13,000. Government contracts, especially military orders, enabled this metal works, located on the southern edge of the city, to become the largest single factory in St. Petersburg.[12]

The working conditions in these factories were brutal. Emancipation of the serfs, which increased the labor supply, and the subsequent industrialization did not improve the workers' lot. The working day was long, beginning at 5 a.m. and rarely ending before 8 p.m. These long hours, as can be seen in Table II, existed for all major industries and there was no improvement over the next decade. Only a few factory workers voluntarily improved the conditions. For example, Ludwig

---

[11] S. Peterburg po perepisi 10 dekabria 1869 goda (St. Petersburg, 1872), part I, p. 46; and also S. Peterburg po perepisi 15 dekabria 1890 goda (St. Petersburg, 1892), part II, p. 23.

[12] A. Antipov, Obzor pravitel' stvennykh meropriiatiiu po razvitiiu v Rossii metallicheskoi promyshlennosti, (St. Petersburg, 1879), p. 38.

Nobel, the owner of a large metal works and a major oil producer in the Black Sea coast, introduced a 10.5 hour work day as early as the 1860's.[13]

On the other hand, wages for St. Petersburg were high in comparison to the rest of Russia. Textile and metal workers averaged 18-20 rubles per month, while highly skilled metal workers received 25-35 rubles per month. Most workers outside St. Petersburg earned much less; their salaries averaged 9-12 rubles per month. Women were paid about one-half that of men; children, who formed quite a sizeable amount of the Russian work force, were paid only one-third the salary of an adult male. In this period the salaries varied from a maximum of 606 rubles a year to a minimum of 90 rubles a year in the city of St. Petersburg.[14] As bad as these wage figures seemed, they were much worse in the Urals, the Donets Basin, and the Baku oil fields where workers did not receive a regular salary.

---

[13] Pazhitnov, *Polozhenie rabochego*, Vol. II, p. 73.

[14] D. Kol'tsov, "Rabochee dvizhenie v 1890-1904 gg.," *Obshchestvennoe dvizhenie v Rossii v nachale xx veka*, Vol. I. (St. Petersburg, 1909), pp. 196-198.

A shortage of inexpensive housing, or any housing at all suitable for factory workers, was a perennial fact of life in the capital from the mid-nineteenth century on. Traditionally, factory owners provided some basic dormitory facilities for workers. Yet after 1860 the housing of workers in factory dormitories, where most workers had resided, steadily decreased to under 20% of the work force because a rapidly growing labor supply prevented the owners from housing all workers who needed a bed, and because fear of inevitable government supervision led the owners to close their factory dormitories.[15] Factory labor agitators found factory housing an ideal environment for organizing and educating workers. The worst overcrowding was in cellar and attic apartments which averaged over two people per room.[16] Cellars were considered the least desirable place to live because they would often be flooded with inches of water, dirt, and grime for months on end, especially during the fall. Flooding was not only uncomfortable but unsanitary because it allowed the spreading of diseases such as typhus and

---

[15] V.V. Sviatlovskii, Zhilishchnyi vopros v Rossii (St. Petersburg, 1902), p. 245.

[16] F. Erisman, "Podval'nye zhilishcha v Peterburge," Arkhiv sudebnoi meditsiny obshchestvennoi gigieny, VII. 1871, p. 60.

cholera. The overcrowding was especially severe in the Aleksandro-Nevskaia and Vyborgskaia boroughs, both predominantly working class, but overcrowding existed throughout the city. The combination of a housing shortage and high rents forced many single people and families to live in a corner (ugol) of a room. Often six or more unrelated people lived in one room. Many apartments, including the hallways and kitchens, were subdivided into den-like quarters. Sanitary norms were ignored; in 1890 only 48% had toilets; 10% had baths; and only 60% had washing facilities of any type.[17] As these figures were an average for the city as a whole, some predominantly working class wards were much worse.

While the conditions of housing became worse during this period, rents for apartments, rooms, and even sections of rooms (ugol), always at a high level, rose even higher. Rents for a basic two room apartment without a kitchen or running water rose to 25 to 36 rubles a month in the 1890's. Even the often flooded cellar apartments rented for an average of 222 rubles a year. The rent for a basic single room ranged from a low of sixty-five rubles a year up to three hundred rubles a

---

[17] Pokrovskii, Statisticheskii, pp. 14-15.

year, depending on the location.[18] Considering the average salary for a worker was about 20 rubles a month, with many workers earning half that, it is no wonder that many workers had to share their apartments or rooms. Highly skilled workers, who were paid relatively well, mentioned their rooms, rarely their apartments in their memoirs. Factory barracks or dormitories, where they existed, often had sixty people sleeping in one room. Yet they usually had running water and basic sanitary facilities. Thus, while wages were relatively high in St. Petersburg, so was the cost of living, food, and shelter in the city.

Basically the urban environment in St. Petersburg was pestilential. Municipal water and sewage services were in a poor state especially during the spring and summer months. The very cold temperatures, at least, kept disease from spreading out of the open sewers. The city government had few financial resources available because it had a small tax base. Thus it could do little to look after the needs of a rapidly growing population. There were few hospitals, zemstvo facilities, or other medical facilities within the factories

---

[18] S. Peterburg po perepisi 15 dekabria 1881 goda, Vol. II (St. Petersburg, 1884), pp. 2-3.

or within the working class wards of the city.[19] Among the obvious signs of the abject poverty within the city were widespread prostitution, venereal disease, illegitimacy, and drunkenness. All in all, the terrible urban environment could build up to an explosive point.

Table III shows an accelerating increase in the population of St. Petersburg from the mid-nineteenth century on. In little over thirty years, the population doubled. In the next decade, 1890-1900, the population increased by over a third. The growth was mainly due to the migration of peasants into the city for jobs, usually in the factories. They became the heart of the work force. In 1900 it was estimated that over half the population, 718,410, were born outside the city as peasants.[20] These workers, often characterized as "peasants in overalls," were marked by a high degree of itineracy. During the winter months, they would work in factories in the city, and during the

---

[19] In the Petergofskii section, there was only one hospital for the 13,000 workers in the Putilov factory which had only two doctors, two fel'dshers, one pharmacy, and few beds. For further information refer to A.N. Rubel', "Zhilishcha bednogo naseleniia g.S. Peterburga" in the Vestnik obshchestvennoi gigieny, April 1899, p. 4.

[20] S. Bernshtein-Kogan, Chislennost', p. 123.

rest of the year these peasants would till the land in their rural commune. One indication of their lack of commitment to the city is the relatively small percentages of workers who had their families with them. In 1897, workers living in St. Petersburg with their families varied from .4% to 38.2%. Printers, who were all highly skilled, had the greatest percentage; 31% of married metal workers maintained families in the capital; 13% of the textile workers; with the carrier trades maintaining the smallest percentage.[21] There was a definite correlation between degree of skills and commitment to the city. The peasants' sojourn in the city was still governed by the commune, because the commune issued the necessary passport required for residence within the capital city. This situation made long-range plans uncertain.

Most of these peasant workers were semi-skilled at best, were employed in the poorest occupations, and earned the worst pay. As the nineteenth century progressed, a hierarchy of workers developed with the peasant at the bottom. In a factory the peasant might earn 9 to 12 rubles a month while the highly skilled worker in the same factory might earn 40 rubles a month.

---

[21] Ibid., p. 56.

Table I. IMPORTANT INDUSTRIES IN ST. PETERSBURG, 1879-1894[21a]

1879 Type	No. of Factories	No. of Workers	Values of Production(1000r)
Textile	81	18,727	34,790
Cotton Spinning	29	3,102	4,469
Chemical	14	457	1,694
Tanneries	32	2,620	11,346
Silicate	62	8,984	2,961
Metallurgical	93	27,902	47,826
Wax	6	770	7,914
Total	317	62,562	111,000

1894 Type	No. of Factories	No. of Workers	Values of Production(1000r)
Textile	70	26,637	52,079
Cotton Spinning	35	4,347	9,343
Chemical	23	2,059	5,705
Tanneries	27	3,476	8,862
Silicate	42	4,262	1,871
Metallurgical	148	36,000	63,000
Wax	8	577	4,277
Total	353	77,358	145,137

[21a] Kochakov, <u>Ocherki istorii Leningrada</u>, v. II, p. 83.

Table II. HOURS OF WORK, 1885 and 1894[21b]

Selected Factories	Hours - 1885	Hours - 1894-95
Cotton	13¾-15	13½-15½
Dye and Print	13½	13½-15
Wool	13½-14	13 -14½
Tobacco	12 -14	14
Chemical	12½-14	13 -14

TABLE III. POPULATION GROWTH, MALE-FEMALE PERCENTAGES[21c]

Year	Male	% of Population	Female	% of Population	Total	%
1858	318,336	62.2	176,320	35.8	496,656	100.0
1869	377,380	56.7	289,827	43.3	667,207	130.1
1881	473,380	54.6	388,074	45.4	861,303	173.4
1890	512,718	53.8	441,682	46.7	954,400	192.0
1900	680,144	54.4	567,978	45.6	1,248,122	251.0

[21b] A.V. Pogozhev, Uchet chislennosti i sostava rabochikh v Rossii (St. Petersburg, 1906), p.75. These hours of work included slightly more than one hour for lunch.

[21c] Kochakov, Ocherki istorii Leningrada, v. II, p. 173.

Peasant workers were mostly employed in tobacco factories, cotton mills, weaving, and dye working. Despite these poor wages and working conditions, peasants flocked to St. Petersburg for what they thought were good wages. During the winter months there were few ways to earn money in the commune. Even though the cost of living was high in St. Petersburg, these peasant workers always managed to send some money either weekly or monthly to their families. Thus, by 1890 St. Petersburg gave the superficial impression of being a large, modern, cosmopolitan European city; underneath the surface the city was very poor and quite rural. While it was clearly the case that a rapidly growing segment of the peasantry was settling permanently in the city and becoming urbanized, many of the huge number of migrants who remained sustained the traditional peasant customs right up to World War I.

The Formation of the Labor Movement in Russia

By the last decade of the nineteenth century, the Russian Empire had already embarked on the path toward industrialization, a path rapid but uneven. Both the number of factories and industrial workers grew. In the mid-1860's, European Russia had no more than 2,500 to 3,000 factories in which 509,000 people worked. However, by 1890 the number of factories more than doubled to approximately 6,000, while the number of workers increased by 65% to 840,000.[22] This industrialization had several characteristics and effects which contributed to the development of a labor movement. A relatively few factories became huge installations employing thousands of people. Those huge factories employed most of the Russian industrial labor force. This concentration of labor in relatively few cities and plants made it easier for activists to organize workers in particular cities and industries. At the same time, workers' wages and hours did not improve. If anything, they got worse. In the face of such worsening conditions, more and more workers were willing to risk the loss of their jobs and insist on improvements. "It is impossible for our position to be any worse," declared Fedor Kozlov, a weaver who spoke out at a strike meeting at the large Morozov mill in Nikolskaia-Zueva about 60 miles northeast of Moscow in

---

[22] Kochakov, *Ocherki istorii Leningrada*, Vol. II, p. 124.

1885. "It has become impossible to live."[23] These sentiments proved ripe soil for a labor movement.

While the emerging group of Russian industrialists were products of the great economic changes, they remained immune to any demands for improvements by their factory employers. Only a few industrialists tried to better the wretched conditions under which their employees lived and worked. Both Savva Timofeievich Morozov and Pavel Mikhailovich Tretiakov were notable examples of enlightened industrial lords who were genuinely concerned about their workers.[24] Most factory owners granted only very reluctantly a minimum of better wages and working conditions. Their unyielding practices fostered a labor movement which they opposed with all their political power.

Simultaneously, the Russian government had a contradictory attitude. The tsars and most of their ministers recognized that industrialization was bene-

---

[23] Iu. Z. Polevoi, "Na puti soedineniia s sotsializmom," in *Istoriia rabochego klassa Rossii, 1861-1900*, ed. L.M. Ivanov (Moscow, 1972), p. 134.

[24] For further information about these two remarkable men, see Valentine T. Bill, *The Forgotten Class: The Russian Bourgeoisie from the Earliest Beginnings to 1900* (New York, 1959) and A.P. Botkina, *Pavel Mikhailovich Tret'iakov v zhizni i iskusstve* (Moscow, 1960).

ficial for Russia as the nation required modernization to catch up with Western Europe. The government enacted several measures to encourage industrialization and foreign investment. Yet they wanted economic change to be controlled with order and stability maintained. Nevertheless, economic change could not occur in a vacuum. It had repercussions all over the political and social landscape. Almost consistently the Russian government took the side of factory owners in any management-worker confrontation. Frequently, the police or Cossack troops entered the factory grounds to suppress strikes.[25] As early as 1870 the government banned strikes, and in subsequent years it tightened the penalties against strikers. A few laws were enacted during the 1880's to remove the worst abuses of child labor and night work. Yet the laws were usually not enforced sufficiently and many of the worst abuses continued. Thus, various factors combined to cause an increase in workers' dissatisfaction in the late nineteenth century; Russia faced a great increase of workers who lived and worked in worsening conditions; factory owners and managers who refused to compromise and a government

---

[25] V.I. Nevskii, "K voprosu o rabochem dvizhenii v 70-e gody," Istorik-marksist, 1927, no. 4, pp. 130-150.

which sought industrialization and yet would not support the economic improvement of the workers which came out of that industrialization. As a result, social and economic tensions rose.

Given the above situation, all that was needed to light this powderkeg were individuals and organizations to support the advancement of industrial workers, both economically and politically. In the 1870's such a labor movement started. The primary ideology for most opponents of the government was Populism. Russian Populists believed that the narod or the peasant masses would one day become the bearers of revolution in Russia.[26] Most Populists believed that the intelligentsia should spur the narod to taking arms against the government through education, agitation, and even terror. In fact Russian Populists were called Narodniki as a symbol of their deep admiration and devotion to the Russian peasantry. While Populism was a rural oriented movement, a number of highly skilled and educated workers, who recently emerged out of the Industrial Revolution, joined it. These workers were quite respon-

---

[26] The classic and still the best source for Russian Populism is Franco Venturi, Roots of Revolution: A History of the Populist and Socialist Movements in Nineteenth Century Russia (New York, 1960).

sive to many of the economic and political demands of the Narodniki. As early as 1863, Yakov Ushakov, a Populist propagandist, received four years in prison for propaganda activity among some workers in St. Petersburg.[27] The Populists believed that revolution or merely change in Russia had to come from the bulk of the population, the peasantry. Therefore their goal for the urban workers was either they became propagandists for the countryside, or else, when possible, revolutionary terrorists. For example, one of the recruits from St. Petersburg's workers, Stepan Khalturin, was employed as a cabinet maker in the Winter Palace in 1879-1880. He subsequently directed a plot to bomb a section of the Winter Palace hoping to murder Tsar Alexander II in 1880. Most Populists could not believe that the relatively small proletariat in Russia's cities could ever be the vanguard for a revolution. The tiny working class had to play a much more subordinate role to the much more numerous peasantry. Nevertheless, some Populists spent the bulk of their time among the workers. For example, Georgii Plekhanov, then a

---

[27] V.I. Nevskii, Ocherki po istorii Rossiiskoi Kommunisticheskoi Partii (Moscow, 1925), p. 48.

Populist organizer among St. Petersburg's workers, stated that while the peasants in the countryside were under the influence of the "more conservative and timorous members of the peasant family, the city workers. . .constitute the most mobile, the most susceptible to propaganda, the most easily revolutionized stratum of the population."[28] These Populists, who formed Chernyi Peredel (Black Repartition) in 1879, had greater faith in the workers as a group and even encouraged workers to organize their own groups. As a result of these Populists' efforts, two major groups emerged in the 1870's to become the first widespread organizations manned by workers in Russia, the Northern and the Southern Unions of Russian Workers.

In 1872, E.O. Zaslavskii, a teacher from an old gentry background in Saratov, founded the Southern Workers Union in the Black Sea port of Odessa.[29] It was the first large-scale organization in Russia, composed predominantly of workers, which was devoted toward aiding the working class. The members, mostly railway

---

[28] G.V. Plekhanov, Sochineniia, Vol. III, "Russkii rabochii v revoliutsionnom dvizhenii," (Moscow, 1923), pp. 67-70.

[29] Iu. Z. Polevoi, Zarozhdeniie Marksizma v Rossii (Moscow, 1959), p. 111.

operators, printers, foundry workers, and telegraph operators, were part of the tiny but growing skilled and educated segment of the working class.[30] The Southern Union had a nucleus of fifty to sixty people, and could depend upon another one hundred and fifty to two hundred factory workers and university students for support. The organization collected weekly dues of twenty-five kopeks which went for the maintenance both of a library and a treasury to help the workers. The organization soon spread from Odessa to other cities in southern Russia such as Kharkov, Rostov, and Taganrog. While primarily an educational and cultural organization, the Southern Union organized a few strikes in Odessa in 1875.[31]

The program of the Southern Union sought a unification of all the workers of southern Russia to struggle against the existing economic and political system. It stated:

---

[30] Nevskii, Ocherki, p.56.

[31] V. Dembo, Pervaia massovaia organizatsiia rabochikh v Rossii k letiiu 'Iuzhno-rossiiskii soiuz rabochikh, 1874-1875,' (Khar'kov, 1925), pp. 48-52.

1. We must be conscious that the workers can reach recognition of their rights only by means of violent struggle, which will obliterate the privileges and the advantages of the existing ruling class.

2. This struggle can occur only by convincing all fully conscious workers of their desperate position.

3. We the workers of the southern Russian region create in one union named the 'Southern Russian Workers Union' and formulate the following goals:

    a. To propagate the ideas of liberty of the workers from the yoke of capitalism and class privileges.

    b. To unite the workers of the southern Russian region.[32]

This was the first program in Russia directed at the industrial working class by any group. Nevertheless, the primary goal of the Southern Union was to get recruits from the working class to go out into the countryside to propagandize among the peasantry. The organization was fairly short lived. In 1877, the police arrested some fifty-nine members, mostly workers, of the Southern Union. They were tried and sentenced to either long prison terms or exile in isolated regions

---

[32] V.I. Nevskii, _Pervaia klassovaia sotsialisticheskaia organizatsiia v Rossii_ (Moscow, 1929), pp. 73-74.

in Siberia.[33] These arrests effectively broke up the Southern Union.

While Zaslavskii played a leading role in the Southern Union, he was assisted by Viktor Obnorskii, a remarkable example of the new breed of skilled workers in Russia. Obnorskii was born in 1852, the son of a retired noncommissioned officer. Since his parents were very poor, Obnorskii received only an elementary education, but subsequently he read a great deal and became quite educated.[34] Obnorskii became a blacksmith and a mechanic. In 1869, Obnorskii went to St. Petersburg where he worked in the Nobel metal works. In the factory, he joined a reading club operated by workers. In 1872, Obnorskii joined the Chaikovskii group, a Populist organization concentrating on propaganda among the city's workers. Soon Obnorskii participated in the organization of the group's library.[35] Both at work and at meetings of the organiza-

---

[33] Nevskii, Ocherki, p. 67, and Pervaia klassovaia, pp. 82-83.

[34] V.O. Levitskii, Viktor Obnorskii, osnovatel' "Severnogo soiuza russkikh rabochikh," (Moskow, 1929), p. 3.

[35] N. Baturin, Ocherki istorii sotsial-demokratii v Rossii (Moscow, 1906), p. 45.

tion, Obnorskii agitated for strikes which he hoped would involve much of the working class population of St. Petersburg. In 1873, narrowly escaping arrests, which destroyed the bulk of the Chaikovskii group, Obnorskii fled to Odessa. In Odessa, Obnorskii took on a number of skilled jobs at a gas works, in a water works, and finally a railway factory. There Obnorskii organized a small circle which he soon affiliated with the Southern Workers Union, in which he took an increasingly important role. Noting his eagerness to learn, Zaslavskii urged Obnorskii to go abroad. In 1874, Obnorskii left for England, France, and finally Switzerland.[36] In all these countries, Obnorskii met various Russian emigres. In late 1875 Obnorskii returned to Russia, but only for a short time. Soon he returned to Western Europe, this time to Germany, where he studied the methods of German Social Democracy.[37] By 1878, Obnorskii returned again to St. Petersburg where he became an active member of the Northern Union of Russian Workers. In Obnorskii, one can see many of the characteristics which came to typify

---

[36] Levitskii, *Viktor Obnorskii*, pp. 32-37.
[37] *Ibid.*, p. 55.

members of the workers' elite: little formal education but a great deal of self-education; highly skilled occupations; and most importantly an eagerness to learn about what was happening outside of Russia.

The Northern Union of Russian Workers, founded in late 1877 in St. Petersburg, was even more of a working class organization than the Southern Union, because both its leaders, Viktor Obnorskii and Stepan Khalturin, and all of its members, were workers. Khalturin had only three years of formal education in a district school near his home in Vyatka province.[38] Like Obnorskii, he also desired to learn much more and then to see the outside world. Like Obnorskii, Khalturin became a mechanic and a blacksmith, both highly skilled occupations. Since he was not happy with his plight in Russia, Khalturin decided to emigrate to America. However, by the time he arrived in St. Petersburg, he had run out of money, and was forced to remain in the city to get a job.[39] In the early 1870's,

---

[38] E.A. Korolchuk, "Severnyi soiuz russkikh rabochikh" i revoliutsionnoe rabochee dvizhenie 70-kh godov XIX-v Peterburga (Leningrad, 1946), p. 22.

[39] S.M. Stepniak-Kravchinskii, Stepan Khalturin (St. Petersburg, 1908), pp. 68-70.

Khalturin made contact with the Chaikovskii group, and proceeded to organize workers in his factory. In 1877, he became one of the founders of the Northern Union. Georgii Plekhanov described Khalturin as a man who, "aided the workers by teaching them, and procuring books for them. When those workers quarrelled, Khalturin made peace among them. The secret of the enormous influence of Khalturin lay in the tireless attention which he devoted to each single thing."[40] Kahlturin thought economic improvement for the working class could only come about only through violent change. The tactic to employ to achieve that violent change would be terrorism. Both Khalturin and Obnorskii attempted assassinations, the former of a tsarist official, the latter of the tsar himself.

The program of the Northern Union also contained a number of Populist features. It advocated political, economic, and social change and improvement for both workers and peasants. The program called for:

1. The overthrow of the existing political and economic state order.

---

[40] Baturin, *Ocherki*, pp. 60-61.

2. The establishment of a free popular decentralized society with full political rights and internal self-government.

3. The removal of land from the gentry and its distribution to those who till it.

4. The fruits of labor in the hands of those who produce it.[41]

Point three of the program was directed solely at alleviating the plight of the peasantry. Point four was directed at both workers and peasants. Points one and two came almost word for word from the political program of Zemlia i Volia (Land and Freedom), which was then the main organization for the Populist movement.[42] The Northern Union was closely affiliated with Zemlia i Volia, which thought that successful change could only come from a mass peasant uprising.

Nevertheless the Northern Union did undertake a number of activities directed solely at its fellow workers. At its height the Northern Union had some two

---

[41] V. Burtsev, "Severnyi soiuz russkikh rabochikh," Byloe, no. 17, 1906, pp. 172-173.

[42] The program of Zemlia i Volia advocated: "1. The transference of all land into the hands of the agricultural working class, 2. The breaking up of the Russian Empire according to local desires, 3. The need for violent revolution to bring about their demands." This program is cited in A.P. Pribyleva-Korba and V.N. Figner, Narodovolets Aleksandr Dmitrievich Mikhailov (Leningrad, 1925), p. 145.

hundred members, a mutual assistance treasury, and a library. It even attempted to print a newspaper, Racochaia Zaria (Worker's Dawn), which would have become the first workers' paper in Russia. But before the first copy could be made, the police discovered the printing press and arrested the people present there.[43] Along with propaganda activities among workers, the Northern Union agitated in different factories, and participated in various strikes in St. Petersburg in 1878 and 1879.[44] Arrests in 1879 and 1880 destroyed the organization and with it, for a decade, much of the leadership of these actively involved skilled workers.

A Description of the Workers' Elite

The working class can be described, at least for the purposes of this dissertation, as those people who are employed to do physical work for wages.[45] This is a very general definition. Certainly the working class

---

[43] K.M. Takhtarev, Rabochee dvizhenie v Peterburge, 1893-1903 (Moscow, 1924), p. 12.

[44] Nevskii, Pervaia klassovaia, pp. 85-90.

[45] David B. Guralnik, ed., Webster's New World Dictionary of the American Language, second edition (New York, 1980), p. 1638.

was hardly a monolithic group and should more accurately be described as working classes without necessarily any class consciousness. They were divided into industrial workers, those people who worked in factories or at crafts in an urban area; and agricultural laborers who earned their living on the land in the rural communes. In Russia there was considerable mixing between the two groups. After the harvest numerous peasants came to the city to work in the factories during the winter months to supplement their meager income. In the springtime they would usually return to the countryside in time for planting. These peasant-workers were thus very seasonal. However, in the course of the nineteenth century there developed groups of workers who lived and worked year round in the cities. Frequently they were second or even third generation descendants of other workers. Often they never saw the rural commune that they were still technically attached to. Thus their ties were with the cities rather than with the countryside. Through the latter part of the nineteenth century there was a decreased demand for seasonal labor by the factory owners and managers because as industry developed and became more complex, the peasantry as a work force gradually lost its utility as skill requirements rose.

From the growing number of full time urban workers there developed a workers' elite. This expression referred to those workers who possessed the new skills needed in various trades and in the iron, engineering, and manufacturing industries. They were usually young, with an average age of between twenty and thirty.[46] The workers' elite was divided into two groups: crafts, and employees of large specialized enterprises. Typical members of the craft trades were carpenters, bricklayers, printers, bookbinders, tailors, and shoemakers. They generally still operated in an apprenticeship system.[47] With the development of sophisticated machinery these trades often required new skills and knowledge. Large specialized enterprises requiring skilled educated employees to operate the newly developed complex machinery were machine works, steel mills, railway shops, and paper mills. Two prime examples of these factories in St. Petersburg were the

---

[46] Valk, *Istoriia rabochikh Leningrada*, Vol. I, p. 167.

[47] The apprenticeship system is a system in which there are several stages of learning before one acquires all the skill of the trade. In all of these stages the apprentice is working for someone who is called a master. The modern Ph.D. program can be seen as such a system.

large Baltic machine construction plant, located on Vasilyevskii Island, which was owned and operated by the state; and the Putilov metal works on the southwest side of the city. While there were a wide variety of occupations, the total number of workers who could be described as members of the workers' elite was very small. Out of a total industrial work force in St. Petersburg numbering 77,000 in 1890 perhaps only one thousand workers could properly be categorized as members of the workers' elite.[48] While these members of the "labor aristocracy" often worked in the same factory with the ordinary workers, the opinion of the workers' elite about the ordinary worker was often very negative. Genrikh Fisher, a metal worker, ridiculed a fellow worker, Sergei Funikov, by stating, "In him there was none of that urban polishing present in us. He still had a lot of the country in him."[49] In the meantime many ordinary workers had little respect or liking for members of the workers' elite. Thus while having the same appearance as the ordinary urban

---

[48] V. Bartenev, "Iz vospominanii peterburzhtsa vo vtoroi polovine 80-kh godov," Minuvshie gody, 1908, no. 10, p. 185.

[49] G.M. Fisher, V Rossii i v Anglii (Moscow, 1922), p. 25.

workers, the attitudes and other characteristics of members of the workers' elite made them a separate group.

The characteristics which distinguished members of the workers' elite as a separate group from the rest of the urban working class were the degree of literacy, standard of living, social traits, economic and political positions, and finally and most important, a strong urge to discover the outside world.

The members of the workers' elite were more literate than their fellow workers. According to the 1897 census, the general literacy rates for Russian urban workers was 23% for males and 13% for females. Yet certain occupations had a very high rate of literacy. The highest percentage, of course, was among the printers, with males having a 93% literacy rate and females 70%. The metal workers, food workers, and woodcutters all had literacy rates of 70% or better. Young workers, aged seventeen to thirty, had even higher rates of literacy. For example, male metal workers between the ages of seventeen and nineteen had a literacy rate of 84%.[50] Workers had increased opportunities to read and write from attending classes at Sunday and evening schools, which met at the only times the workers had off from their jobs. V.A. Shelgunov, a mechanic, recounted how, "the workers' elite loafed around second hand book stores, browsing and purchasing old books."[51] I.I. Timofeev, a metal worker, managed to obtain custody of the library of the Tochisskii Circle, an intellectual and worker educational and discussion group with some 1,000 volumes of old books and journals. His library became quite well known in St. Petersburg by not only members of the workers' elite but by intellectuals as well. He loaned his books whenever asked by a fellow worker.[52] Because a worker could not frequently afford to purchase his own copies of books, the workers often pooled their

---

[50] Valk, *Istoriia rabochikh Leningrada*, Vol. I, pp. 184-185. Valk explained that despite these high figures, one has to remember that in Russia the standards for literacy were very low. They just required a very basic knowledge of reading and writing. Often if an individual could sign his name he was classified as literate.

[51] V.A. Shel'gunov, "Rabochie na puti k Marksizmu," *Staryi bol'shevik*, 1933, no. 2, p. 99.

[52] Kochakov, *Ocherki istorii Leningrada*, Vol. II, p. 383.

limited financial resources and purchased books and journals collectively.

Economically, while the members of the workers' elite were by no means well off, they still earned significantly more than their fellow workers. Since their occupations required greater skills and more responsibility regarding the operations of some rather complex machines, their salaries were proportionately greater. The Ministry of Finance reported in 1894 that the salaries for highly skilled metal craftsmen and lathe operators were nearly 700 rubles a year, while an unskilled worker in the same factory earned less than 200 rubles a year.[53] These wages enabled the workers' elite, despite the high cost of living in St. Petersburg, to spend money on their education. Though ordinary workers might have the desire to learn how to read and write, their low salaries were used solely for food, rent, and clothing. Thus it was very difficult for one of these workers to try to improve his lot because without education they were unable to obtain the necessary skilled positions; but without these skilled occupations they could not afford the

---

[53] Valk, *Istoriia rabochikh Leningrada*, Vol. I, p. 185.

education. While the number of members of the workers' elite grew in the latter part of the nineteenth century, it grew from a base of apprentices and children of the highly skilled.

A significant portion of the workers' elite were non-Russians. Ethnically St. Petersburg was a Russian city, but to find work thousands of Finns, Poles, and Lithuanians came to the city.[54] All were from the most economically and culturally advanced western part of the Russian Empire. These non-Russians had higher literacy and skills proportionately, and they were able to fill some of the best jobs. Most important, these non-Russians had always maintained ties with Western and Central Europe, in particular with their labor movement. In this way the non-Russians were able to supply information about developments outside Russia to the skilled Russian workers.

A very significant characteristic of the workers' elite was that they were hungry for information about the world outside Russia. Viktor Obnorskii was hardly unique in traveling to Western Europe where he saw

---

[54]Pokrovskii, Statisticheskii, p. 7.

developments among the British, French, and especially the German workers. The major drawback to travel was the lack of money to make the journey. For instance, Stepan Khalturin was not alone in wanting to travel, in his case to America, which he thought was far better economically to its workers. But he was prevented from making the trip by a lack of money. These workers avidly read accounts of Western Europe and the United States in newspapers such as Russkie Vedomosti, Russkoe Bogatsvo, and Severnyi Vestnik.[55] This curiosity about the outside world would be a major reason many members of the workers' elite formed circles to exchange information and news about latest developments in the West.

Generally the members of the workers' elite were apolitical. They sought merely a cultural and economic improvement of their present situation.[56] Through formal education and self-improvement by books, journals, and lectures, the workers hoped to follow the example of their Western contemporaries of bettering themselves. The workers believed that through education

---

[55] Nevskii, Ocherki, pp. 149-150.

[56] V.A. Shel'gunov, "Vospominaniia," Ot gruppy Blagoeva k "Soiuzu Bor'by" 1886-1894 gg. (Rostov-on-Don, 1921), p. 54.

they could raise their economic standard of living by acquiring better skills so that they could get a better paying position. Secondly, through further education the workers' elite could attain a greater cultural life. They enjoyed attending lectures, reading anything they could find, and discussing amongst themselves philosophical issues. "We workers can reach consciousness of our miserable position by means of obtaining better books, newspapers--to render to one another mutual favors,"[57] concluded one railway workers after a discussion. The furtherance of their education became, perhaps, the central goal for the workers' elite.

Some members of the workers' elite realized that self-education would only benefit themselves. They decided to teach other members of the workers' elite through the formation of discussion groups, also known as circles. Sometimes they also attempted to teach the less skilled workers. These workers formed the "workers' intelligentsia."

Educational Opportunities for the Workers

Education was an important attainment in the life of a member of the workers' elite. It was their method

---

[57]Nevskii, Ocherki, p. 184.

for economic and cultural advancement. Without some education, the workers would be unable to operate the increasingly complex machinery required for their jobs. Yet for some of the workers' elite the basic formal education received in factory and in Sunday schools was just a necessary beginning. In every spare moment such workers visited second-hand book shops, attended public lectures and attended defenses of doctoral dissertations which were always public in Russia. Thus, the workers' movement must be perceived as a very broad intellectual one of always striving for education and for advancement.

The government pursued a contradictory policy toward the education of workers. On the one hand, prominent members of the government such as Sergei Witte[58] recognized a skilled labor force was essential

---

[58] Sergei Witte acted as government advisor to both Alexander III and Nicholas II. While acting as Minister of Finance he pursued policies close to the interests of business. He believed that foreign capital was indispensible to Russia's economic development and thus spared no effort to attract foreign investors. He strongly backed a policy aimed at the increased intervention of the state in the economic affairs of the nation when the result of that policy would be increased industrialization and modernization of the Russian Empire.

for the industrialization and modernization of Russia. On the other hand, various government leaders feared that educated workers would eventually try to strive for political gains which would threaten the autocratic basis of the Russian government. The government unsuccessfully attempted to compromise. It hoped that any schools opened for the workers would instill in them a belief in the traditional autocracy and in Russian Orthodox teachings.[59] Yet instead of the psalms, some teachers taught Pushkin; and instead of the precepts of the autocracy, some teachers read Chernyshevskii. When the government learned of these things, it closed some of the schools.

A group which both strongly urged the government to open schools and which provided major financial support to the schools were the industrialists. In 1870 industrial leaders of the St. Petersburg community, recognizing the need for skilled labor, decided to open technical schools to train foremen for their factories.[60] They also asked zemstvos and the city government to direct Sunday and evening schools. Within ten

---

[59] Ia. V. Abramov, Nashi voskresnye shkoly (St. Petersburg, 1900), pp. 103-104.

[60] Valk, Istoriia rabochikh Leningrada, Vol. I, p. 46.

years there was a large network of these schools at most of the major factories in St. Petersburg. All of these schools were directed by the Russian Technical Society, an association of industrialists who provided services to the workers and to the poor of St. Petersburg in areas such as education and housing for the homeless. One manufacturer, V.P. Vargunin, was not only interested in educating his workers so that they could properly run his machinery, but he was also genuinely interested in raising the cultural level of both his workers and their children. Vargunin founded a daily school for the children of the workers, and a Sunday school for his employees. Sunday was the only day off from work for most workers, so this was the only day classes could regularly be held, which was very indicative of this great desire for learning. Varginin and his two sons, Nikolai and Vladimir, established a library for the workers at their Nevskaia paper mill. This factory, founded in 1839 in Shlisselburg, south of St. Petersburg, employed around 300 people. The technically advanced plant produced very high quality paper for government use. Vargunin was politically liberal and through education he sought to promote the working class as an ally to oppose the autocracy.[61] Most industrialists were not of Vargunin's political persuasion, but they still encouraged some education for their workers because a skilled work force would raise their productivity. By 1895 thirty-five schools were organized in the factories.[62]

These factory schools not only held classes on Sundays but during the evenings as well. Work in the factories usually ended at 8 p.m. in St. Petersburg, and by 8:15 or 8:30 classes began two or three evenings a week.[63] It was quite an achievement for workers to want to attend classes after working fourteen hours in a day. It seemed as if every spare moment the workers had was absorbed in either learning or in studying. One teacher commented, "All these people, working from 5 am to night, then manage to come here to look at their lessons. It's very exhausting."[64] Each one of these evening and Sunday schools had between thirty and

---

[61] All the information on V. Vargunin and his aspirations was given in K.M. Takhtarev, Rabochee dvizhenie, pp. 28-29.

[62] Uchebnye zavedeniia Ministerstva narodnogo prosveshcheniia (St. Petersburg, 1895), pp. 384-391.

[63] A. El'nitskii, Istoriia rabochego dvizheniia v Rossii (Moscow, 1925), p. 143.

[64] Takhtarev, Rabochee dvizhenie, p. 32.

and one hundred workers enrolled in them. Most students remained in the schools for two or three years. Most were young; their ages ranging from eighteen to thirty. By 1893, 7,293 workers were enrolled in various schools throughout the city.[65] One-half of the students were enrolled in schools controlled by the Russian Technical Society. The other one-half of the students were enrolled in schools directly organized by the factory owners. In 1884 the first women's Sunday schools were opened and they also spread rapidly throughout the factories.

 Students who wanted work to supplement their income while they attended the University or the Technical Institute were usually the teachers. Even some professors came into the factories to teach, and once in a while a worker learned enough to be able to teach his fellow workers in one of the Sunday or evening schools. The subjects taught to the workers were reading and writing, basic arithmetic and elementary drawing. After that very basic stage, many workers were taught Russian history and geography, sciences such as biology, geology, and physics, geometry, and political

---

[65]Pokrovskii, Statisticheskii, p. 28.

economy. The workers read various newspapers, particularly Russkie Vedomosti, which gave extensive treatment to foreign developments, the works of authors such as Gogol, Pushkin, and Nekrasov, and Darwin's theory of evolution.[66] In fact, the subjects discussed at these schools became quite involved. Intellectual dissidents used their instruction in the schools as a forum to arouse the workers to politically oppose the government. Yet they were far from being completely successful. Many workers resented the mixing of politics with education. For example, K. Norinskii, who entered a vocational school in the Baltic machine construction plant, mentioned that, out of his forty classmates, only ten subsequently participated in any political or dissident activity.[67]

The Sunday and evening schools faced a number of obstacles. First, a number of government departments, such as the Ministry of Internal Security and the Ministry of Internal Affairs, opposed the schools because in their eyes the schools formented revolution. Their opposition prevented any national funding and

---

[66] Abramov, Nashi, p. 110.

[67] K. Norinskii, "Moi vospominaniia," Ot gruppy Blagoeva, p. 11.

allowed only minimal local funding of the various schools. Thus the schools were dependent on factory owners, who could at any time terminate funds. Most factory owners wanted the schools solely to teach the workers the requisite skills needed to raise the productivity in their factories. When some factory owners became alarmed over some of the political slants of the teaching, they either closed the schools or extensively cut the funding. The schools needed money for salaries of teachers, and for the purchase of books and other materials. One problem which affected most schools continually was the lack of funds for their teachers. To partially remedy the problem of funds, many schools charged workers two rubles a month for tuition and materials.[68] Space for classrooms was another problem. Often factory grounds or even teachers' apartments had to be used. Despite these obstacles, factory, evening, and Sunday schools played a major role in raising the literacy of the St. Petersburg worker, and provided the worker with at least basic skills in reading, writing, and arithmetic. It was the most important and wide-

---

[68]Kochakov, *Ocherki istorii Leningrada*, Vol. II, pp. 678-679.

spread effort on the part of educated society to alter the fate of the urban worker.

CHAPTER II

INTELLECTUAL AND WORKERS' GROUPS IN
ST. PETERSBURG THROUGH 1890

<u>Survey of Student Intellectual Groups in St. Petersburg</u>

St. Petersburg was one of the centers of student dissident activities. There were many factors which explained the prominence of St. Petersburg. First, St. Petersburg was the site of two of Russia's highest quality institutions of higher education: the University and the Technical Institute. Both attracted excellent graduates of <u>gymnasiums</u> from all over Russia. They were prime candidates for opposition forums due to their intellectual caliber. Both attracted leading faculty. Second, as the center of Russia's governmental institutions, the city attracted some of the brightest minds in the land. Third, the city was one of the most westernized in the Russian Empire because of its geographical proximity to the Baltic Sea and its large ports, attracting not only Western commerce but Western ideas as well. Fourth, of all Russian cities, St. Petersburg had one of the largest populations of non-Russians. According to the 1869 census, 38,000 non-Russians lived in St. Petersburg.[1] Yet, foreigners assumed a significance far beyond their size for the city's commerce and trade. Thus, cross currents of ideas, both Western and Russian, flowed within the salons, the lecture halls, and the apartments in this large and rapidly expanding city. From 1870 to 1900, the city doubled in size from three-quarters of a million inhabitants to nearly 1.5 million people.[2]

Intellectual and dissident activity, including the student population, has already been amply researched in Russian history. It is not the purpose of this section to summarize that huge body of writing. What is necessary here is to place the student intelligentsia in the framework of the labor movement, especially among the "workers' intelligentsia" of the late nineteenth century. Intellectuals, for purpose of this study, were people who considered themselves well educated, enlightened, and often became very critical of the autocratic government in Russia. The student intelligentsia were simply those intellectuals who were still in high school or in institutions of higher

---

[1] Sanktpeterburg po perepisi 1C dekabria 1869 goda, part 1 (St. Petersburg, 1872), pp. 110-111.

[2] S. Peterburg po perepisi 15 dekabria 1900 goda, part 1 (St. Petersburg, 1903), pp. 6-10.

education. Which student groups or circles conducted propaganda and other activities among the workers in the 1880's and the 1890's, and why? What was the attitude of circle members toward the workers and toward their role in workers' activities? Were contacts between students and workers extensive or rare? Did non-Russians play a large role in the formation and the development of circles?

During the 1860's and 1870's Russian intellectuals concentrated almost solely on the peasantry as the soldiers for the future revolution. As the vast bulk of the Russian population was peasants, anyone who believed that revolutions could only succeed with the support of the population, had to place his faith in the peasantry. Populism, which espoused the doctrine of an agrarian revolution, was the paramount ideology of the mid- and late-nineteenth century Russian revolutionary movement. Even though the majority of the intellectuals lived in the cities, they rarely thought of urban areas as centers for revolution. However, the growing industrialization of Russia after 1860 could no longer be ignored. St. Petersburg became the main industrial center of Russia. Granted that many of these workers were first generation off the land. However, student intellectuals had to admit that these peasant-workers were acquiring a new and different mentality by living in the cities. For example, A.V. Nizovkin, a university student active in the Chaikovskii Circle, noted in the early 1870's that the metal workers had already been marked by urban civilization. They dressed better; they no longer lived communally; and the traditions of the artel were dying out among them.[3] The numbers of workers in St. Petersburg rapidly increased after the emancipation of the serfs in 1861, which allowed many peasants to migrate to the cities for work. Many intellectuals saw themselves as a bridge between the villages and the factories. Prince Petr Kropotkin, one of Russia's leading anarchists, was involved in feverish propaganda activity among urban workers for two years during the 1870's. Kropotkin gave a vivid picture in his memoirs.

> My sympathies were mainly for the textile workers and in general the workers in the factories. There were thousands of this kind of workers in St. Petersburg and every summer they returned to their villages to farm the land. These half-

---

[3] Sh. M. Levin, "Kruzhok chaikovtsev i propaganda sredi peterburgskikh rabochikh v nachale 1870-kh godov," Katorga i ssylka, 1929, no. 12, p. 191.

peasants and half-workers brought with them into town the spirit of the Russian mir (commune). Among them revolutionary propaganda met with considerable success.[4]

During the early 1870's, the Chaikovskii group became the first major Populist organization to actively organize among the urban working class of St. Petersburg. Their intention was not to promote the urban workers as the nucleus for revolutionary action. Rather, the Chaikovskii group sought recruits from the urban working class to go and propagandize among the rural working class. The rural working class was those peasants who worked on someone else's land for a salary. They assumed that there was a natural link between the urban and the rural working classes. Almost against their own inclinations, they had close links with factories. The Chaikovskii group was the first large Populist organization to present the ideas of Populism to factory workers. It was founded in 1869 by Mark Natanson, who later became a Social Revolutionary leader.[5] After Natanson's arrest and exile in

---

[4] P.A. Kropotkin, Zapiski revoliutsionera (Leningrad, 1933), p. 199.

[5] Mark Natanson (1851-1919), a former student at St. Petersburg's School of Medicine, became a founder of the Populist group Zemlia i Volia. Later, he became one of the leaders of the Social Revolutionary Party, and served on the S. R. Central Committee.

1871, Nikolai Chaikovskii took over the leadership. Kropotkin was the most famous leader of the group. The Chaikovskii group formed a circle of twelve people, each of whom taught three to five workers to read, to write, and to have a basic knowledge of history, geography, and the sciences. Their work was centered in the Vyborg district of the capital.[6] Their propaganda and educational activity proved successful. Numerous workers cited the educational contributions the Chaikovskii group made in their lives. That group founded a library for workers, who contributed a small percentage of their wages for the library's upkeep. In April 1873, the Chaikovskii group helped establish a mutual aid bank among the well paid and highly skilled workers in the Nobel armaments plant. It was managed by workers, in particular, V.P. Obnorskii, an early member of the "workers' intelligentsia."[7]

Yet the very success of the Chaikovskii group proved their undoing. As contacts between the

---

[6] L. Shishko, S.M. Kravchinskii i kruzhok chaikovtsev (St. Petersburg, 1906), p. 30.

[7] V.O. Levitskii, Viktor Obnorskii, osnovatel' "Severnogo soiuza russkikh rabochikh," (Moscow, 1929), p.58.

Chaikovskii group and the workers increased, the police discovered their activities. Abruptly, a series of arrests during the latter half of 1873 mortally crippled the organization. By the winter of 1873, the Chaikovskii group no longer existed as an organized body. Nevertheless, their contribution to the Russian labor movement would be a permanent one. With the Chaikovskii group, we had the first genuine interaction between intellectuals and workers. Several workers escaped arrest and continued to organize activities among their fellow workers. The noted Italian historian Franco Venturi concluded:

> The Chaikovskii group was the first to plant the seeds of a genuine working class organization. . . . It was the Chaikovskii group which provided the impulse for a working class movement which, despite its original limitations and the violence of the persecutions it had to face always thereafter maintained some measure of continuity and which grew in scope and influence as revolutionary Populism developed during the 'seventies.[8]

The 1870's was a decade of feverish activity by Russian Populists. Though active organizing among the urban workers virtually ceased with the destruction

---

[8] Venturi, Roots of Revolution, p. 507.

of the Chaikovskii group, Populists went into the countryside in the "v narod" ("to the people") movement to propagandize among their primary targets, the peasantry. Distrust by the peasantry and intense police surveillance quickly destroyed that idyllic movement. Then Populism abandoned mass recruitment, turned inward, and toward terrorism. A few highly skilled members of the urban working class, such as V.P. Obnorskii and Stepan Khalturin, were recruited into the Populist group Narodnaia Volia (People's Will), but only as individual agents to conduct assassination attempts against tsarist officials, not as leaders for a working class movement. The campaign of terror finally culminated with the assassination of Tsar Alexander II on March 1, 1881. Following his assassination mass arrests and repression crushed the Narodnaia Volia.

Leading observers of Russia in the 1880's characterized the decade as a gloomy, hopeless, cheerless one. One leading Populist, M.S. Olminskii, who was active as a propagandist in the St. Petersburg labor movement in the 1880's and 1890's stated: "The 1880's were a very tragic, unhopeful and pessimistic period."[9] Intellectuals felt frustrated. The veteran Populist journalist, Nikolai Mikhailovskii declared that the intellectuals lacked any sense of purpose or direction. They wanted to serve but did not know how.[10] Revolutionary activity met with little support from the very people it was supposed to serve. Populists were confused and disillusioned. After the assassination of the Tsar in 1881, they fully expected a national uprising by the peasantry of Russia. Instead, the population remained quiet. The alleged revolutionary masses were hardly revolutionary. All mass and individual tactics to provoke revolution--both the "v narod" movement to spread anti-government activities and terrorism to eliminate tsarist officials--clearly failed.

In 1884-85, in St. Petersburg, a successor organization to the Narodnaia Volia, tried to revive

---

[9] M.S. Ol'minskii (Aleksandrov), "'Gruppa narodovol'-tsev' (1891-94 gg.)" Byloe, no. 11, 1906, pp. 1-3. Similar words have been recounted in the following works: V. Ivanov-Razumnik, Istoriia russkoi obshchestvennoi mysli, Vol. II (St. Petersburg, 1908), pp. 291-333; V. Bartenev, "Vospominaniia Peterburzhtsa o vtoroi polovine 80-kh godakh," Minuvshie gody, 1908, no. 10, p. 119; and O.M. Govorukhin, "Vospominaniia," Golos minuvshago, 1926, no. 16, p. 215.

[10] N.K. Mikhailovskii, "Literatura i zhizn'," Russkaia mysl', 1892, no. 6, p. 41.

the tactic of terrorism. Its most famous member was Aleksandr Ulianov, the older brother of Vladimir Lenin. It was an old idea revived by desperate people who wanted to accomplish something.[11] The group plotted to murder Tsar Alexander III. Right from the start the police knew of its plans. Before anything serious could occur, police arrested the conspirators on March 1, 1887 right on the Nevskii Prospekt in St. Petersburg. Five people, including Ulianov, were hanged. Intellectuals sought service to the people but again it was a service without any sense of purpose. The gloom and doom atmosphere deepened later in the 1880's. A symbol of this pessimism occurred when Lev Tikhomirov, one of the few members of the Executive Committee of the old Narodnaia Volia still at large, renounced revolutionary activity and returned to Russia from exile as an apologist for the reactionary tsarist policies.

Many dissident intellectuals abandoned any attempts at large scale revolutionary activities. Instead they conducted propaganda, in what they them-

---

[11] Ol'minskii, "Gruppa narodovol'tsev," p. 8.

selves characterized as a "small deeds atmosphere."[12] Propaganda was essentially education, teaching the workers the fundamentals of language, science, history and literature. These intellectuals conducted evening classes to provide the workers a basic education along with a sense of self-esteem. The teachers intended that the workers should learn that their counterparts in Western Europe had lived in similar conditions earlier.[13] But those workers had not resigned themselves to abject poverty. Instead they organized trade unions to press for improvements in their wages, working hours, and basic living conditions. Anti-government intellectuals sought to make Russian industrial workers aware of their potential strength. While it was important to give these workers a sense of pride, the major focus of these "small deeds" was basic education. Workers needed and, in fact, many craved the rudiments of reading and writing. For example, one lathe operator, I.V. Krutov, declared, "I sometimes do not sleep the entire night for I am

---

[12] V. Golubev, "Stranichka iz istorii rabochego dvizheniia," Byloe, no. 12, 1906, p. 107.

[13] Takhtarev, Rabochee Dvizhenie, p. 20.

thinking of ways to improve our lives."[14] These workers believed that the principal vehicle to improve their lives was education. Intellectuals were pleased at the responsiveness of workers to these educational activities. These "small deed" activities tended to be met favorably by workers. Yet, here too, often the intellectuals tended to be overzealous, which caused the results for the intellectuals to be mixed.[15]

Yet the characterization of the 1880's as a decade of frustration, drift, alienation, and despair is only part of the picture. Below the surface, young intellectuals, usually attending St. Petersburg University, the Technical Institute, and the _gymnasiums_, formed circles. They were groups of six to eight people who often met as much as three times a week in the evenings and on Sundays to educate each other. Circles were rarely composed of students from different institutions.[16] Thus, one circle had students from the university, another was composed of students from the Technical Institute; while a third may have had its

---

[14]Bartenev, "Vospominaniia," _Minuvshie gody_, p. 172.

[15]Takhtarev, _Rabochee dvizhenie_, p. 24.

[16]V.V. Sviatlovskii, "Na zare Rossiiskoi sotsial-demokratii," _Byloe_, no. 19, 1922, pp. 150-152.

members from a particular gymnasium. Circles appeared at the start of each academic year. In the members' opinions, these circles filled gaps in their formal education. During meetings members read Western writers such as Herbert Spencer and John Stuart Mill and Russian authors such as Nikolai Chernyshevskii and Petr Lavrov.[17] Then, as a group, the members discussed these authors. Other times they debated major controversies of the day such as Charles Darwin's theory of evolution or the political philosophies of liberalism, radicalism and socialism. Discussions often ran for hours. Not only were legally obtainable books read, but illegal works were read as well, such as those by Aleksandr Herzen and Petr Lavrov, two leading Russian socialists; the works of French utopian socialists, Count St. Simon and Charles Fourier and the first two volumes of Karl Marx's Das Kapital. Sometimes, circles obtained illegal editions written by Russian emigres who were members of the old organization Narodnaia Volia.[18] Circles often made systematic studies of political economic theorists and contempo-

---

[17] Ibid., p. 158.

[18] L.B. Krasin, "Dela davno minuvshikh dnei, 1887-1892," Proletarskaia revoliutsiia, 1923, p. 52.

rary Russian literature, particularly the works of Count Lev Tolstoi. Usually libraries of legal and illegal works were collected for members of the circles to use. For the purchase of books, each member would donate a small sum such as ten kopeks a week.[19] Yet these activities were generally of a very small scale. Thus, circle members essentially educated each other in areas not formally offered in school. For most members the purpose was purely to supplement their education at secondary school or university. Only after arrests by the ever vigilant police did these students turn to illegal and revolutionary activities.[20]

At the same time personal ties with workers were minimal. In fact, the later propagandist K.M. Takhtarev conceded: "About ties with the workers and our participation in the workers' movement, we only dreamt. We constantly discussed the workers but that was all. Any work among the workers was very risky for both the student and the worker."[21] In fact, from most of these young intellectuals we get a real sense

---

[19]Ol'minskii, "Gruppa narodovol'tsev," p. 14.
[20]Sviatlovskii, "Na zare," p. 158.
[21]Takhtarev, *Rabochee dvizhenie*, p. 21.

of emptiness. "They badly wanted to know some genuine workers. Yet they did not know how to find them," commented one student.[22] If they were successful and began significant ties with workers, both the intellectual and the worker were fearful of arrest. Thus, intellectuals faced a bitter dilemma. They yearned for ties with workers, yet feared the probable consequences of these ties. Few intellectuals knew how to resolve this dilemma.

Nevertheless, the 1880's were not a complete failure in the eyes of some young intellectuals. Circles of dedicated, radical students, already highly politicized, formed in the educational institutions of St. Petersburg. Many of them sought contact with factory workers and were successful in their efforts. Among these groups, one of the first was the Blagoev Circle, named for its leader Dimitŭr Blagoev. Blagoev was a Bulgarian who arrived in St. Petersburg in 1880 where he entered the university. Blagoev read both Marx and Ferdinand Lassalle, both of whom greatly

---

[22] M.I. Brusnev, "Vozniknovenie pervykh sotsial-demokraticheskikh organizatsii," <u>Proletarskaia revoliutsiia</u>, no. 2, 1923, p. 21.

influenced his political philosophy.[23] He had many arguments with Populists, who despite the repression and the disillusionment after the assassination of Alexander II, remained the ideological leader of the Russian dissidents. Blagoev drifted toward a tiny but growing group of Russian Marxists, people who had been in the Chernyi Peredel group. Blagoev engaged in propaganda activities among several of the workers' circles in St. Petersburg. He noticed the receptiveness with which workers listened to him.[24] In early 1884, Blagoev and several other students at the university formed the "Party of Russian Social Democracy" to increase and to coordinate propaganda among the workers' circles. Despite the claim of being Russia's first Social Democratic group, the party was actually a hybrid of ideologies focused, not only around Marx, but also around Petr Lavrov and Ferdinand Lassalle.[25] The purpose of the group's propaganda work

---

[23] Baturin, Ocherki, p. 6. Ferdinand Lassalle (1825-64), a German socialist and one of the founders of the German Social Democratic Party, favored organizing cooperative associations for workers. Workers' cooperatives became popular in Russia, and Lassalle's ideas became an inspiration for Russian socialists.

[24] Nevskii, Ocherki, p. 72.

[25] El'nitskii, Istoriia, p. 82.

was to increase the number of educated and politically conscious workers, who could then propagandize among other workers. The goal of the organization was to create a small but cohesive cadre of workers. The members of the group did not think in terms of a mass politically conscious proletariat for Russia, at least not for the foreseeable future. The role of the intellectual was to educate the worker, not to attempt to take over the leadership of the workers' circles. They were educators and propagandists, not agitators. Their ties with members of the workers' elite were significant and made a lasting impression on several workers.[26] Yet actual working class members within Blagoev's group were few, three out of a total membership of twelve to fifteen. Their names were P.I. Ashulov, A.A. Gerasimov, and D.I. Shatko.[27] All three were engineers, people who operated or supervised the operation of engines or technical equipment. None would play significant future roles in the workers' movement. The rest were either students at the university or at the medical academy, both of which came

---

[26] Nevskii, Ocherki, p. 79.
[27] Ibid., p. 81.

largely from the upper classes, and would have had little real contact with workers, given their class origins. The Blagoev group organized a library including both legal and illegal books, journals and pamphlets. In 1884, the group decided they had to found their own newspaper to present the group's own solutions to the major issues of the day. The first and only issue of Rabochii (Worker) appeared in January 1885. With the appearance of that issue, the police became very concerned over this tiny group.[28] In March 1885, Blagoev was arrested and was soon deported back to Bulgaria where he later became one of the founders of the Bulgarian Communist Party. On January 27, 1886, police destroyed the rest of the organization, arresting many of its members and seizing the printing press of Rabochii.[29] Some intellectuals escaped arrest, and subsequently entered Tochisskii's and Brusnev's groups. While a tiny group, Blagoev's circle was the first quasi-Marxist organization, and the first to catch the attention of the

---

[28] Baturin, Ocherki, p. 10. A complete account of Blagoev's newspaper can be found in N.L. Sergievskii, Rabochii; gazeta partii russkikh sotsial-demokratov (Blagoevtsev) 1885 (Leningrad, 1928).

[29] N. Baturin, Sochineniia (Moscow, 1930), p. 48.

nascent emigre Marxist group, the Emancipation of Labor, then existing in Switzerland. Cooperative ties brought about exchanges of materials and information useful for both groups.[30]

Another foreign student, Tochisskii, the son of a Polish colonel, founded the next significant Marxist intellectual circle in St. Petersburg. Pavel Varfolomeevich Tochisskii was born in 1864 in the city of Ekaterinburg (which later became Sverdlovsk) of upper class gentry parents. His mother was an educated, westernized liberal who had read biographies of various French revolutionaries such as Jean-Paul Marat, Maximilien Robespierre, and Georges-Jacques Danton. She conveyed their radical ideas to her children, influencing significantly both Tochisskii and his sister, Maria.[31] In contrast to his liberal mother, Tochisskii's father was a conservative defender of the tsarist regime, and was the warden of the prison in Ekaterinburg. Father and son relations were never close.[32] In 1883, while completing a course at the

---

[30] N.L. Sergievskii, "Plekhanov i Gruppa Blagoeva," Proletarskaia revoliutsiia, 1928, no. 8, pp. 55-58.

[31] A. Breitfus, "Tochisskii i ego kruzhok," Krasnaia letopis', 1923, no. 7, p. 320.

[32] Ibid., p. 321.

local _gymnasium_ in Ekaterinburg, Tochisskii organized a circle of self-education in which he and his fellow gymnasium students read and discussed works by N.A. Dobroliubov, D.I. Pisarev, V.V. Bervi-Flerovskii, and F. Lassalle. Quickly, his father and the headmaster of the _gymnasium_ discovered the circles' existence. Both clashed with Tochisskii. Bitterly, Tochisskii broke with his father, dropped out of school, and went to work in a factory near Nizhni Tagil as a blacksmith. Then, Tochisskii returned for a short time to Ekaterinburg to work in a railway plant. Not only had Tochisskii broken with his family; he also broke from his social middle class origins. This fact proved very significant for Tochisskii's political views. Throughout the rest of his life. Tochisskii greatly respected the individual worker's political consciousness and the worker's need to control his own decision making. That view was virtually unknown among other student intellectuals. Tochisskii applied that attitude when he insisted the workers maintain their own organization associated with his own circle of intellectuals. By now he was a committed revolutionary. In the summer of 1884, Tochisskii and his sister Maria went to St. Petersburg where they entered an artisan course to study metal crafts at the Trade School of the Russian

Technical Society.[33] There he met numerous highly skilled workers, and also began his acquaintance with Marxist literature. For example, he read Marx's Communist Manifesto and Plekhanov's Our Differences. These works impelled Tochisskii to become a Social Democrat.

Tochisskii's political philosophy evolved. He considered the urban proletariat to be Russia's only revolutionary class. He completely broke with Populism and its reliance on the peasantry as the army of the revolution.[34] The Populists had declared that the overthrow of the autocracy or the political struggle must take precedence over all other activities. Yet, Tochisskii recognized the relatively tiny number of urban workers in Russia and that the bulk of them were still first generation workers who lacked any political consciousness.[35] Simply, Russia was not as economically developed as Western Europe. Therefore, the workers needed assistance from members of the intelligentsia, people such as Tochisskii. The intelligen-

---

[33] V.V. Sviatlovskii, "Na zare," p. 145.

[34] Nevskii, Ocherki, p. 85.

[35] M. Lebedeva (Tochisskaia) "K biografii Tochisskogo, vospominaniia sestry," Istoriko-revoliutsionnyi sbornik, Vol. III, 1926, pp. 296-297.

tsia would help lead and organize receptive workers. Yet the intelligentsia would serve only a temporary role. In fact, Tochisskii declared that the intelligentsia would be no more than "mere guests" in any revolution.[36] They should not be allowed any leadership role at all. The workers should be very cautious of the intelligentsia at all stages of their political and cultural development as they always remained bourgeois. Therefore, the intelligentsia inherently and ultimately will work for bourgeois interests rather than the real interests of workers. Thus, Tochisskii essentially rebuffed members of his own social class. His distrust of the intelligentsia and his fear that the intelligentsia would try to dominate any real leadership of the revolutionary movement remained a cardinal principle of Tochisskii's political philosophy. The relationship between the working class and the intelligentsia foreshadowed a perennial dispute among Marxists. What should the true role for the proletariat be? Who should have the real control over the working class movement? The fact that most members of the intelligentsia, including Lenin, insisted on their own control caused major tension between them

---

[36]Nevskii, *Ocherki*, p. 86.

and members of the "workers' intelligentsia." Tochisskii's extreme caution regarding the role and power of the intelligentsia explained the dual structural organization for his group which was soon set up.

By 1885 Tochisskii established solid ties with workers of the Nevskii Gates region. In fact, he found work near the Nevskii Gates in the artillery arsenal on the Vyborg side of St. Petersburg where he attended a metal worker's school.[37] By summer, his plans to organize a circle ripened. Tochisskii's goal was to raise the intellectual and moral level of the workers.[38] Secretly, a library and a mutual aid fund were organized. The fund would aid workers who were out on strike or were locked out by their employers. It would also serve as a basic supplementary allowance to aid, at least minimally, the poorest workers. Mutual aid funds strengthened bonds among workers.[39] In a sense, groups with such mutual aid features were embryonic trade unions allowing workers

---

[37] Breitfus, "Tochisskii," p. 323.
[38] Nevskii, Ocherki, p. 87.
[39] Breitfus, "Tochisskii," p. 332.

to think in terms of collective interests and problems in an organizational format. Thus, collecting these funds raised political consciousness among the workers.

Through a mutual decision by the workers and by the intellectuals in the Tochisskii Circle, circles composed solely of workers were formed to raise their cultural level. They provided both self-education by the workers and propaganda by intellectuals. By 1886, Tochisskii, his sister Maria, and another intellectual, Dmitrii Lazarev, formed a circle.[40] To establish ties with workers, Lazarev entered the Vysshee Technical School. Upon completion of his course, Lazarev became a lathe operator at the factory. Appropriately enough, these intellectuals and artisans gave as their official name for the circle the Association of St. Petersburg Artisans. To purchase books and to fund the mutual assistance treasury, each member had to contribute twenty-five kopeks a month. As the average skilled worker was paid a ruble a day, this was not an insignificant amount. The group's intention was to enlist workers as members in the circle, not keep it solely composed of intellectuals. Three highly skilled

---

[40] V. Nevskii, "K istorii 'Partii russkikh sotsial-demokratov' v 1884-1886 gg.," Byloe, 1918, no. 13, p. 219.

workers quickly tied themselves to the group. They were Egor (Klimanov) Afanasev, Vasilii Shelgunov, and Nil Vasiliev.[41] While a greater emphasis than ever before was placed on workers, the organization remained primarily composed of intellectuals.

Tochisskii drew up the positions, principles, duties and the organizational structure for the circle. In fall 1886 during the first full meeting, the circle approved Tochisskii's recommendations. The central cadre of the Association was divided into two parts-- a workers' section and an intellectual one.[42] To further ensure security from arrests, only a small group of active members, the cadre, learned the composition of the organization. The maintenance of security was critical because all revolutionary groups in Russia faced an ever present police surveillance of dissident intellectuals. Therefore, Tochisskii thought it was imperative that only a very small number of members would know the identity of other members, the location of the group's library, and the ties the group had with other groups in factories. All people outside

---

[41]Breitfus, "Tochisskii," p. 337.
[42]Breitfus, "Tochisskii," p. 331.

this central cadre, who were called sympathizers, collected money for the purchase of books for the library and for the mutual aid fund from other workers and students. In addition, the sympathizers paid twenty-five kopeks a month dues.[43] The central cadre distributed the various responsibilities to each other, and to elect the meeting's *starosta* or elder. Initially, the *starosta* was Tochisskii himself. His duties were to call and to preside over the meetings, to collect the membership dues, to keep the group's regulations and accounts, to prepare each meeting's agenda, and to notify all the members of the time and place for meetings.[44] The members elected the association's librarian and the treasurer of the mutual aid fund. Meetings of the society were held regularly once a month. To tighten security even further, the meetings occurred in different flats or rooms of the members. Thus, the Tochisskii group maintained a characteristic of Russian dissident groups in the late nineteenth century. Its organizational structure was extremely tightly knit and highly centralized. This

---

[43] R.A. Kazakevich, *Sotsial-demokraticheskie organizatsii Peterburga kontsa 80-kh--nachala 90-kh gg.* (Leningrad, 1960), p. 41.

[44] Nevskii, "K istorii," p. 223.

structure had the positive effect of lessening the dangers of police discovery and arrest. At the same time, this structure tended to isolate the members from the rest of society.

During meetings, the group discussed the entry of new members into the Association and also the financial condition of the organization. The group distributed money to purchase new books and journals for the library, and allocated various duties to each member. Again, for security purposes, each member had a pseudonym. For example, Tochisskii was called "Sentiabr." His sister Maria had two pseudonyms: "Aproska" and "Dochka." Dmitrii Lazarev was simply called "Momo."[45] At the same time the workers' section of the Association was separate but parallel. For example, each worker had a pseudonym. The members of the group's intellectual section never knew the real names of the workers. The leadership carefully guarded the workers' section of the organization, even preventing the intelligentsia and the workers from ever meeting together as one group. Tochisskii realized that the student intelligentsia was much more likely to be

---

[45] Kazakevich, Sotsial-demokraticheskie organizatsii, p. 43.

arrested than workers' members, who melt more easily into the general population. By keeping the two groups separate, he sought to prevent the workers from possible arrest and police surveillance. That measure, just like his other regulations, certainly strengthened the security of the group. As an illustration of security methods, each member of the Association would only be able to communicate personally with two other members outside of meetings. One member could only pass on instructions to one other. Tochisskii's circle was very careful in its recruitment of new members. Only close acquaintances of current members would be considered, and then, only after a number of preparatory meetings during which the candidate's reliability was evaluated.[46]

Rapidly, Tochissii's group established ties throughout St. Petersburg. For example, in the Nevskii Gates area, they had connections in the Aleksandrov factory, the Obukhov factory, the Vargunin factory, and the Kartochnaia factory. On Vasilyevskii Island, an active and highly skilled worker, I.I. Timofeev conducted propaganda on behalf of the group at the large

---

[46]Nevskii, Ocherki, p. 92.

Baltiiskii Armaments plant. Several women, who were sympathetic to the group, were active at the Laferm Tobacco factory, an industry which largely employed women. Tochisskii and Lazarev both worked at the Berda factory. Egor (Klimanov) Afanasev propagandized at his place of work, the Ekspedtsii Paper Mill Factory. Nil Vasiliev propagandized at the Arsenal. Tochisskii was the principal orator, propagandist, and organizer of the circle. Next to him, Lazarev was the most active.[47] Thus, one or two of the group's members propagandized a much larger group of workers at the member's place of employment. One of the members' main purposes was to get acquainted with as many workers as possible, and to organize workers' circles. These circles met at the flats of workers and were mainly for self-education. When workers were sufficiently educated and politicized in the eyes of the circle, then they would read theoretical tracts including those of Marx and Engels.[48] Circle members then noted which workers were most gifted. Then, they were, when possible, induced to become propagandists for

---

[47] Kazakevich, <u>Sotsial-demokraticheskie organizatsii</u>, p. 45.

[48] Breitfus, "Tochisskii," p. 340.

their fellow workers. In this way, for example, Leonid Breitfus, who subsequently wrote a worker's memoir of the period, became acquainted with I.I. Timofeev. Timofeev was placed in charge of several hundred of the group's library books, and later became one of the founders of the Central Workers' Circle. Members of the organization distributed among the workers books from the library they had created. Maria Tochisskaia was placed in charge of the intellectual's section of the library. From Tochisskaia's and from Timofeev's sections, books were readily distributed to the most advanced workers. Often the workers read and discussed their books or journals during their meetings. Sometimes an intellectual attended to explain the more difficult books. Not only were educational and propaganda activities conducted among women workers, but also, quite significantly, among some units in the army. For example, books and brochures were given by Ivan Shalevskii to troops of the Novorossiisk regiment billeted at the Okhtinskii gunpowder works.[49] Unlike the Blagoev circle, the Tochisskii group never was able to obtain a printing press to

---

[49] E. Korolchuk and E. Sokolova (eds.), **Khronika revoliutsionnogo rabochego dvizheniia v Peterburge**, Vol. I, (Leningrad, 1940), p. 135.

print their own brochures and leaflets. They were forced to rely on their ideological partners, the Populists, to print all their materials for them. Both Social Democratic and Populist materials of a legal and an illegal nature were distributed.

Membership dues were used not only to purchase books, but to establish a mutual aid fund. The purpose of the fund was to help workers who were out on strike, or who were arrested and held in prison, or to aid exiles. Yet the amount of money in the fund was too small to do much good to fulfill the purposes of the fund.[50] Egor Afanasev, a highly qualified blacksmith, was placed in charge. The rest of the dues was used to acquire books, journals, brochures, and newspapers. There were two distinct parts of the Tochisskii group's library--one for legal books and one for illegal books. The latter ones, again for security purposes, were isolated in their own library. Andrei Breitfus succeeded Maria Tochisskaia as director of the illegal section. Tochisskii insisted that the selection of books be geared to the lower educational level of the workers.[51] Books should serve the needs of the basic

---

[50]Nevskii, Ocherki, p. 95.

[51]Kazakevich, Sotsial-demokraticheskie organizatsii, p. 45.

readers, rather than the highly educated intellectuals. Timofeev and other workers kept most of the legal books. Timofeev accumulated at his apartment a collection of nearly seven hundred volumes.[52] The size of that collection is quite remarkable for a worker with little formal education and who had a twelve hour a day job. That collection included works of classic and contemporary literature, economics, history along with journals and newspapers such as Russkaia Mysl, Severnyi Vestnik, Russkoe Bogatsvo, Russkie Vedomosti and Moskovskie Vedomosti. Each book had a number. Unfortunately, the catalogue of books was never preserved. In 1888 it was destroyed while the police conducted a search.[53] The illegal collection was subdivided into two parts. One part consisted of pamphlets and brochures to be read and kept in different workers' flats and then returned after being read. The collection of illegal books, such as works by Marx and Plekhanov, were kept and were not to leave Breitfus' apartment.

---

[52] K. Norinskii, "Moi vospominaniia," Ot gruppy Blagoeva, p. 10.

[53] N.L. Sergievskii, "K voprosy o vozraste Leningradskoi organizatsii VKP," Krasnaia letopis', 1930, no. 2, p. 15.

The ideology of Tochisskii's group was a confused amalgam of Populism and Social Democracy. To illustrate that point, numerous Narodnaia Volia tracts were kept as well as the Marxist ones. Tochisskii wanted to maintain solely Marxist works. Nevertheless, on this point, he was overruled by the membership of the Circle, which insisted the group not be directed by any specific ideology to the exclusion of another.[54]

The Tochisskii circle was primarily concerned with the education of workers so that they could form a cadre of highly educated and politicized workers. It never formed a political program. Had the group attempted such a program, they would have floundered on disagreements between Populists and Social Democrats. They most likely decided for that reason not to devise a program. The group viewed themselves solely as teachers and as guides for the working class, not as leaders of the workers. The group believed workers should lead other workers.[55] The Tochisskii circle never engaged in political activities, or led strikes. The group was geared only to the most receptive members of the working class, the workers' elite. Thus, while the number of

---

[54]Breitfus, "Tochisskii," p. 330.

[55]Ibid., p. 326.

workers influenced by Tochisskii's circle was very small, those workers formed the nucleus of the "workers' intelligentsia" which soon emerged as an independent and influential force.

Tochisskii's circle existed up to the end of 1888. Yet in March 1888 arrests began. The reasons for the collapse of the group were: 1) arrests of Narodniki or Populists led police to the Tochisskii group; 2) the police tracked down Tochisskii and other key members. The tsarist government feared the Populists more than the Marxists. After all, a Populist organization, Narodnaia Volia, successfully assassinated Tsar Alexander II in 1881. Another attempt on the life of a tsar, Alexander III, had been made just the previous year. The government was not really certain whether or not Narodnaia Volia was really dead, or was still powerful. Therefore, the police kept particular surveillance over all Populist groups. The members of Tochisskii's group became aware of police surveillance which foreshadowed their imminent arrest. For that reason, they sought to preserve the library. In that task they were largely successful. Most of the library survived the destruction of the organization. Tochisskii, Lazarev and Breitfus were the first to be arrested. Tochisskii and Lazarev were exiled to

Zhitomir, while Breitfus was exiled to Tver.[56] The police continued to follow other members. Soon more arrests followed. Yet, Tochisskii's concern with the security of the worker's section proved successful. The workers' network, numbering four to six circles, escaped detection, for the most part, and continued its operations. These groups eventually formed the Central Workers' Circle within a year.

Another Polish student, Gabriel Rodziewicz (Gavril Rodzevich), who attended the St. Petersburg Technical Institute, formed a circle in 1887.[57] This circle was dominated by Poles, who formed two-thirds of the membership and who taught numerous techniques of Social Democratic propaganda to the Russians. St. Petersburg contained many Poles in both the universities and in the factories. Poland industrialized sooner than Russia, and Poles organized sooner than the Russians in trade unions and had organized a Social Democratic party about a generation earlier than the Russian party, in 1879. Both successes and failures in trade union organizing were experienced by Polish activists--both

---

[56]Korolchuk and Sokolova, *Khronika*, p. 144.
[57]Golubev, "Stranichka," p. 108.

workers and intellectuals. They were more than willing to offer their experiences to the Russians. Interaction between Poles and Russians was frequent.[58] The Rodzevich Circle met secretly to discuss socialist literature. Not only did it function as a self-education group, but it also established contacts within St. Petersburg with factory workers, first Poles and then Russians. The circle functioned until 1889 when most of its members entered the Brusnev Circle.[59] Rodzevich's Circle was illustrative that Poles exerted a powerful and direct influence on the Russian Social Democratic and labor movements.

The year 1887 was a disastrous year for intellectual dissidents in Russia. Aleksandr Ulianov's Populist group, plotting to assassinate the Tsar, was discovered. Four conspirators, including Ulianov, were hanged. Arrests destroyed Tochisskii's circle. Students could not trust one another. It seemed that as soon as a circle was formed, a student informer would cause the arrest of its members. Populism seemed to go nowhere. The mood among students was depression.

---

[58] L. Vasil'evskii, "Pol'skaia s.d. partiia 'Proletariat' 1882-1886," Byloe, no. 4, 1906, pp. 193-207.

[59] Brusnev, "Vozniknovenie," p. 18.

It was very dangerous for anyone to read illegal literature. The state appeared all powerful to those students. As a result, student dissident activities declined. Soon, though, by 1888 student circles started to reappear. However, this time, they were much more concerned with self-education and were solely student concerns.[60] Many students were just too frightened to have contacts with factory workers. Nevertheless, a relatively small number of students, about forty to fifty, became actively involved in circles.[61] Of that small number, only a relatively few people were concerned with propagandizing workers. Circles were scattered throughout St. Petersburg's five higher educational institutions. Most, however, were associated with two places--the University and the Technical Institute. Unlike the University, whose members were mostly from the upper and middle classes (landowners, professionals, high government officials), the Technical Institute had students from the lower middle class and non-Russians such as Ukrainians and Poles. As their backgrounds were closer to workers, the students at the Technical Institute carried on much

---

[60] Ibid., p. 28.

[61] Bartenev, "Vospominaniia," p. 170.

more effective propaganda than did students at the University.

In 1885, Mikhail Ivanov Brusnev arrived from Stavropol to enter the St. Petersburg Technical Institute.[62] During his first two years, Brusnev was politically inactive but aware of the student circles at the Institute. He also was sympathetic toward Populism.[63] By 1887, Brusnev formed a self-education circle where the members informally read and discussed illegal books and pamphlets. Soon, leaders of the various circles, including Brusnev's, discussed the need to unify and better organize the disparate student circles throughout St. Petersburg. By March 1888, at a meeting in the flat of V.N. Ivanov, a Technical Institute student, Rodziewicz (Rodzevich) formally proposed that all the student circles merge into one organization.[64] Discussions ensued at that meeting and at subsequent meetings. Students argued whether the orientation of the group should be Social Democratic or Populist. One particular point of controversy was

---

[62] Sviatlovskii, "Na zare," p. 144.

[63] Brusnev, "Vozniknovenie," pp. 26-28.

[64] A.M. Orekhov, Pervye marksisty v Rossii, Peterburgskii 'Rabochii Soiuz', 1882-1893 gg. (Moscow, 1979), p. 27.

whether or not they should support terrorism. Ultimately, the group which attended the meetings rejected terrorism because they believed it would be unproductive and would only strengthen the government.[65] Rather than a small tight-knit monolithic organization, the students decided that the proposed central organization would be a broad coalition of student radicals holding differing views, both ideologically and tactically. Furthermore, in the course of meetings, they also decided that the proposed group should be primarily concerned with student issues. Propaganda work among the workers was secondary.[66] Brusnev conceded that only a minority of the students were able to work with the workers. Most were either unprepared or unwilling.[67] By the beginning of 1889, they agreed to form a central organization, which they logically called the "Central Student Circle."

Thus, by the late 1880's, in St. Petersburg there were two parallel processes going on simultaneously. Student circles consolidated into an intellectual center which they called the "Central Student Circle." At

---

[65] Bartenev, "Vospominaniia," p. 172.

[66] *Ibid.*, p. 173.

[67] Brusnev, "Vozniknovenie," p. 19.

the same time, workers' circles became scattered in factories. Throughout the city, workers, on their own initiative and direction, formed their own central organization, the "Central Workers' Circle." While the Central Student Circle had representatives from all five educational institutions in the city, it mainly was composed of students from three schools: The Technical Institute, the University, and the School of Forestry. From the Technical Institute, there were five poles (B. Lelewel, W. Cywiński, G. Pietrowski, Ch. Bankowski, and G. Kosinski) and four Russians (V.N. Ivanov, M.I. Brusnev, and the brothers L.B. and G.B. Krasin). From the University there were three Russians (V.S. Golubev, D.V. Stranden, and V.V. Sviatlovskii) and one Pole, G. Rodziewicz (Rodzevich). From the School of Forestry there was only one representative, N. Sivokinin. Reflecting the liberal arts and academic nature of their education, the University members showed a far better grounding in political theory, mostly Marxism. Over the next decade or two, the University supplied many of Russia's early Marxist theoreticians. Again reflecting their educational curriculum, the members from the Technical Institute were not as concerned with theory, but with more practical or daily concerns. The Institute members conducted far more agitation and propaganda among the workers than did the people from the University. Finally, the representative from the Forestry School was not a Social Democrat at all, but a Populist or Narodnik.[68] Thus, by the end of the decade, organized but clandestine activity by the students on behalf of themselves and workers resumed in St. Petersburg.

Formation of the Central Workers' Circle

While workers lived throughout St. Petersburg, one of the major concentrations was in the northern part of the city. One area, the Nevskii Gates played a major role in the history of St. Petersburg's labor movement. Many of the city's huge factories such as the Nevskii (formerly the Semiannikov) shipyards, the Aleksandrov metal works, the Obukhov metal works, and the Palia and Maksvelia candle factories were located there. Each had thousands of people employed within its walls. In the Nevskii Gates, "the streets were muddy and in bad condition. Housing was dense, often averaging six to

---

[68]Nevskii, Ocherki, p. 88.

ten people per room.[69] The population was young with a majority of the area's population under thirty, predominantly male and unmarried. The Nevskii Gates was filled with traktirs (taverns), beer bars, churches, but had few cultural places. For the area's estimated population of 60,000, there were all of two run-down theaters.[70] In its crowded streets occurred many fights, especially after payday when workers had money to buy vodka and beer and get drunk. Workers were beaten and even murdered. Yet the police on the whole did little to preserve law and order. Most workers, regardless of their economic position, hated the police.[71]

Located next to the Nevskii Gates region was Narva Gates area, another huge workers' region. From early morning it resounded with factory whistles calling its inhabitants to work. The center of this section was the Putilov metal works which had over 13,000 employees. "In the evening, masses of people filled the streets. Traders pressed through the crowds selling

---

[69] Sanktpeterburg po perepisi 10 dekabria 1869 goda, pp. 74-75.

[70] F. Kon', Iz istorii moego byt'ia (Khar'kov, 1924), p. 79.

[71] Ibid., p. 80.

cheap icons, cloth or food items. These workers' raions (regions) seemed like one organism, filled with thousands of noises of voices and steps."[72] Many potential workers entered the city through these gates and the surrounding regions. Then they immediately confronted St. Petersburg's hugeness and noise, along with its masses of people. A.M. Buiko, a worker at the Putilov factory, exclaimed: "In my native village, I knew everyone. In the capital, I saw crowds of unknown and indifferent people who do not talk to each other, who know only their own affairs, and who hurry everywhere."[73] Buiko was hardly unique in feeling isolated and alienated in this huge, noisy, dirty, drunken and uncultured environment. Many workers, such as Buiko, searched desperately for some way to escape this drab, unfeeling emptiness, and to find some companionship of like-minded people.

There were several vehicles for escape, and most of them depended on education. Some workers enrolled in factory or artisan schools. Other workers went to evening or Sunday schools run by philanthropic

---

[72] A.M. Buiko, "Put' rabochego, zapiski starogo bol'-shevika," Staryi bol'shevik, 1934, no. 6, p. 10.

[73] Buiko, Put' rabochego, p. 11.

associations. At these schools, workers not only learned a trade but also the rudiments of reading and writing. Once they acquired this basic knowledge, many tried to expand it by enrolling in one of the city's libraries, by visiting the city's reading rooms, by attending public lectures, or by reading newspapers such as the liberal Russkie Vedomosti or Severnyi Vestnik. These workers often looked at the foreign sections of these newspapers for information about workers' movements in the West.[74] Thus through these methods, these workers, who formed the "workers' intelligentsia," exhibited a definite curiosity about the world outside their small raions, their city and even their country. From facilities such as schools, libraries, public lectures, and reading rooms, workers met and then organized circles to further their self-education and to find some companionship.

Some of these workers were quite remarkable. T.T. Samokhin was a pattern maker at a copper factory. While still quite young, he became interested in the workers' question. Samokhin read all the legal books on the subject of workers' rights that could be found in St.

---

[74] S.I. Mitskevich, Na zare rabochego dvizheniia (Moscow, 1924), p. 10.

Petersburg's libraries. Then, he studied Esperanto and French so that he could correspond with foreign workers.[75] Soon, he formed a successful circle consisting of pattern workers. The members of the circle mastered the laws and regulations governing workers' hours and pay. Fedor Poliakov, a young weaver, worked at the chemical section of the Ramenskoi factory. He borrowed books from the factory doctor, which enabled him to learn some medicine, natural science, and philosophy. Poliakov even learned basic Latin, necessary then for medicine.[76] D.I. Konstantinov, a blacksmith at the Brest railway plant, had been active since the early 1870's. He led discussions among his fellow workers. Finally, S.I. Prokofiev, a very intelligent lathe operator, worked at the Veizeldt factory. He read many books and newspapers. He even learned English. Eventually, he traveled to England, illustrating that some of these members of the "workers' intelligentsia" managed to successfully escape their stultifying environment.[77] All these workers became quite educated,

---

[76] Mitskevich, Na zare, p. 17.
[77] Ibid., p. 24.
[78] Ibid., p. 24.

often learned foreign languages, and became very interested in the West.

These very intelligent, educated, cultured workers met their fellow workers in their factories. Slowly and carefully, they discovered the most sympathetic and intelligent ones. Once a friendship had been established, these workers then offered newspapers with interesting articles, or even some books. Using such methods, they were able to test the basis of their previous ideas about each person.[78] Once a worker had established ties with several workers, he then organized them into an informal group or circle. Workers' circles were the principal institutional expression for the emergence of the "workers' intelligentsia." Each circle was quite small, numbering six to eight workers. Each was established spontaneously by a worker with no assistance by any intellectuals. The circles were designed to improve the members' own educational background, and to provide a social alternative to the dreary <u>traktirs</u> and beer bars. By the end of the 1880's, circles had spread throughout the city with an estimated

---

[78] K.M. Takhtarev (Peterburzhets), <u>Ocherk peterburgskogo rabochego dvizheniia 90-kh godov</u> (London, 1902), p. 15.

several hundred workers belonging to them.[79] Members of these circles included joiners, blacksmiths, printers, lithographers, artisans, iron workers, weavers and other skilled occupations. Some workers accepted membership into circles very readily. Many, however, left the circles to return to the brawling bars of the fellow workers. Usually workers' circles met secretly once a week in a member's room or flat. In good weather, they often gathered in meadows or parks. Usually, one worker led the group by reading a section of a book, a journal article, or a part of the daily newspaper. Then he conducted a discussion about the issues raised in that book or article. Sometimes the discussion became quite intense.[80] Thus, circles were spontaneous and generally nonpolitical. Basically they were both an educational activity and a social diversion, and only consisted of a tiny percentage of the total industrial working class in St. Petersburg.

Once circles were established, the members of one circles set various qualifications for potential new members. For example, members had to be at least twenty years old. Youthful workers were often regarded

---

[79] Sviatlovskii, "Na zare," p. 150.
[80] Takhtarev, Ocherk, p. 17.

by their fellow workers as often still immature and consequently not very cautious. They might tell their friends about their circle which could then lead to police surveillance. Secondly, before a candidate could become a full member, he had to wait at least two years. This intervening time allowed the members of the circle to carefully scrutinize a candidate's motivations for joining as well as a candidate's character. They did not want an impulsive member, or a member who might turn out to be a police agent.[81] These were elitist groups of workers, who despite their often lively discussions on issues, were generally of like-minded character with similar goals for the group. Throughout the 1880's workers' circles were tiny groups serving their own particular advancement--educationally, culturally, and socially--rather than the advancement of the Russian working class as a whole.

The main purpose for workers' circles was self-education so that they could advance themselves economically and culturally. The main vehicle for self-education was through reading and the subsequent discussion of books. Some workers thought about

---

[81] F. Kon', *Istoriia revoliutsionnogo dvizheniia v Rossii*, Vol. I (Khar'kov, 1929), p. 95.

politics, but even these workers usually regarded politics as "a dream because life pushed us toward more practical levels such as hours of work, wage increases and better living conditions."[82] Despite his meager wages, Ivan Krutov was so devoted to his circle that he rented a separate room for the circle to meet. His family, consisting of his wife and four children, lived in another room. Krutov was so concerned over security that circle members during meetings had to walk barefoot and talk softly.[83] The circles gathered over cups of hot tea and plates of zakuski (hors d'oeuvres). Often they got some vodka to satisfy any potential police observers that their circles were innocuous. Egor Afanasev, a very educated and skilled blacksmith, led a circle of seven men. A young student, V.V. Sviatlovskii, described a typical meeting of that circle. Soon after his arrival, a worker, Aniushkevich, began a lecture on chemistry. To the author's astonishment, everyone present listened for an hour and a half with "considerable attention." At the end of that lecture, a discussion covering a wide range of subjects ensued for the rest of the evening. A couple of times

---

[82]Fisher, V Rossii, p. 8.

[83]V.B. Bartenev, "Vospominaniia," p. 173.

Sviatlovskii tried to steer the conversation to politics. Right away the workers returned to discussions on chemistry, geography, and history. Later Sviatlovskii prepared a lecture on geology, a very nonpolitical field, so that he "could then draw closer to the workers."[84]

Workers' circles read works by Russian Populist writers such as N.G. Chernyshevskii, N.A. Dobroliubov, M.E. Saltykov-Shchedrin, D.I. Pisarev, N.V. Shelgunov, and N. Mikhailovskii. Sometimes they read foreign authors such as Charles Dickens, Emile Zola, and Edward Bellamy. Their works enlightened Russian workers on Western workers' conditions. Selections from Russian journals such as <u>Sovremmenik</u>, <u>Russkoe Slovo</u>, and <u>Otechestvennye Zapiski</u> were read and discussed. In some circles reports about the French Revolution or the Paris Commune were read. These often gave the radical intellectuals present the opportunity to raise issues and questions which affected the working class. Iulii Martov, the future leader of the Mensheviks, conceded the great importance of books for the workers he dealt with in Vilnius. Martov declared, "For all these poor workers, our circles opened new worlds of inner

---

[84]Sviatlovskii, "Na zare," p. 158.

experiences and intellectual culture."[85] Martov conceded that education was the alpha and the omega of the workers' movement.

Members of the workers' elite were quite interested in descriptions of their own working and living conditions. During the 1880's there were a number of reports published by factory inspectors which gave illustrations of conditions inside Russian factories. The best known was by Dr. F.F. Erisman.[86] Those reports gave the leaders of workers' circles the opportunity to discuss low wages and the long work day, along with the poor hygiene of Russian factories. Yet, even in these discussions, workers demanded factual descriptions rather than political propaganda. Sometimes Polish brochures published in Western Europe were read and then discussed. Some examples of these titles

---

[85] Iu. Martov, *Zapiski Sotsial-demokrata* (Berlin, 1922), p. 127.

[86] Dr. F.F. Erisman was a leading Russian hygienist during the last half of the nineteenth century. He began the development of hygiene for workers' residences and for their factories. His sanitary studies created the Russian school of public health. Erisman examined the very poorest segments of St. Petersburg's population. The workers read his articles published in the journal of public health, the *Arkhiv sudebnoi meditsiny i obshchestvennoi gigieny*.

were "About Competition," "The Worker's Day," and "What each worker must know and understand." Sometimes simplified versions of works by Karl Marx and Ferdinand Lassalle were read and discussed as to how they could be applied to Russian life. While intellectuals led many of those discussions, workers were reluctant about intellectuals trying to maintain a major role in their circles. They insisted that the members of the workers' circles be self-reliant and that they control their own circles. Finally, they realized that there was a direct connection between intellectuals' activities and police surveillance. S.I. Prokofiev, a leader of workers' circles, conceded that he avoided contacts with intellectuals because he feared inevitable arrest.[87]

During the 1880's, not all circles were composed of highly skilled workers. In St. Petersburg there were a few circles of unskilled workers. Often their meetings began by reading psalms.[88] Religion was still a major part of the lives of all Russian workers except some of the members of the "workers' intelligentsia." Intellectuals dominated those circles much more than the

---

[87] S.I. Prokof'ev, Iz perezhitogo (Moscow, 1922), p. 110.
[88] Ibid., p. 112.

circles composed of the workers' elite. Initially they taught its members selections from the Bible, prayers, and psalms. Only very gradually, in fact, imperceptibly, did these circles move on to nonreligious subjects.

Other circles were conducted by established philanthropic professionals. For example, every Sunday afternoon, Doctor M.I. Pokrovskaia, a woman physician and author of several articles on St. Petersburg's women workers, conducted a large circle of very young, unskilled, poor women. The goals of this circle were multipurpose. The women wanted to learn the basics of reading, writing, and arithmetic, just like the "workers' intelligentsia." The women showed a great desire for learning. One girl commented:

> All day I am in the factory sewing from morning to night. I come home completely exhausted. My father is always drunk, while my mother seems continually sick. Only here (at these assemblies) can I study.[89]

For these women the Sunday assemblies represented an escape from an otherwise very dreary life. The women were recruited for these circles in various ways.

---

[89] Dr. M.I. Pokrovskaia, "Peterburgskie voskresnye sobraniia dlia rabotnitsy," *Mir bozhii*, March 1899, p. 1.

Sometimes the employer provided the incentive. One girl, Sasha, a sixteen year old servant, said her employer, a lawyer, read about the assemblies in the newspaper. Then he urged that she should attend the circle to improve herself. Not only did they learn the basics of education, but they also learned sewing and embroidering. The group had a small library containing novels by Mikhail Lermontov, Nikolai Gogol, and Ivan Turgenev. It also had books on hygiene and on both the physical and natural sciences. Dr. Pokrovskaia mentioned how as time went on more and more girls became interested in serious books. In fact, several women spent their whole time on Sundays reading.[90] The library also contained several illustrated journals.

The subject matter in these circles was even less political than in the circles the workers operated themselves. The circle was established by a philanthrophic group, the "Association for the Care of Young Girls in St. Petersburg." The Association's goals were twofold. First, it was to preserve young girls, primarily of the working class, from "harmful actions." Second, the meetings were to assist in the girls' moral development

---

[90]Pokrovskaia, "Peterburgskie voskresnye," p. 7.

and attitude. Many people in St. Petersburg wanted to reverse an increase in teenage pregnancy and prostitution among young girls. The streets were not a good moral environment for young working girls. Third, the group would train the girls to become self-reliant, to stand on their own feet, and to give them a sense of self-esteem.[91] These goals would not only be accomplished by reading, but by singing, playing games, and by dancing. No men were allowed because their attendance might divert the assembly's members. Unlike workers' circles, these circles were paternalistic, almost in the sense of a modern day summer camp with its relationship of camper and counselor. All of the girls' time was regulated. Instead of being encouraged as in workers' circles, arguments were not allowed. These assemblies were a diverse group of girls including cigarette factory workers, paper mill operators, dress makers, maids and a few cooks. These circles provided a needed release from the tension and depression found in their homes and factories. Along with reading and playing games, physical exercise was also stressed. Just like the workers' circles, this group had a self-help treasury providing, at least, a little money to members who became

---

[91] Ibid., p. 4.

unemployed or ill. The women participated in the operation of the treasury. That was to teach them thrift. Religion played a role at these Sunday gatherings. Each room had icons in the corner. During the afternoon, a priest conducted a service and then delivered a sermon. But these activities were not required of the women. Dr. Pokrovskaia conceded that not all present wanted to hear the priest.[92]

An important part of these Sunday Assemblies was social interaction. Women passed the time drinking tea, eating bread and sausage, and often just talking to each other. At 5 p.m., most of the girls gathered in the largest room for public readings. Dr. Pokrovskaia commented that public readings were very common among young workers.[93] This was quite logical as most workers had difficulty reading. Public readings were a major aspect in workers' circles as well. After the public readings, the women danced for a while as both physical exercise and social interaction. After dancing, the women rested by drinking water or by singing mostly coarse factory songs. Sometimes, the director read

---

[92] Pokrovskaia, "Petersburgskie voskresnye," p. 10.
[93] Ibid., p. 4.

comedies to the workers. Finally, around 9 p.m. the weekly assembly ended.

There were many differences between these Sunday assemblies and workers' circles: The former were paternalistically run and controlled by doctors and city employees. The assemblies were completely apolitical, and contained a great deal of physical exercise. A major purpose focused on moral, as well as intellectual development. They had at least government toleration, if not approval. Yet there were several striking similarities! For both groups, workers attended to improve themselves, culturally and educationally. They wanted to gain a sense of self-esteem. Just like the male workers in circles, these women wanted to escape a cold, alienating and hostile environment. These circles were a release for both groups of workers. Reading and public lectures were central features in both groups. These Sunday assemblies were certainly less political than the workers' circles, but the end goal, the desire to learn, remained the same. Therefore, these circles should be included, along with the circles run by workers, because both types contributed to the development of an educated and skilled working class.

Yet, all these circles faced an almost staggering set of problems. First, they faced a shortage of funds. Money was needed to purchase books. Nikolai Bogdanov, a railway worker and labor leader, noted that with their meager sums of money, members of circles went to second-hand book markets in the city. Yet there was never enough money to satisfy their demand or need for books.[94] The workers always had a shortage of reading matter. Books were always circulated from person to person. Very often, workers clipped articles from newspapers. Then they pasted them in books and circulated them.[95] Self-help treasuries were viewed by the members as critical to aid each other in times of illness or unemployment. Yet, here too, the funds were never enough. As an illustration of the importance of these activities, workers' circles generally each had a treasurer and a librarian. To purchase books and to supplement the mutual aid fund, money was obtained by several methods. Each circle member had to contribute a membership fee varying from twenty-five to fifty kopeks a month. Friends or sympathizers from the

---

[94] M. Ol'minskii, "O vospominaniiakh N.D. Bogdanova," Ot gruppy Blagoeva, p. 42.

[95] Prokof'ev, Iz perezhitogo, p. 110.

intelligentsia gave some money. Yet many of the intelligentsia were students living on a subsistence level. A few more affluent and concerned residents of St. Petersburg did donate money. Some of the girls formed the Sunday Assembly and then raised funds by selling cookies or their embroidery products.[96] Yet, again, the sums did not reach nearly enough the demand for books or for the treasury.

Another obvious problem was that members of circles, regardless of their political orientation or lack of orientation, faced the opposition of the government. Until the organization of police unions in the early 1900's, the so-called Zubatov unions, no governmental agencies ever favored the organization of workers into groups to better themselves.[97] They regarded all

---

[96] Pokrovskaia, "Peterburgskie voskresnye," p. 7.

[97] Zubatov unions were named after their initiator, Sergei Zubatov. Zubatov was a colonel in the tsarist secret police in Moscow from 1896 to 1902. Zubatov believed that to prevent further infiltration of the workers by revolutionaries, the government should allow them to express their economic demands. This would be accomplished by the promulgation of legal and pro-government workers' organization, all under the control of the secret police. They attracted a large portion of Moscow's working class. Their very success led to their demise. In 1902, Zubatov was transferred, and then dismissed and exiled. During the February Revolution, fearing that he would be tried by the new Provisional Government, Zubatov shot himself. For further information, see Jeremiah Schneiderman, Sergei Zubatov and Revolutionary Marxism (Ithaca, 1976).

groups as potentially subversive. For example, the government did all it could to discourage the Sunday Assemblies. They planted informers in workers' circles. All of them faced the threat of police surveillance, which could at any time, destroy one or more of the circles.

Another problem that members of the workers' circles faced was where to meet. While the workers' elite was better paid than the rest of the working class, they still lived in very cramped quarters. It was quite common for a family of four to be crowded into one room. That room was needed for cooking, eating, and sleeping. A worker needed a particularly understanding wife and family before they allowed him to take over their room for several hours a week. If the family was accommodating, the worker risked getting his family implicated in his illegal activities. Therefore, usually a worker carefully thought out and weighed the various factors before he allowed his room to be used as a meeting site. Often that problem was alleviated by having the meeting sites rotated from member to member so that everyone shared the responsibility. Thus the responsibility fell on a particular family only once a month or even less. Rarely could a worker or the circle itself afford to rent a room to be used solely for meetings. I.V. Krutov was very much the exception.[98] Thus, meeting sites proved a major obstacle for workers attempting to form circles.

Another critical problem for circles was a basic lack of good teachers for the circle. While most of the workers involved in circles had a great desire to increase their learning, most did not possess the necessary knowledge to convey it to others. They were excellent learners, but not good teachers. Despite the risks involved, that fact forced many workers' circles to search for potential teachers out of the intelligentsia. They were reluctant to have assistance from the intelligentsia because that gave radical students a role and power over the workers they otherwise would not have had. Members of the intelligentsia knew they were in great demand. Sometimes they took advantage of that situation to make demands such as the type of reading matter, or the direction of discussions at circle meetings. As a result, in most cases, ties between the intelligentsia and workers were very limited and were only of a purely educational type.[99] Virtually all

---

[98] Bartenev, "Vospominaniia," p. 170.

[99] M.N. Liadov, Istoriia Rossiiskoi Sotsialdemokraticheskoi Rabochei Partii (St. Petersburg, 1906), p. 14.

circles had some objections to close collaboration with intellectuals. They carefully guarded their organizational independence and control. Despite the great need for teachers, a few workers' circles, known by other workers as dikie (shy or unsociable), did not allow any intellectuals to come near their groups.[100]

By the late 1880's the circle movement had made great progress. There were about twenty circles organized and led by workers. The circles were located in the Nevskii and Narvskii Gates regions in the southern part of the city, on Vasilyevskii Island on the Vyborg side on the northeast section, and in the central part of the city. Many of the city's major factories such as the Obukhov, Baltiiskii, Putilov, Kartochnaia, Voronin, the State Paper Mill, and the Galernoi Tobacco plant, all had at least one circle operating within their walls. The most significant circles were the following: 1) V.F. Klopov's circle, composed of workers from the Obukhov works. Its student teacher was B.F. Lelewel, a Polish student at the Technical Institute. 2) I.I. Timofeev's circle, composed of workers from the Baltiiskii factory. Its

---

[100]Takhtarev, Rabochee dvizhenie, pp. 45-46.

members were I.A. Fomin, I. Egorov, M. and P. Iakovlev, I. Belgaev, and P. Kaizo. It began in 1887, and quickly formed ties with the intelligentsia, specficially members from the predominantly Polish Rodzevich circle of which Lelewel was a member. 3) I.V. Krutov's circle, which was also composed of workers from the Baltiiskii metal works. For a labor activist, he was rather old (around forty), and a former peasant from Vologoda province who became a lathe operator.[101] Its student teacher was P.A. Golubev, a Russian who was also a member of the Rodzevich circle. 4) N.D. Bogdanov's circle, composed of workers at the Warsaw Railway plant. His circle formed in 1886 and subsequently met in the Obnorskii Canal area. Bogdanov, an excellent orator with a good education and a library, had little need for intellectual assistance. Only after two years of his circle's existence did Bogdanov agree to an intellectual, V. Pereverzin, even attending the meetings. He only allowed that because Pereverzin was a moderate and quiet person who would not interfere in Bogdanov's circle activities.[102] 5) G.A. Mefodiev's circle named after another labor activist at the Warsaw

---

[101]Bartenev, "Vospominaniia," p. 170.
[102]Nevskii, Ocherki, p. 273.

Railway Plant. Mefodiev, pseudonymed "Gamia," was a very active and popular orator. His circle met on Sivkovsk Lane in the central part of St. Petersburg. The intellectual teacher for his group was G. Pietrowski, another Polish student at the Technical Institute who was also a member of the Rodzevich Circle. 6) The last major circle was the Shelgunov-Afanasev circle. This circle had two outstanding labor leaders, V.A. Shelgunov and E.A. Afanasev.

Vasilii Andreevich Shelgunov, born in 1867 of peasant parents near Pskov, became one of the outstanding leaders of the workers' elite. At the age of nine Shelgunov went to St. Petersburg to seek work. He was very eager for an education and frequented evening classes, where he received a decent general education. At the age of thirteen Shelgunov worked at a bookbindery, where he would read many of the books. While there Shelgunov once collided with the censor stationed at the factory over the withdrawal of a book. He questioned this action and this incident led Shelgunov to read other illegal works.[103] Further education for both himself and his friends became a preoccupation

---

[103]Nevskii, <u>Ocherki</u>, p. 146.

throughout Shelgunov's life. In 1885 he enrolled at a technical school, and attended numerous public lectures, even some doctoral defenses at the University. At the Baltiiskii Machine Construction Plant, he became one of the leaders of a self-education discussion group. His partner as leader was Egor Afanasev, also pseudonymed "Klimanov." He was born in 1866, and while still a teenager became a blacksmith at the large State Paper Mill Factory in St. Petersburg. There he attended the technical school attached to the factory to raise his intellectual and cultural level.[104] E. Afanasev first became involved with the Blagoev circle and then with the Tochisskii circle. For both people their careers as political activists were just beginning. Their circle and the five other workers' circles became the core for the formation for the Central Workers' Circle.

Yet these circles were basically isolated and locked into their own cells for self-knowledge. They were isolated not only between regions ion the city, but also between factories. For example, there was no coordination between Bogdanov's and Mefodiev's circles, even though both consisted of workers in the same

---

[104] Ibid., p. 195.

factory, the Warsaw Railway Plant. The few ties were irregular and accidental. While it was true that teachers for the circles came from groups such as the Rodzevich Circle, these intellectuals tended to act as individuals. By this time, some of the workers' leaders began to consider the need to unify the disparate workers' circles throughout St. Petersburg. Many of the students thought the intelligentsia should be the leaders of any unified workers' group. Yet that idea was hotly opposed by other students. For example, Mikhail Brusnev, a Russian student at the Technical Institute, declared that the workers' movement must be directed and controlled by the workers themselves.[105] He believed that student groups were too unstable due to the risk of arrests. He also questioned the commitment of the intellectuals. For example, frequently, once summer arrived, students left St. Petersburg and dispersed to their parents' homes in the countryside. The workers did not have the pleasant option of taking summer vacations. More than one worker sarcastically declared, "Every summer the revolution scattered to the

---

[105] Kazakevich, Sotsial-demokraticheskie organizatsii, p. 82. The information is based on unpublished sources from the Leningrad archives.

dachas."[106] That fact did not engender respect by the workers for their student teachers. Mikhail Brusnev recognized the reality that workers' leaders would never accept direction by students.

During 1889 leaders of a few workers' circles decided to organize a meeting to try to centralize their operations. In the latter part of the year, three workers, E.A. Afanasev, G.A. Mefodiev, and N.D. Bogdanov, each the director of a circle, established a headquarters to hold regular meetings of circle representatives.[107] Early in 1890 these leaders organized a much larger, more representative meeting of leaders from workers' circles. That meeting was secretly held at I.A. Fomin's room in the Harbor section of the city. He also set up a committee composed of seven workers: Egor Afanasev, his brother Fedor, Bogdanov, Mefodiev, P.N. Evgrafov, V.V. Buianov, and I.A. Fomin. Each member represented the combined circles from his raion (region) in St. Petersburg, or from his factory. There was no chairman of the group.

---

[106] Shel'gunov, "Vospominaniia," Ot gruppy Blagoeva, p. 57; and N.D. Bogdanov, "Na zare sotsial-demokratii (Vospominaniia)" Ozvobozhdenie truda (Voronezh, 1918), p. 8.

[107] Korolchuk and Sokolova, Khronika, p. 147. The information is based on unpublished sources from the Leningrad archives.

It would be collectively run, and would coordinate the current circles, and try to create new circles.[108]

During the 1880's, St. Petersburg had a parallel network of workers' and intelligentsia circles. For much of the decade each network had little coordination or direction within itself or with any other network regarding activities of any type. By the end of the decade each network, on its own initiative, formed a central circle to more effectively conduct activities among the intelligentsia and the workers' elite.

---

[108] Ol'minskii, "O vospominaniiakh N.D. Bogdanova," Ot gruppy Blagoeva, p. 41.

Two brothers who were leaders of workers' circles: F.A. Afanasev (left) and E.A. Afanasev (right).

Ф. А. Афанасьев («Отец»)

Е. А. Климанов

Another photograph of F.A. Afanasev (left) along with Mikhail Silvin, a student at the Technical Institute (right).

MICHAEL SILVIN

FEDOR AFANASEV

Two student representatives on the Central Workers' Circle: M.I. Brusnev (left) and V.S. Golubev (right).

MICHAEL BRUSNEV

В. С. Голубев

A noted workers' leader: Vasilii Shelgunov (left) and a leading Social Democratic propagandist: Stepan Radchenko (right).

STEPAN RADCHENKO

VASSILY SHELGUNOV

Two leading student leaders who both had frequent contacts with workers: Konstantin Takhtarev (left) and M.S. Olminskii (right).

KONSTANTIN TAKHTAREV

М. С. Александров
(Ольминский)

Pavel Tochisskii (left) and Leonid Krasin (right), two student activists from the period.

LEONID KRASIN

PAUL TOCHISKY

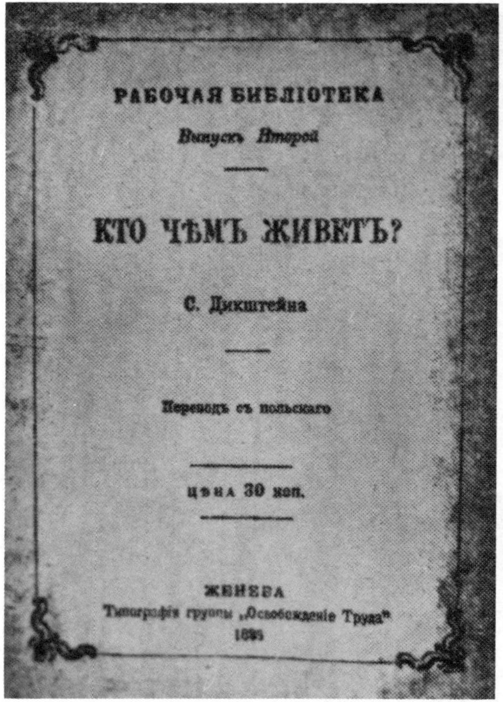

(Left): The resolution from the Paris Congress organizing May Day and the title page of a frequently read book, S. Dikshtein's Who lives by what?

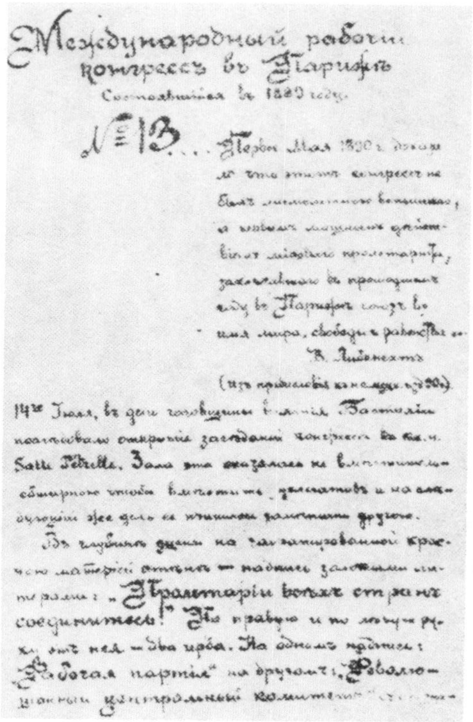

ST. PETERSBURG LABOR LEADERS (*c.* 1917). (1) M. Kniazev; (2) N. D. Bogdanov; (3) V. M. Karelina; (4) Egor Afanasev; (5) A. E. Karelin; (6) I. I. Iakovlev; (7) A. P. Ilin; (8) N. Kaizer; (9) T. V. Razuvaeva.

Some workers' leaders from the 1890's
(from a photograph about 1917)

CHAPTER III

THE MEMBERSHIP OF THE CENTRAL WORKERS' CIRCLE

The Background of Members of the Central Workers' Circle

The Central Workers' Circle was formed in late 1889 and lasted for over four years until it collapsed due to the arrest of its leading figures in 1894. Its members were the most highly skilled, most educated and most politicized in the Russian urban working class. Later, according to Marxist-Leninist theory, the urban working class, with the assistance of the radical intelligentsia, would carry out any future Socialist revolution. During the formative years of Russia's industrialization, the Central Workers' Circle was a worker-controlled organization having a political and cultural program designed to benefit the working class. They represented most of the workers' circles in St. Petersburg. Later, according to Marxist-Leninist theory that organization should have become a nucleus for revolutionary activities. After all, its members were the elite of the working class. In any future revolution, their organization should have provided the generals for the armies of workers trying to overthrow the tsarist autocracy and subsequently to inaugurate a dictatorship of the proletariat. Yet, the organization lasted only for four short years. Nothing comparable replaced it in the Russian labor movement. Most members of the Central Workers' Circle faded into obscurity. Few played major roles in either the 1904 or the 1917 revolutions. The workers' movement became dominated by middle class intellectuals. The author believes that one failure of the Central Workers' Circle is partially due to a seeming irony that only in the earliest, the least developed years of Russia's industrialization did the labor movement have a relatively united worker-directed organization crossing factory lines, occupations, nationalities, and sexes. Through the membership of the Central Workers' Circle, perhaps a composite portrait of the leadership of the Central Workers' Circle can explain this paradox in Russian history. Had the workers retained control over their movement, the course of Russian history might have been very different.

There is no complete list of members of St. Petersburg's workers' intelligentsia for the late nineteenth century, or for that matter, any period of time. Several authors have estimated the workers' intelligentsia as about 1% of the working class in the city.[1] According to the 1897 census of St. Petersburg, there were about 100,000 workers in the factories and plants. Therefore, roughly 1,000 of them were members of the workers' intelligentsia. Yet out of that number only eight to ten workers composed the Central Workers' Circle. That number is too small to draw any conclusions concerning the background and attitudes of the Central Workers' Circle. To expand this list it was necessary to use a great deal of subjective judgment. After consulting various sources, both memoirs and secondary ones, the author expanded the list of workers who were members of circles associated with the Central Workers' Circle to roughly forty

---

[1] In discussing the workers' intelligentsia most authors are vague as to the percentage or the exact number of workers who are part of that segment of the working class. However, a few recent sources such as Richard Pipes' Social Democracy and the St. Petersburg Labor Movement (1963), and R.A. Kazakevich's Sotsial Demokraticheskie Organizatsii Peterburga (1960) mention between several hundred to 1,000 workers as belonging to the workers' intelligentsia. The early Soviet historian K.M. Takhtarev in his memoir account, Rabochee dvizhenie v Peterburge, 1893-1901 gg. (1924) mentioned that about 1% of the workers in St. Petersburg were part of that group. A few other contemporary authors such as G. Rubakin in his short article, "Iz zhizni rabochei intelligentsii" published in Mir bozhii (March 1896) mentioned the group as a new phenomenon distinct from the rest of the working class.

people.[2] Admittedly, that sample is still very small. However, the list does provide us with a representative sample of the Central Workers' Circle. Certainly the Central Workers' Circle's membership cannot be equated with the workers' intelligentsia, except that all its members came from that segment of the working class. Nevertheless, the reader can draw some indirect ideas

---

[2]The sources for the list are the following: R.A. Kazakevich, Sotsial-demokraticheskie organizatsii Peterburga (1960); V.V. Sviatlovskii, "Na zare Rossi- iskoi sotsial-demokratii," Byloe (1922); V. Nevskii, Ocherki po istorii Rossiiskoi Kommunisticheskoi Partii (1925); and K.M. Takhtarev, Rabochee dvizhenie v Peterburge, 1893-1901 gg. (1924).

List of Members of the Central Workers' Circle

1. N. Bogdanov
2. F.A. Afanas'ev
3. K. Norinskii
4. I.I. Timofeev
5. V.A. Shel'gunov
6. V.V. Buianov
7. G.A. Mefodiev
8. V. Fomin
9. S. Funtikov
10. G.A. Fisher
11. V. Proshin
12. A. Karelin
13. V. Karelina
14. I. Egorov
15. I. Zhel'abin
16. N.G. Poletaev
17. M.P. Kniazev
18. E. Tumanov
19. V. Poroshin
20. D. Nikitin
21. P. Evgrafov
22. A.S. Filimonov
23. V. Ivanov
24. N. Grigor'eva
25. S. Maklakov
26. Y. Maiorov
27. S. Kuchin
28. E.A. Afanas'ev
29. P. Kaizo
30. T. Stefanenkov
31. I. Iakovskii
32. I.V. Krutov
33. N. Babushkin
34. S. Kanatchikov
35. E.I. Nemchinov
36. M.P. Petrov
37. A.M. Buiko
38. A.S. Shapovalov

concerning the characteristics of the workers' intelligentsia.

Most of the members were born between 1860 and 1875. By the early 1890's their average age was twenty-two. Out of the sample of sixteen workers whose birthdates could be determined, twelve were under twenty-five. When a worker was significantly older, into his thirties or forties, that fact was distinctly commented on by his colleagues. For example, V.V. Bartenev, a student active in worker circles, commented, "The spirit of the circle was I.V. Krutov, an old man, forty years of age."[3] Thus the workers' intelligentsia was a group composed of the young.

The members associated with the Central Workers' Circle were predominantly male. Out of the thirty people examined, only four were women. This fact is hardly surprising. The rate of literacy among women workers was much lower than that of male workers, which in itself was not high. It was about 40%.[4] Usually women workers did not have the opportunity for education except at a rudimentary level. They tended to be

---

[3] Bartenev, "Vospominaniia," p. 175.
[4] Bernshtein-Kogan, Chislennost', p. 64.

clustered in the least skilled industries such as dressmaking, tobacco, and textiles. Many male workers regarded women workers as essentially a lower order who were incapable of struggling for ideals. One member of the workers' intelligentsia, S. Kanatchikov, commented that he, "was very surprised when I met two conscious women workers who listened and discussed as we (male workers) would."[5] Thus, women who might against all obstacles, have the necessary high skills and education to join the Central Workers' Circle found a great bias against them among their male counterparts.

Only two members of the Central Workers' Circle were born in St. Petersburg. Most were born in the countryside in tiny villages consisting of peasants. Only one activist, E.I. Nemchinov, who later became a deputy in the 1905 Soviet, declared that his parents were lower middle class; and even he came from a small village.[6] These villages were located in provinces near St. Petersburg, usually St. Petersburg and Pskov provinces. M.P. Petrov mentioned that his grandparents

---

[5] S. Kanatchikov, *Iz istorii moego byt'ia* (Moscow, 1929), p. 85.

[6] E.I. Nemchinov, *Vospominaniia starogo rabochego* (Moscow-Petrograd, 1924), pp. 12-14.

were household serfs. He believed that his family's existence was pitiful. "When during the times his parents were unemployed, they literally had nothing to eat, not even a crust of bread."[7] Generally their families were very large. Many members commented that they had six, eight or ten brothers and sisters. To raise these huge families, both the quality and the quantity of land was poor and insufficient, often just a couple of hectares (one hectare is nearly 2.5 acres). Thus, at an early age these future workers believed they had little future on their families' plots. In their eyes, they had absolutely nothing to stay in the countryside for. Most left their villages when they were still children, usually twelve to fourteen years old. Thus, while the members of the Central Workers' Circle came from rural backgrounds, they realized the countryside held little for them. Their future lay in the city. Having faced great poverty in their early years, these young workers were determined to economically succeed in the cities. Reading their memoirs and autobiographies gives a person the impression that these workers were extremely intelligent and

---

[7] M.P. Petrov, Moi vospominaniia (Moscow, 1932), p. 184.

ambitious. Unlike most Russian workers who frequently returned to their native countryside often at harvest time, members of the Central Workers' Circle never returned to their rural roots. Their rural background became part of their past; yet it would not be a forgotten past.

Desperate poverty helped create a very sad home life during their childhood. Frequently one or both parents died when the future Central Workers' Circle's members were still very young. Many workers commented in their memoirs that their fathers were despotic and alcoholic. Another labor leader active in the Central Workers' Circle, V.A. Shelgunov, declared that "his father drank a lot, and he acted scandalously toward my mother. He beat her and even drove her out of the house." Specifically, he described his father as despotic and insulting. His mother died when Vasilii was just eight years old.[8] At this stage of Shelgunov's life, the family had already moved to St. Petersburg. At the age of nine, Shelgunov entered an iron foundry where he received sixty-five kopeks a day for eleven hours of work. His father never approved of the efforts

---

[8] Shel'gunov, "Vospominaniia," Ot gruppy Blagoeva, p. 54.

of young Shelgunov to get ahead, such as through schooling. By the time Shelgunov was thirteen, his father left him altogether. Shelgunov was on his own while he was a young adolescent. Other workers' memoirs mention that their fathers were alcoholics. Sometimes, a father's alcoholism became so bad he was forced to enter a hospital for treatment. Alcoholism led to an early death for many fathers, and also helped create the conditions for wife beating and child abuse. The frequency of parental alcoholism had several consequences for the lives and attitudes of the members of the Central Workers' Circle. They strongly opposed drinking, declared drinking was terrible for any Russian to do. They were never close to their fathers. In their memoirs only a few wrote positively about their fathers. For most of these workers, their father's advice was something not to be considered. Poor relations with their fathers only added to a miserable childhood of poverty, hunger, and a lack of clothing. Their parents were often quite conservative. Thus, many members turn to political radicalism was a reaction against their deplorable early family life. There was a definite generation gap among Russian workers. Fathers and sons had very different outlooks, and often bitter relationships.[9]

On the other hand relations with their mothers were very different. In their memoirs and autobiographies, numerous workers commented how they owed a great deal to their mothers. Mothers provided the discipline to keep the family afloat in its dire straits. Not one worker's memoir mentioned that a mother was a heavy drinker, much less an alcoholic. As fathers often died at an early age from alcoholism, mothers became the providers for the large family. She was the unifying force. M.P. Petrov mentioned how his mother dreamed of her children getting an education.[10] Other workers commented that the roots for their urge for an education went back to their mothers. Mothers often gave them the impetus not to accept their poverty, but to try to succeed. In fact, these workers' mothers were often the only positive experience in their otherwise miserable childhood.

At an early age future members of the Central Workers' Circle regarded education as the major source

---

[9] K. Mironov, *Iz vospominanii rabochego* (Moscow, 1906), p. 22.

[10] Petrov, *Moi vospominaniia*, p. 72.

for a release from their destitution. At seven or eight, most members of this sample of the Central Workers' Circle attended zemstvo or village schools near their homes. All of these future workers regarded this education as inadequate. At school they learned reading, writing, arithmetic, and religion. The facilities, supplies, and funding were inadequate to fulfill the primary purpose of providing a basic literacy to peasant children. Many village schools had priests as teachers. Few workers wrote favorably of the priest-teachers. Most commented that the priests were not well educated, were strict disciplinarians, and spent most of the time teaching religion rather than the other subjects. A.M. Buiko gave a fairly common account when he wrote: "Especially severe as a priest-teacher was Orlov who taught us Religion or Catechism. The priest unexpectedly and sadistically loved to grab the students by their hair."[11] Other workers in their memoirs commented that their teachers drank constantly and even appeared in class tipsy. One is amazed that these children's love for learning survived these schools except for an early resentment toward religion, a

---

[11] A.M. Buiko, "Put' rabochego," p. 7.

resentment that was maintained for the rest of their lives.

It would only be later, after these future members of the Central Workers' Circle arrived in the city, that they received a genuine formal education. Virtually all entered factory or technical schools to learn a trade. With great energy they entered the courses even though classes began after a long work day in the factory. Sometimes this schedule was too much for these young workers. "During the first hour, we sat cheerfully and vigilantly, but by the third hour, we began to nod out from the tiredness of the long day."[12] Yet most survived two or three years in the factory schools under these trying conditions. The level of knowledge learned in their previous village schools determined the class they entered in the factory or technical schools. If they had no knowledge, the young workers entered the first class. If they retained the basic "four R's," they entered either the second or the third class. Most factory schools contained four to six classes. While education was important for their jobs, few factories provided many incentives for attend-

---

[12] Kanatchikov, *Iz istorii*, p. 93.

ing school. Several workers commented that their attendance deprived them of overtime work and the money which they needed. Some of these evening schools taught advanced subjects such as physics, chemistry, geometry, and geography. At the conclusion of the year course students had to pass examinations given by the Ministry of Education in Russian language, arithmetic, penmanship, and religion.[13]

Unlike the village schools, in the factory schools the workers often wrote favorably about the teachers. These teachers were easy to follow, and had interesting teaching methods. For example, they read interesting stories to their students. Nevertheless, many teachers were just as keen in spreading radical political ideas as in teaching academic subjects. In the sample most workers initially became politicized through contact with such teachers. After getting to know various students, teachers often passed illegal books or brochures to them. Frequently this was the first time these students saw any materials which criticized the government. Other teachers discussed Russian revolutionary figures or distributed anti-religious tracts to

---

[13] Shel'gunov, "Vospominaniia," Ot gruppy Blagoeva, p. 61.

their potential disciples. The teachers were not always successful mixing propaganda with education. Sometimes a student resented the socialist propaganda. Yet this student rarely protested, because he needed and wanted an education.[14]

These workers' cravings for further education made this formal after-work schooling insufficient. To supplement it, sometimes they visited the museums in St. Petersburg, especially the Hermitage, where they examined the art and statues. Other times they walked in the city's parks or along its canals thinking and absorbing the day's lessons. Frequently they attended libraries or public lectures. Many read the city's liberal newspapers such as Russkie Vedomosti, where they avidly read the foreign press section.[15] Other times at work, journals or newspapers were passed out from worker to worker. Thus, formal schooling was just the foundation for these workers' education. As their teachers were frequently political radicals, many workers became initially politically conscious in this way. Books opened a new world of hope for these workers and became their passion. The desire to further their

---

[14] A.S. Shapovalov, V bor'be za sotsializm (Moscow, 1934), p. 58.

[15] Nevskii, Ocherki, p. 85.

education remained with the members of the Central Workers' Circle for the rest of their lives.

Most of the Central Workers' Circle's members were metal workers. In fact, out of the sample of thirty workers, eighteen were metal workers of one type or another. Very often, when the workers initially arrived in St. Petersburg they started off with terribly low paying jobs, getting as little as thirty to fifty kopeks a day. E.I. Nemchinov mentioned that the conditions were terrible in the factory he initially worked in. The sleeping quarters there were filthy, and each worker had to share his bed with at least one other person.[17] Fedor Afanasev declared that in his factory conditions were horrible.

> We had fourteen hour days, with a fifty-five minute break for lunch which was not included in our day. The workers lived in specially built barracks; the rent of which was deducted from our salaries. Conditions in the factory and in the barracks were unsanitary and unhygienic. In a room built for five lived twenty-five to thirty people. Children were virtually slaves until they became twenty-one years old. They were supposed to get three to eight rubles a month salary. However after rent and clothes were deducted, their salary was usually nil.[18]

---

[17] Nemchinov, *Vospominaniia*, p. 20.

[18] I.I. Vlasov, *Tkach Fedor Afanas'ev, 1859-1905* (Ivanovo-Voznesensk, 1925), p. 36.

Yet due to their penchant for an education, these workers did not remain at these factories for long. They moved to better paying and more skilled jobs as soon as they could. A few were lathe workers, which required a great intelligence and an understanding of technical drawings along with a knowledge of arithmetic. Other jobs also required some knowledge of more advanced mathematics. Members of the Central Workers' Circle acquired the necessary skills for positions such as locksmiths, blacksmiths, lathe operators, and bookbinders. These workers became the elite of Russia's working class. The members of the Central Workers' Circle formed an upwardly mobile group. Sometimes they even complained about poor wages when their salary reached over eighty rubles a month.[19] This was at a time when the average worker made thirty or less rubles a month. The members were highly ambitious, and were never satisfied with their current position. Revolutionary activity is rarely begun by people who are locked into a group, but by those people who are either upwardly rising or sliding

---

[19] Ol'minskii, "Moi vospominaniia," *Ot gruppy Blagoeva*, p. 9.

downward on the social and economic ladder.[20] Members of the Central Workers' Circle certainly formed a group of dissatisfied upwardly mobile people. In their factories, they stood out among their fellow workers. Fedor Afanasev was called the "apostle" among his fellow workers.[21] Logically these workers filled a leadership role among their fellow workers. In this context, it was inevitable that they would form circles of self-education and discussion.

Here then is a composite portrait of the membership of the Central Workers' Circle. They were descended from poor peasant families in villages near St. Petersburg, and were reared in deeply religious but often single parent homes with many brothers and sisters. Although they were initially educated mainly for jobs, reading for its own sake became a passion for them. Forced to leave home at a very early age, sometimes twelve or thirteen, these young boys and a few

---

[20] Lawrence, Stone, "Theories of Revolution," in Bruce Mazlich, David B. Ralston, and Arthur D. Kaledin, eds., Revolution, A Reader (New York, 1971), pp. 52-55; Joseph Greenbaum and Leonard Pearlin, "Vertical Mobility and Prejudice," in Reinhard Bendix and Seymour Lipset, eds., Class, Status and Power (Glencoe, Ill., 1953), pp. 480-491.

[21] M. Morshanskaia, Tkach Fedor Afanas'ev (Moscow, 1924), p. 11.

girls, faced a strange and hostile world. Expecting
to lead, these young people found few followers among
their fellow workers. They were an elite without a
function. The young women felt equally lost. Upward
mobility became a key to understanding their tremendous
ambitions and desires for political and economic
changes. Their background, unhappy and confused,
shaped their attitudes toward religion, drinking, the
less skilled and unskilled workers, politics, intellectuals, and finally toward each other as an elite of the
working class. Membership in the Central Workers'
Circle and its affiliated circles offered the workers
an opportunity to reassert their values, in association
with others of their kind. Thus, the Central Workers'
Circle represented an aggrieved group, alienated against
a world they never made.

The Attitudes and Values of the Membership

The attitudes and values of members of the Central
Workers' Circle were critical to understand the group's
purposes and priorities. Uneducated and unskilled
workers usually blamed their poverty on themselves or
on factors over which they had no control. For example,
they agreed that conditions in their home villages and

in their factories were bad, but those bad conditions were their own fault because, "they were drunkards and had forgotten God."[22] However the more intellectually inclined workers tended to link their own personal experiences to social and economic questions. For example a drunken and corrupt village priest made a future member of the Central Workers' Circle doubt religion and even God. A tyrannical factory owner turned many members of the Central Workers' Circle against capitalism. Intellectually inclined Russian workers, from which the Central Workers' Circle came, went from the specific to the general, from the simple to the complex. Their particular experiences shaped their broad perspectives on issues affecting them. Experience shaped theory for those workers.

Until the late nineteenth century, religion was a central feature in the lives of poor Russians. For many centuries the peasantry has been religious, but some observers commented that its religiosity was only superficial. For example, the Scotsman Sir Donald MacKenzie Wallace, a keen observer of nineteenth century Russia, declared:

---

[22] A.O. Lukachevich, "V narod," Byloe, March 1907, p. 12.

> It must be admitted that the Russian people
> are in a certain sense religious. They go
> regularly to church on Sundays and holy days,
> cross themselves repeatedly when they pass a
> church or icon, take the Holy Communion at
> stated seasons, rigorously abstain from
> animal foods not only on Wednesdays and
> Fridays, but also during Lent and the other
> long fasts, make occasional pilgrimages to
> holy shrines, and in a word, fulfill punc-
> tiliously the ceremonial observances which
> they suppose necessary for salvation. But
> here their religiousness ends. They are
> generally profoundly ignorant of religious
> doctrine, and know little or nothing of Holy
> Writ.[23]

While the "Old Believers" made inroads among the peasantry, most peasants retained their allegiance to the established Orthodox Church, which was subservient to and a defender of the tsarist government. The peasants' personal link with the church was through the village priest, often as uneducated and as poor as the peasant himself was. Many priests were notorious for drunkenness or loose living, and therefore frequently became objects of scorn and amusement, rather than respect. A secret governmental report asked: "Can the people respect the clergy when they hear how one priest stole money from below the pillow of a dying man at the moment of confession; how another was publicly dragged

---

[23] Donald M. Wallace, Russia: On the Eve of War and Revolution, Cyril Black, ed., (New York, 1961), p. 385.

out of a house of ill-fame?"[24] Despite these examples most peasants remained religious and committed to Orthodoxy. Village churches were crowded on Sundays and on religious festivals. While the peasant may not have understood religious dogmas and doctrines, he retained a deep belief in God and in the ritual aspects of Orthodoxy. The icon on the walls in peasant *izbas* (huts) remained an eternal reminder of their basic religiosity.

After the Emancipation of the serfs, the Orthodox Church recognized the growing urbanization in Russian life. The Church provided inexpensive housing for the urban poor. The Church recognized that these people had to be served by the Church, or quite possibly be forever lost to its commandments. According to the 1869 census, over 85% of St. Petersburg's population was Orthodox.[25] The rest were distinct Catholic-Uniate, Protestant, Jewish, and Moslem minorities. The Church owned a great deal of property, mostly churches, convents, and abbeys.

---

[24] Ibid., p. 379.

[25] *Vseobshchaia Adresnaia Kniga S. Peterburga* (St. Petersburg, 1867-8), pp. 72-85.

The Church organized a special association to conduct religious teachings among the workers. It was called the "Society for the Spread of Religious-Orthodox Enlightenment." Discussions were often conducted in the dining areas of factories.[26] These religious associations were supported by the government and factory owners, frequently to partially offset anti-religious propaganda conducted by radical students. These religious discussions were popular among the workers. Priests led sessions of religious poetry, Bible readings, and prayers. Often priests denounced drinking, and would not allow any alcoholic beverages at these meetings. In fact, the Church took an active role in St. Petersburg's Temperance Associations. These religious sessions struck a responsive chord among most workers.

Another indication of the strength of religion was in the workers' folklore. Their songs, stories, and poetry had many religious themes. Numerous autobiographies and memoirs written by workers also indicated that religion was tightly connected with the emotional side of people's lives. Their judgments on

---

[26] V.F. Shishkin, "Propaganda russkimi sotsial-demodratami proletarskoi morali v kontse XIX-nachale XX v.," Ezhegodnik muzeia istorii religii i ateizma, VII, Moscow, 1964, p. 26.

right and wrong reflected church pronouncements. Thus, right up through the end of the nineteenth century, most Russian urban workers reflected their peasant roots in the degree of their religiousness. For example, the well known labor leader, K.M. Norinskii, remarked that his family habitually went to night service each Saturday, and on Sundays went to all services. He furthermore said that he was deeply religious until the age of eighteen or nineteen.[27]

Nevertheless, the membership of the Central Workers' Circle had dramatically different attitudes from the rest of the working class on the subject of religion. Virtually all were like Norinskii, religious until young adulthood. Through practical living experiences, they lost religion. For example, Petr Moiseenko, a long time labor activist, said: "Such was our amazement when we knew that the monks brought to the woods women and raped them there. . .any belief was lost not only in monks and priests but in God as well."[28] This incident illustrates how observed abuses

---

[27] K. Norinskii, "Moi vospominaniia," Ot gruppy Blagoeva, p. 17.

[28] M.M. Persii, "Avtobiografii rabochikh kak istochnik izucheniia ateizma v. rabochem dvizhenii," Voprosy istorii religii i ateizma, sbornik statei, VIII, Moscow, 1960, p. 116.

destroyed their faith in religion. Members of the Central Workers' Circle believed that priests and monks should serve a good example. Instead priests and monks often acted like the worst members of the community they served. A.M. Buiko remarked that when he was young, he noticed the priests' drunkenness and other unsavory practices. Buiko asked, "If they are representative of God, then what good is God?"[29] Thus, when the worker was young, a negative experience helped turn that worker against religion. Later, when the worker attended school, readings in science books often strengthened that worker's doubts about religion.

The differing attitude over religion caused great hostility between the members of the Central Workers' Circle and the rest of the working class. The former was never known for patience or tolerance. They told their religious co-workers that they were "blind, sheep, or imbeciles." Obviously, this name calling did not make their propaganda efforts very effective. K. Mironov recounted a discussion he had with several workers at the large machine construction plant he was employed in. One worker replied that Christ was a man

---

[29]Buiko, Put' rabochego, p. 117.

who lived among the people, and who suffered what the people did. Then ensued a debate over whether or not Christ was a man or God. As a result of Mironov's outspoken views, another worker threatened then to go to the police and report Mironov for blasphemy and socialist "contamination."[30]

Sometimes these threats led to actual arrests. It was vey unusual for a worker not to have an icon in his room, a fact illustrating the general religiosity of most workers. Mironov mentioned that the room of two members of the Central Workers' Circle had no icons in it. The landlord saw this, and placed one of his icons in their room. The tenants told him to remove it. An argument resulted between the two workers and their landlord. Fearing they were atheists, and therefore socialists, the landlord reported them to the police. Accurately or otherwise, nonbelieving workers became associated with political radicalism and subversion.[31]

In their memoirs, many workers confirmed that their religious doubts led them to political doubts. Nevertheless, their anti-religious ideas found few

---

[30] Mironov, *Iz vospominanii*, p. 9.
[31] *Ibid.*, p. 23.

followers. A.S. Shapovalov said his fellow workers recoiled from him as if he was infected with the plague. One worker said: "Previously, when you believed in God, you looked like an angel. Your eyes were good and your face was clean. Now your face is darkened and you resemble a devil. You are damned, Sashka."[32] Thus, anti-religious feeling separated members of the Central Workers' Circle from their fellow workers, and, in fact, embittered their relations considerably. A major break between this tiny group and the rest of the working class over the question of religion threatened.

On the question of religion, poor relations not only occurred among workers, but also between the membership and their families. Funtikov, a treasurer for the organization, had a tremendous row with his wife over religion. The struggle lasted two to three years. At one point he threatened to throw all the family's icons into the stove. Neither Funtikov nor his wife gave in. Finally, he left his wife, and broke all ties with his family.[33] Another incident occurred

---

[32]Shapovalov, V bor'be za sotsializm, p. 63.
[33]Ol'minskii, "Moi vospominaniia," Ot gruppy Blagoeva, p. 13.

between a blacksmith, Skylar, and his wife. For a long time they argued over religion. One Saturday evening he went home, and noticed a vigil lamp before the icon. Then Skylar cursed God, and threw his boot at the icon smashing both the lamp and the icon. His wife replied, "God will punish you for what you have done." Skylar replied, "There is no God. All this is your stupidity. Bring me a thousand of your icons and I will destroy them all."[34] Religion not only created a gap between husband and wife, but also between father and son. Doubts over religion isolated the young workers. Their propaganda efforts met with little success. Two workers mentioned that they could not disturb the religious tradition among their fellow workers. If anything, all their efforts did was to widen the gap between the Central Workers' Circle and the rest of the working class. The members frequently dismissed their fellow co-workers' arguments as the "ignorance of the dark and the undeveloped."[35] Their propaganda methods tended to lack consideration and patience. These methods only led to increased police

---

[34] Buiko, "Put' rabochego," p. 17.

[35] Shapovalov, V bor'be za sotsializm, p. 70.

surveillance of them. A few members of the Circle were turned into the police by their fellow workers. Thus, the Central Workers' Circle struggled for the soul of bulk of the workers in a competition with the Church.

While overindulgence in alcohol has been characteristic of the Russian population for centuries, the rate of intoxication among the population increased significantly after the middle of the nineteenth century. By 1870, there were 2,700 drinking establishments in St. Petersburg alone. In 1869 more than 34,600 drunks were arrested.[36] Numerous workers commented in their memoirs that when they entered the city, what greeted them were churches and bars. There were numerous factors which explained the increase in drinking, most of which were attributed to the growing influx of villagers into the city for work. Most were lonely, having just left their families behind. They felt alienated in what they regarded as a huge, crowded, and impersonal city, which contrasted to their small personalized villages. They lived in depressing conditions in dormitories or in rooms, and worked long hours in often monotoncus jobs. Alcohol provided a

---

[36] V. Mikhnevich, Petersburg: ves' na ladoni (St. Petersburg, 1874), pp. 291-93.

release and an escape from these dreary conditions. For a while the government did little except restrict the sale of alcohol on Sundays and on public holidays. Drunks still sprawled on the sidewalks of the city. Finally, toward the end of the century, the government, in conjunction with the Church, sponsored Temperance Associations to curb the increase in alcoholic drinking in St. Petersburg. Among workers, alcohol consumption crossed income lines. In fact, it seemed the greater the salary of a worker, the more developed was his appetite for alcohol.[37] On paydays the rate of drinking was huge. Many workers spent the bulk of their salaries in bars. Neighborhoods were packed with drunk people. In contrast, almost to a man, members of the Central Workers' Circle opposed an indulgence in alcohol. For one thing they recognized that alcohol abuse ruined people's lives. Secondly, cultural and educational work could not be conducted while workers were drunk. Members of the group tended to be very serious and moralistic. Yet they opposed the Temperance Associations, one of the few groups actually combatting drinking among the workers. They thought Temperance Associations were a trap to lure

---

[37] Petrov, _Moi vospominaniia_, p. 185.

workers into supporting the government and the Church. Their memoir accounts minimized the temperance aspects of the Associations, and maximized the pro-government and religious aspects of them. Thus, while the Central Workers' Circle's membership opposed drinking, the group refused to join or aid the one major organization which combatted alcoholism.

As has already been stated, members of the Central Workers' Circle frequently had unhappy personal backgrounds through single parent homes, alcoholic fathers, or child abuse. These unhappy childhoods carried over into adulthood. Many members married but few marriages succeeded. Their apartments or rooms were crowded, affording little privacy. Members of the Circle tended to be an isolated group. They related poorly with everyone except other members of the Circle or prospective members. Frequently conflicts arose with their wives, who sought basic material needs. One wife commented that her husband's expenditures on books were wasteful as they needed food on the table. Other wives complained that their husbands' activities brought a danger of arrest. An arrest would lose them not only a husband, but also the main breadwinner for the family. Conflicts arose over religion, and over political activities. Wives tended to be more religious and politically conservative than their husbands. Couples lacked communication with each other. One wife, in fact, said: "He (my husband) was a good person, but then he became a socialist." Frequently members of the Central Workers' Circle were pleased when the marriage of one of their colleagues failed. "Now he writes a lot, he was married."[38] (underlining is mine) According to their memoirs, most members of the Central Workers' Circle lost their wives when they reached the age of twenty-five to thirty years. After a divorce, they became immersed in the activities of the circle they belonged to. After an unsuccessful personal life, they became married to their circles.

Just like their attitudes on other subjects such as religion, the political views of the members of the Central Workers' Circle were shaped from personal experiences instead of from a conceptual framework. For example, seeing examples of poverty all around him often turned the worker against the system which apparently allowed that poverty. Only later did the worker read radical tracts which confirmed his conceptions. A member of the Central Workers' Circle

---

[38]Mironov, Iz vospominanii, p. 23.

frequently developed his political views completely on his own. Initially, he rarely knew any radical intelligentsia. A.S. Shapovalov is an example of a worker who became politically conscious without any help of the intelligentsia. After discovering "socialism" by reading radical books and brochures, he resolved to search out members of the socialist intelligentsia. Nevertheless, he had no idea where to find them.[39] Just as their personal lives were lonely, their political views remained isolated, and alienated them from the rest of their fellow workers.

Their conceptions of socialism were hazy, lacking the political theorization developed in books. Rather than a fixed program, socialism for the members of the Central Workers' Circle was an attitude--an attitude of curiosity. They wanted to discover other workers, or perhaps student intellectuals who believed as they did. Yet neither person was easy to find. Most of their co-workers in the factory, the "grey mass," did not see the advantages of achieving political freedom.[40] Why would this be the case when their fellow workers came

---

[39] Shapovalov, V bor'be za sotsializm, p. 65.
[40] Takhtarev, Rabochee dvizhenie, p. 13.

from similar backgrounds? Most likely this was due to their own rising expectations.

Members of the Central Workers' Circle were upwardly mobile. As they developed into an elite they had less and less in common with their fellow workers. One such unskilled worker, K. Langelid, told S. Kanatchikov, an expert pattern maker: "To love music and poetry are all good things, but to us workers (underlining is mine), they are idle, parasitic, and have no activity. You (S. Kanatchikov) closely resemble the idle intelligentsia. You do not understand nor do you feel as we (ordinary workers) do."[41] Thus, the Central Workers' Circle formed a subgroup cut off by its ambition, its expectations and its critical curiosity from the other workers and even from most of the middle class intelligentsia.

Once members of the Central Workers' Circle arrived at a political framework, hazy as that might be, then they frequently repudiated both their own past attitudes and even Russia's past. This, again, was understandable, as Russia, for them, represented arbitrariness, intolerance, and backwardness. They

---

[41] Kanatchikov, Iz istorii, p. 89.

embraced the West, or at least what they thought the West was. Memoir accounts indicate that they read initially any newspaper reports on developments in Western Europe and the United States. Many learned western languages, including English. A few, such as Genrikh Fisher, a metal worker active in the Central Workers' Circle, even emigrated to the West. Fisher lived in England until 1921 when he returned to Russia where he lived until his death in 1935. Often the break with old Russia often became complete. Members of the Central Workers' Circle repudiated rural Russia with its huge peasantry. Fisher himself declared concerning the peasantry: "We recognize their pitiful conditions. But the peasantry will not play a great historical role. For us they are a backward mass, unorganized, having little in common but desiring more land. We (urban workers) want to act completely independently of the peasantry."[42] These statements were echoed by other members of the Central Workers' Circle. The potential significance of these statements was huge because these sentiments by members of the Central Workers' Circle foresaw that little

---

[42] Fisher, V Rossii i v Anglii, p. 16.

cooperation between educated urban workers and Russia's huge peasantry would ever develop.

We have seen that workers' circles had many ties with members of the student intelligentsia, mostly as advisors and teachers. However that relationship always remained an ambivalent one. Since the main purpose of forming circles was to increase the educational development of its members, they received instruction from whomever would give it. Radical intellectuals eagerly acted as teachers and discussion leaders for the workers. Yet, at the same time, workers noticed that the intellectuals' offers were basically two edged. In particular, the <u>Narodniki</u> (Populists) regarded the urban workers as revolutionary pioneers who should after their education go out into the country to agitate. It was true that in the late nineteenth century most Russian workers still had strong ties with the countryside. Each summer many workers returned to their native villages to work on the land. Ever since the days of the <u>Zemlia i Volia</u> and the Chaikovskii circle in the 1870's, the Populists had agitated among the industrial workers. In contrast, Social Democratic students conducted a much more gradual and milder campaign of propaganda among workers. They favored the creation of a cadre of labor leaders, and only later did they favor direct agitation. Many workers who were involved in circles, realized that agitation would only get them into trouble with the authorities. In fact, one worker declared, "They (Narodniki) stir us up, you (the Social Democrats) teach us what we should know. To listen to the Narodniki, you would become involved with hatred toward the government, and get a rebellious (buntarist) soul."[43] Thus, Marxists represented education, moderation and relative safety to these workers; while Populists represented agitation and rebellion to them. The workers were not so much attracted to the ideology of the Marxists as to their methods. They wanted an education, and the Marxists were more willing to provide them with that education than the Populists were.

In their search for western opinions the members of the Central Workers' Circle had a difficult time relating to students. Several workers mentioned in their memoirs that summers were an excellent time to organize circles and to hold meetings, as they could be outdoors, in parks and in the woods, instead of in their crowded rooms. Nevertheless student intellectuals were

---

[43] Liadov, Istoriia, p. 65.

not present during summers as they were generally at their parents' homes. The absence of student intellectuals taught the workers they had to be self-reliant. The Central Workers' Circle then became determined to utilize their own talented members. As a result, the program of the Central Workers' Circle stated that student intellectuals needed the circle's permission to enter its affiliated workers' circles. Furthermore, those intellectuals must accept the views of the Central Workers' Circle.[44]

Even then, members did not fully trust the student intelligentsia. They stated that representatives of the Central Workers' Circle would attend meetings of affiliated circles to ensure the intellectuals present did not overstep their bounds. The workers said the intellectuals must serve only an auxiliary role such as responding to the needs of workers or aiding in the composition of brochures. The members clearly stated: "The liberation of the workers must be the affair of the workers themselves."[45] The development of the workers' movement had to be achieved

---

[44] R.G. Lapsina and G.S. Zhuikov, "Novoe o deiatel'nosti grupp Blagoeva, Tochisskogo i Brusneva," Voprosy istorii KPSS, 1971, no. 7, p. 78.

[45] Nevskii, Ocherki, p. 303.

from the point of view of the Central Workers' Circle. Even with these precautions, a few workers' circles, not affiliated with the Central Workers' Circle, refused to allow any ties with intellectuals. Thus, there was an underlying basis of distrust between the members of the Central Workers' Circle and members of the student intelligentsia.[46]

Then, too, members of the Central Workers' Circle had different interests from students. Workers tended to be very practical. While they eagerly sought more education, their personal tastes remained quite simple. Sometimes members of the student intelligentsia brought to workers a few tickets to a concert or to a play. The workers neither understood nor liked the entertainment. They called it "lordly and too upperclass."[47] Shortly afterwards, a few workers met some affluent liberal professionals. The discussions were forced and strained. The workers thought they were being treated condescendingly. Student discussions tended to be highly theoretical discourses, or also heated arguments. The practical minded workers did not understand most of the discussions and did not find them particularly

---

[46]Takhtarev, *Rabochee dvizhenie*, p. 45.

[47]Kanatchikov, *Iz istorii*, p. 88.

relevant to the reality of daily poverty faced by most people in Russia. Workers saw little point in these arguments. To them it seemed as though the intellectuals did not know themselves what was necessary to do for Russia. Arguments and theoretical discussions only confused these down-to-earth people.

Finally, workers and students had different purposes for their circles. The workers wanted to improve their dreary lives and escape monotonous conditions. Books and education seemed to be the keys for upward mobility and success. For many intellectuals, educating the workers was a means to an end; that was anti-government activity. This different purpose concerning education caused a tremendous conflict between the intellectuals and the members of the Central Workers' Circle. In the mid-1890's the intellectuals decided to switch the focus of activities from educating the members of workers' circles to agitating among the "grey masses" of workers. As a result many educated and highly skilled workers broke completely with the intellectuals, feeling, quite accurately, that the intellectuals abandoned them. This break occurred at about the same time the Central Workers' Circle collapsed due to massive police arrests in 1894.

Within the working class, there was a real contrast between older and younger workers, those under the age of thirty. The younger workers tended to be more skilled, educated, politically developed, and less religious than those of their parents' generation. The generation gap contributed to the basic hostility between the huge mass of ordinary workers and the tiny group of workers' circles. Hostility by the bulk of the older workers toward the workers' circles' membership was particularly sharp on religious and political issues. Intolerantly, members of the workers' circles told their fellow workers to open their eyes, not to be so "blind and stupid." Commonly members of the workers' circles condescendingly called their co-workers "seriye," which may be translated as grey or dull.[48] This pejorative was frequently coupled with other insulting names equivalent to the American word "hick." The members of the workers' circles noted the drinking, arguments, and fights among the rank and file. They wondered how the aggressiveness of the "grey masses" could be directed aginst the government and the system.

Not only did the average worker dislike criticism of religion and the political system, but they also

---

[48] Bogdanov, Na zare, p. 8.

resented the condescending attitude of the membership of the Central Workers' Circle. They knew that "seriye" was a pejorative term. They resented being laughed at for their religious faith, and being called other names such as "barbarians, sheep, and imbeciles." On the other hand, the average worker called members of circles names such as "students," illustrating the bookishness and naivete of members of the Central Workers' Circle. "The grey working mass not only did not like but also detested and could not understand the workers' intelligentsia. The masses considered them wicked and vermin for acting superior."[49] The masses thought when such people criticized the Tsar, that they were "terrorists, scoundrels, and trash."

The gulf between these two elements of the working class transcended social and political issues. I.V. Krutov, a well read machine operator, noted that his workers' audiences could not understand his theoretical discourses on Darwin. They were flatly bewildered.[50] G. Fisher noted that, "factory workers seemed to me another race of workers."[51] While members of the

---

[49] Mironov, Iz vospominanii, p. 20.

[50] Ol'minskii, "Moi vospominaniia," Ot gruppy Blagoeva, p. 12.

[51] Fisher, V Rossii i v Anglii, p. 19.

Central Workers' Circle and the rest of the working class often lived in the same neighborhoods, and worked in the same factories, Fisher was correct in stating they lived in two different worlds. On a basic level they dressed and talked differently, since members of workers' circles often picked up some of the language and customs of their student tutors. Both groups of workers maintained very different social and political values. E.I. Mitskevich was quite accurate when he stated, ". . .From these workers were produced intelligentsia, torn away from the working masses and looking at some of the ordinary workers in a haughty way."[52]

Not only were relations bad between the members of the Central Workers' Circle and the rest of the Russian working class, but they were bad with non-Russian workers as well. St. Petersburg had tens of thousands of non-Russian workers, mostly Finns, Estonians, Latvians, and Poles. Generally, they were better educated, more highly skilled, and politically conscious than Russian workers.[53] On that basis they had many things in common with the members of workers' circles,

---

[52]N. Stepanov, Sotsial-demokratiia v Rossii v kontse XIX i nachale XX vekov (Khar'kov, 1931), p. 29.

[53]Pokrovskii, Statisticheskii, p. 10.

who represented the elite of the Russian working class. On that basis alone, logic would have dictated good relations and ties. Yet S. Kantichikov related that the foreign workers in his metal factory were "all stern, silent, and extraordinarily difficult to meet."[54]

Generally, the foreign workers had contempt for the Russian people as a whole as either inferior or non-Western. Most foreign residents spoke poor Russian, and on that basis alone found it difficult to communicate with Russian workers, who rarely spoke Polish, Finnish, or any of the Baltic languages. They felt alienated in the Russian capital and believed they could only relate with people of their own nationality. The temperament of Finns and Estonians tended to be more inward. Russians did not really understand that. Instead Russians dismissed them as cold and unfriendly.[55] While members of the workers' circles were not, on the whole, prejudiced toward a people of a different nationality, they never understood the traits of other nationalities any better than they understood their fellow workers.

---

[54] Kanatchikov, *Iz istorii*, p. 71.
[55] *Ibid.*, p. 74.

Initially, members of the workers' circles felt very isolated. With unhappy childhoods, they developed a passion for reading. They entered the large, cold, capital alone, but soon married women different from themselves. Their marriages became unhappy affairs. Frequently, they bitterly argued with their wives over issues such as politics or religion, with the wives being much more conservative. Single members rarely dated because they were often reluctant to jeopardize women with the police; arrest could mean their own exile or even death. Friendships outside their own circle were equally shunned both for this reason and for fear of informers. Circle activity absorbed all their free time.

A significant element of the workers' circles were <u>artisans</u>. They either worked individually or in small groups. Thus, their work environment was vastly different from the factory workers. They had an especially privileged position. Did these members form this subgroup mainly for their own advancement, or did they form a "vanguard" for the rest of the proletariat, acting in the interest of the rest of the Russian working class? Many believed they were different. Contempt and dislike for the rest of the working class was common. They had few dealings with them outside the work place. Some even wanted to leave the proletariat class completely, and become teachers, office workers, or statisticians. Essentially they wanted to join the lower elements of the middle class and work for either zemstvos in the countryside or for municipal governments. However, such people formed a minority of the membership of workers' circles in the 1880's and 1890's.[56]

We have reviewed the various characteristics that typified the individuals who belonged to the Central Workers' Circle. While the sample of thirty-eight workers is insufficient to make any broad conclusions about the background and attitudes of a workers' intelligentsia, it is possible to conclude that the members of the Central Workers' Circle were a segment of the workers' intelligentsia. They formed the most vocal and the most politicized subgroup of the workers' intelligentsia. That fact is clear because members of the Central Workers' Circle were the only workers in the 1800's and the 1890's who later wrote memoirs.

While members of the Central Workers' Circle often were isolated socially and culturally from other workers,

---

Liadov, Istoriia, p. 67.

they were not satisfied with that isolation. Slowly, they began to find other workers who shared their ideals. One worker summed up this startling feeling when he declared: "I am not alone; there are many of us, we are as one."[57] Yet for a long time this was a vague idea. They had so many negative experiences to overcome. They slowly learned to trust a few of their co-workers. Once that occurred, then single units from the workers' intelligentsia began to coalesce. N. Rubakin, the learned Russian bibliographer, noted this in an article on the new phenomenon of the workers' intelligentsia when he commented that they "possessed their own Weltschmerz, that is a melancholy over the state of the world, their own principled élan in promoting their own principles."[58] The Central Workers' Circle utilized those ideals in the structure of their group.

---

[57] Buiko, Put' rabochego, p. 14.

[58] N. Rubakin, "Iz zhizni rabochei intelligentsii," Mir bozhii, March 1896, (St. Petersburg, 1896), p. 20.

CHAPTER IV

THE ORGANIZATION AND THE SOCIAL AND CULTURAL ACTIVITIES OF THE CENTRAL WORKERS' CIRCLE

The Organization of the Central Workers' Circle

Following at least two major meetings of representatives from the leading workers' circles in St. Petersburg during the winter of 1889-90, the Central Workers' Circle emerged as the sole organization for most of the workers' intelligentsia.[1] The group lasted in one form or another until 1894 when massive police arrests crippled the organization. The Central Workers' Circle had several purposes. First and perhaps foremost, it raised money to aid its members and their families in times of hardships. Money was also used to purchase books and journals for its own library to further the education of members. The group also established workers' clubs and cooperatives. Furthermore the circle considered that it represented the skilled workers in St. Petersburg when they had con-

---

[1] For further information concerning the formation of the Central Workers' Circle, see pp. 93-94 in chapter two of this dissertation. "The Formation of the Central Workers' Circle." See also Golubev, "Stranichka," pp. 114-116; and also Kazakevich, Sotsial-demokraticheskie, p. 84.

flicts or potential conflicts with governmental and factory authorities. Through libraries, discussions, and the allocation of funds, the group tried to improve the political, economic, and cultural positions of its members. It sought to insure that all activities which pertained to the workers in St. Petersburg were directed by the workers themselves without any interference from intellectuals or any other nonworkers. To accomplish those goals, the dozen or so workers' leaders who gathered in late 1889 and early 1890 recognized that the members of circles needed a centralized organization to direct and coordinate the twenty or so workers' circles in the city. To appreciate properly the impact of the Central Workers' Circle, one needs to deal with the following topics: The type of organization that these workers formed and the democratic nature of the organization. The priorities that the Central Workers' Circle maintained with their intellectual counterparts. The financial resources that the Central Workers' Circle possessed. What the Central Workers' Circle did with those resources to promote the group's interests as well as the interests of the entire workers' intelligentsia. The answers to these topics provide the reader some indications as to the hopes and aspirations of the workers' intelligentsia as embodied in their organization, the Central Workers' Circle.

The Central Workers' Circle had a centralized pyramidal structure. At the top was the Central Workers' Circle itself. Initially it had six to seven members. All the members were young, male, skilled workers, and each came from a different factory or <u>raion</u> (region) in the city. Their names were Nikita Demenkevich Bogdanov and Aleksandr Sergeevich Filimonov, both metal workers; Egor and Fedor Afanasev (Klimanov), brothers, of whom the former was a blacksmith and the latter was a weaver; Gavril Aleksandrovich Mefodiev, another metal worker at the Warsaw Railroad Yard and a former activist in the Tochisskii Circle; Petr Evgrafovich Evgrafov, a worker at the New Admiralty Plant; Vladimir Vasilevich Fomin; a metal worker at the Baltic Plant and the

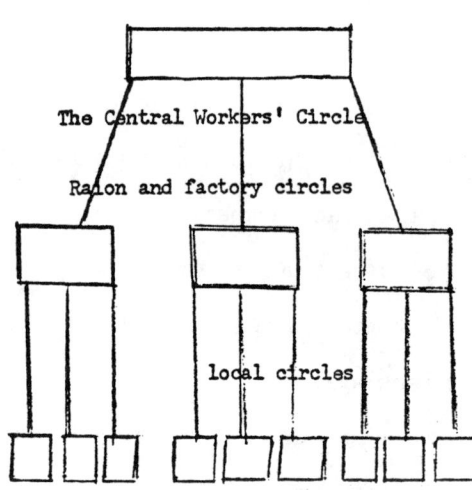

DIAGRAM SHOWING THE INSTITUTIONAL STRUCTURE OF THE CENTRAL WORKERS' CIRCLE

host of the first meetings of the Central Circle; and Vladimir Ilarionovich Proshin, a rubber worker. There were no official leaders of the group, but rapidly Bogdanov and Filimonov emerged as the unacknowledged leaders of the group.[2] Until his arrest in 1891, Egor Afanasev (Klimanov) had the critical position of treasurer. At the two formative meetings, proposals were made that the body of the Central Workers' Circle be elected from the different circles throughout the city. Several workers raised arguments over the issue of group democracy versus the need for security. The advocates of group democracy lost the debate. Their opponents said that frequent police surveillance required that the most active and knowledgeable workers' leaders from the various sections in the city should assume for themselves the various positions on the Central Circle. Advocates of a loosely organized, highly autonomous and democratic organization lost out.

Even after the organization became regularized and consolidated, "representatives were not elected by region, but instead were chosen by the center from a list sent to it."[3] Consequently, members of the Central

---

[2] Ol'minskii, "Gruppa narodovol'tsev," p. 2.

[3] Ibid., p. 5.

Circle did not lose their position through a vote of no confidence or through a defeat in an election. Instead they left only after the police arrested and jailed them. These unplanned removals caused frequent changes in the composition of the group. Despite these frequent changes in membership, the Central Workers' Circle never became a particularly democratic body. The forces for democratization simply never had the votes in meetings to alter the charter. Perhaps an authoritarian government made an authoritarian Central Workers' Circle inevitable.

Directives flowed from the top down. The Central Circle furnished literature to the circles below it. It issued recommendations regarding political and educational activities. Each representative on the Central body became the leader and the organizer for the _raion_ (region) workers' circle, which then transmitted recommendations to the various circles below it. That representative became the liaison between the Central Circle and the regional circle. After often lengthy discussions of the Central Circle's recommendations, the local circle could reject some or all of the recommendations.[4] Thus, recommendations were not

---

[4] Lapsina and Zhuikov, "Novoe," p. 79.

directives. The local circles retained significant autonomy. Decisions throughout the organization from the top Central Circle to lowly factory circles were made on a consensus basis. Voting was informal; generally all members had to go along with a decision for it to be implemented. "The members of the Central Workers' Circle did not have the right to decide significant questions, such as whether or not to participate in a strike, without the approval of all members."[5] In return, the Central Workers' Circle received from the *raion* and factory circles information about events and conditions in factories and plants and heard reports about the progress of all the circles below it.

Each member of these regional circles was supposed to organize as many circles as he could among people at work. He then became the *rukovoditel* (leader) at each circle he established. While one member of the Central Circle could represent more lower circles than another member, he did not have more formal power than anyone else because decision making was conducted in a consensus basis. Informally, some members, due to their persuasive powers, did have more influence than other members. The *rukovoditel* had several obligations. He

---

[5] *Ibid.*, p. 79.

had to remain a member of the raion or factory circle,
and attend its meetings as well as the meetings of his
new circles. These new circles were at the bottom of
the pyramid. They exercised much less democratic
autonomy than either the Central Workers' Circle or the
raion and the factory circles. In the local circles,
the leader decided the group's activities and meeting
agendas. He controlled both the treasury and the
library, two of the circle's most crucial agencies.
The rukovoditel received and then distributed proclamations and leaflets to his members. As the charter for
the Central Workers' Circle indicated, the rukovoditel
for these localized circles even had the power to
approve or veto candidates for new membership. "Each
active member has the right to decide which workers
should become members of circles."[6] Provisions were
made in case of incompetent or weak leadership. In
those situations, the raion or factory circle had the
obligation to remove that individual and install someone else as rukovoditel. Furthermore there was a limit
to mobility in the pyramid. No member in the lowest
circles, except for the rukovoditel, could serve on the
raion and factory circles. The excuse given by the

---

[6] Ibid., p. 79.

charter was to insure security for the organization. Presumably keeping the membership list on this tier of circles secret would keep it out of the hands of police discovery for a longer period. Only the rukovoditel kept the list, and specifically he would have to be arrested for the contents of the list to get divulged to the police.[7] Security was used again to limit democracy in the organization. The need to maintain security determined the membership of the organization in the upper two tiers of the pyramid.

All of the circles were fairly small. They averaged six to eight workers. Only workers could be members. The organizers believed that large circles attracted police attention. The lower circles were concentrated in the largest factories in St. Petersburg, such as the Putilow, the Obukhov, the Baltic, the Warsaw Railroad, the State Paper Mill, the French-Russian co-owned Berda factory, and the New Admiralty. These factories were scattered throughout the city; on Vasilyevskii Island, in the Neva Gates and the Narva Gates regions in the city's south side, in the downtown Obvodnoi Canal area, and the newer Vyborg and Petersburg sections on the north and northeast

---

[7] Ibid., p. 80.

sides of town. Meetings for all circles occurred once a week in the evening after work in a member's room or apartment, often rotating from member to member. Most meetings were devoted to lectures and subsequent discussions based on those lectures. Most people worked until 6 p.m. Circle meetings started an hour later, at seven, and sometimes went on until midnight or 1 a.m. Individuals were not at their freshest at those hours. Petr Kaizo, another labor activist, commented that by 9 p.m., he often dozed off, right during the lecture.[8] On the other hand, the Central Workers' Circle met each Sunday, a better time because most workers had that day free. It had a set place which was a communal apartment held by Gavril Mefodiev, his wife and three other labor activists. The first few meetings of the local circles were devoted to acquainting each member with the other members. They also set up educational goals for the circle as well as a basic format for meetings.

A major goal for all circles, particularly the lower circles, was to further the education of its members usually through lectures. The lectures covered a broad gamut of subjects that might interest the workers. For example, Charles Darwin's theory of evolu-

---

[8] Ol'minskii, "Moi vospominaniia," *Ot gruppy Blagoeva*, p. 11.

tion was a very popular subject. Another subject was an explanation of Das Kapital, the complicated three volume political-economic work by Karl Marx. These subjects had to be delivered by student teachers in an extremely clear, simplified manner often repeating major points. Otherwise the audience would not understand, and would doze off.[9] If a student could not be available for a meeting, then the rukovoditel, who was usually the most educated worker at the meeting, acted as the lecturer and the moderator of the discussion. Other subjects were less academic, and more directly pertinent to the concerns of St. Petersburg workers at that time. For example, workers heard lectures by their tutors on various factory inspectors' reports describing conditions in Russian factories. The lectures often lasted two hours. After the lecture, the members present discussed the subject, often in a heated manner. When there was no formal lecture planned for the meeting, usually a few members brought up an unresolved question or issue. For example, workers frequently discussed the working and living conditions of workers in Western Europe and in the

---

[9] Ol'minskii, "Moi vospominaniia," Ot gruppy Blagoeva, p. 10.

United States, and compared their conditions to those of Russian workers.

Often the source material for those discussions was newspaper articles from Russkie Vedomosti or other quality liberal newspapers.[10] Other times the members utilized materials from the thick political-library journals then popular such as Mir Bozhii. The circles got copies of these journals from the Central Workers' Circle library, or else if funds were adequate, they developed their own libraries. Then they discussed how their salary and working conditions could be improved. Those discussions often led their members to play a more active political role, such as participating in strikes in their factories. As all strikes were illegal in Tsarist Russia, participation in strikes at different factories from which the members were employed was a political statement. Yet rarely, as we will see, were these workers the initiators of such strikes. The members of circles, sometimes even at the lowest level, were from the best educated and informed core of workers. Yet they were not ready to play a leadership role because they feared that exposure led to inevitable

---

[10] M. Morshanskaia, Tkach Fedor Afanas'ev (Moscow, 1924), p. 58.

arrest. Only a few members of the workers' intelligentsia were ready to take that risk.

The safeguarding of security was a prime consideration for the members of circles. They wanted to advance themselves, not become martyrs. As discussions became quite heated at times, members feared that attention from neighbors would be drawn to their meetings. Sometimes, a member played an accordian to cover up the noise from discussions.[11] Vera Karelina also mentioned that her circle met in an apartment located in a haunt of vice. It was a large building where two brothels were located. She said that the local police traditionally closed their eyes to that building.[12] Her apartment was two rooms. The front room gave the appearance of a social gathering. When prospective members attended, the circle gathered in the front room where they danced, and played music. Only later, after the group decided the candidate was trustworthy did they move into the back room where the serious discussions occurred. To further insure the group's security, a worker only became a candidate for member-

---

[11] V. Karelina, "Na zare rabochego dvizheniia v Peterburge," Krasnaia Letopis', no. 4, 1922, p. 16.

[12] Karelina, "Na zare," p. 15.

ship after the recommendation of not one but two current members.[13] Nevertheless, police surveillance and nosy neighbors caused the breakup of most circles after a few years. Circle meetings were a very risky venture, despite all the precautions taken to prevent arrests.

Meetings of the Central Workers' Circle and the raion and the factory circles were not only devoted to lectures and educational forums, but they were also devoted to overseeing the other circles. The leader from the local circle, or the representative from the middle tier of circles, the raion and factory ones, delivered reports on the condition of his circle, affairs that were progressing, and new activities they were considering. Then the circle discussed the report and issued its recommendations. Finally, the Central Workers' Circle and the raion and the factory circles screened prospective candidates for membership in the lowest circles. Thus they had a voice, and often a veto over both the personnel and the agendas of the lower circles. In this way, the organization of workers' circles in St. Petersburg had a centralized structure. A student activist, L.B. Krasin, summarized

---

[13]Nevskii, Ocherki, p. 278.

the purposes of the upper tier circles when he said: "The development of self-knowledge remains in the words of the workers, a necessity in each factory and plant to show the workers their poor position, to organize self-help groups, to work for common interests, and to gradually unify the various circles."[14]

Parallel with the network of workers' circles, two groups of intellectuals formed two centralized structures of circles in St. Petersburg. Coincidentally, these two groups had a similar three tier pyramidal structure: a central circle composed of representatives selected from sections of the city or from educational institutions, which were in turn composed of representatives from local circles. While the two groups had this similar structure, each group--the Central Workers' Circle and the Central Students' Circle--maintained a distinct identity, policies, aims and aspirations completely independent of the other. Just as in the Central Workers' Circle, orders flowed from the top down. One of their main purposes was to coordinate and to regularize contacts with the workers. Soon after the formation of the Central Workers' Circle,

---

[14]Krasin, "Dela davno," p. 14.

a representative from the student intelligentsia attended most of their meetings. Their representatives acted in an advisory capacity. They recommended educational subjects for lectures and discussions. They got books for discussions and aided in activities. Their recommendations were just that, recommendations. They could not make policy. One of the student representatives, Mikhail I. Brusnev, went so far as to say the role of the student intelligentsia was "strictly pedagogical." He made it very clear that the intelligentsia should not try to direct the workers' circles. "The liberation of the workers is an affair of the workers themselves. The role of the intelligentsia should get less and less."[15] He believed that the intelligentsia acted at the behest and at the service of the workers' intelligentsia. Their presence was supposed to be unobtrusive and advisory.

Four students, three of whom veered toward Social Democracy, were attached to the Central Workers' Circle during its four year existence. They were, in order of chronological placement: V.S. Golubev, with a pseudonym of "Diadia Senia," a student at St. Petersburg University; M.I. Brusnev, who had the pseudonym of "Semen

---

[15] Nevskii, *Ocherki*, p. 304.

Petrovich," a student at the Technological Institute; W.F. Cywiński, a Pole who also attended the Technological Institute; and M.S. Olminskii, who also had the pseudonym of "Aleksandrov." The first three served in rapid succession, while Olminskii, a Populist, acted as the intelligentsia's representative for the last half of its existence. None overstepped their roles as advisors. According to Brusnev, "the idea that the liberation of the working class was the task of the workers was inculcated by us in all the workers' circles."[16] They tried to ensure that the other intellectuals aiding in workers' circles did not overstep their advisory role. They acted strictly as teachers. For example, V.V. Sviatlovskii taught chemistry in Egor Afanasev's (Klimanov) circle.[17] Intellectuals aided the workers' circles by obtaining books for reading lessons and discussions. Their goal was to prepare the workers' intelligentsia through education to become potential leaders for the less prepared and educated workers. In the lowest workers'

---

[16] M.I. Brusnev, "Pervye revoliutsionnye shagi L. Krasina," in M.N. Liadov and S.M. Pozner, eds., Leonid Boriscvich Krasin (Moscow-Leningrad, 1928), p. 69.

[17] Kochakov, Ocherki istorii Leningrada, p. 388.

circles, the intellectuals' main task was just to teach basic reading, writing, and arithmetic. At that level it was impossible for them to teach the theories of Marx and Engels.

While there were two separate intellectual organizations at that time in St. Petersburg, they cooperated closely. For example, one organization, the <u>Gruppa Narodovol'tsev</u> (the <u>Narodnaia</u> <u>Volia</u> or People's Will Group) owned a secret printing press, and very willingly published the other organization's materials along with its own. The former organization tended toward Populism, while the latter, the Central Students' Circle, tended toward Social Democracy.[18] Yet these political lines were blurred. For example, item number eleven of the Central Students' Circle's program stated that "the workers must struggle for liberation through the use of political terror. This political terror is recognized as the main instrument in the struggle against the autocracy."[19] The espousal of terror was a cardinal principle of a part of the Populist movement in the late nineteenth century. Georgii Plekhanov, the

---

[18] While this group had the same name and had similar ideas, it was a different organization than its famous namesake of a decade previous.

[19] Kon', <u>Istoriia</u>, p. 193.

father of Russian Marxism, strongly denounced the use of political terror as, "a rash and impetuous movement, which would drain the energy of the revolutionists and provide a government repression so severe as to make any agitation among the masses impossible."[20] By 1890, Plekhanov's views were well known but not often popular with many politically liberal and radical Russians. While remaining organizationally distinct, the two intelligentsia networks had similar goals regarding the workers, did not possess two distinct ideologies and cooperated closely.

The first network to organize was the one that had mostly Social Democratic ideas. In the fall of 1889, several student circles, mostly from the Technological Institute but also including some from the University, united into a city-wide organization.[21] The name of this organization became the Central Students' Circle, a kindred name to the workers' group just then forming. The group met regularly one evening a week to discuss

---

[20] L.B. Deich, G.V. Plekhanov, materialy dlia biografii (Moscow, 1922), p. 45.

[21] For further information on the formation of the Central Students' Circle, sometimes called the Brusnev group, see chapter 2, pp. 87-90. See also the memoir accounts by M.I. Brusnev, "Vozniknovenie," pp. 26-28, and V.B. Bartenev, "Vospominaniia," pp. 170-174.

major problems and their experiences with the other
student circles. Its membership consisted of six
Polish students: G.M. Rodziewicz (Rodzevich) and his
wife, B. Lelewel, W.F. Cywiński, I.K. Buraczewski, and
C. Bankowski; and three Russians: V.N. Ivanov, P.A.
Golubev, and V.S. Golubev. (No relation is known.)
Its goals were to coordinate student intelligentsia
work among the workers' circles and to expand the group's
own educational development. As Brusnev, who joined the
Circle a few months later, stated: "The goal of the
organization was to go to the workers to prepare some
of them to become leaders of the workers."[22] Their
method of training leaders among the workers was to
broaden the education of those workers. The new
organization gradually grew. Besides Brusnev, L.B.
Krasin, a man who made his mark in diplomacy three
decades later, joined the Central Circle. Even though
Brusnev was not one of the founding fathers of the
organization, and was not a leader, many Soviet sources
have called the Central Students' Circle, the Brusnev

---

[22] I. Nikitin, Pervye rabochie soiuzy i sotsial-demo-kraticheskie organizatsii v Rossii (Moscow, 1952), p. 87.

group.[23] The reason is, most likely, that they did not want to name it after a Pole or after a Russian such as V.S. Golubev, who turned away from Marxism. He entered the Central Workers' Circle as the liaison between the organized workers' circle and the organized intellectual groups. With this expansion and newly found recognition, the group formulated a program, defining the group's policies and goals.[24]

At the moment when the Central Student Circle succeeded in conducting numerous activities with the Central Workers' Circle, it was buffeted by several police arrests. During the spring of 1890, St. Petersburg students conducted large scale student demonstrations that were largely nonpolitical. "In spite of our opposition, the demonstrations involved us."[25] The subsequent arrests removed some of the group's leading members. Only V.S. Golubev, Cywiński, and

---

[23] Several Soviet authors have used this confusing designation. For example, R.G. Lapsina and G.S. Zhuikov, "Novoe o deiatel'nosti," *Voprosy istorii KPSS*, 1971, pp. 78-80; and R.A. Kazakevich, *Sotsialdemokraticheskie organizatsii Peterburga*, 1960, pp. 77-82.

[24] For a translation and an explanation of the program of the Central Student' Circle, see the appendix.

[25] Brusnev, "Vozniknovenie," p. 25.

Brusnev survived unscathed. To make the situation worse, a number of Polish activists such as Cywiński left St. Petersburg for Poland, because they regarded their work with Russian workers as merely a preparatory time for activism in Poland. After police attention lessened in the fall of 1890, several student activists such as L.B. Krasin and Cywiński returned to St. Petersburg. With the survivors, they revived the Central Students' Circle and reestablished contacts with the Central Workers' Circle.[26] Problems with the police during the spring persuaded the intellectuals to be very careful in their dealings with the workers so as not to endanger them. For example, they stipulated that students present in workers' circles' meetings must always wear inconspicuous clothing made of poor material similar to what workers wore. Then attention from police agents would not be drawn to them which could become fatal to the entire circle. Everything had to be done in a conspiratorial manner.[27]

A few months later, during the winter of 1890-91, Populist circles started to centralize their disparate groups in St. Petersburg. They called their group, the

---

[26] Golubev, "Stranichka," p. 115.

[27] Brusnev, "Vozniknovenie," p. 28.

Gruppa Narodovol'tsev (the Narodnaia Volia group). They maintained good relations with the Central Students' Circle. Nevertheless, the former never merged with the latter. There exists no record of their program and a few details concerning their organization.[28] It aided the Central Students' Circle in the publication of some of its brochures and leaflets. Its leader M.S. Olminskii (Aleksandrov) became the representative from the intellectuals in the Central Workers' Circle in the summer of 1892, a position he held until 1894.

Thus, while the two major intellectual student organizations in St. Petersburg maintained good relations with the Central Workers' Circle, and had one representative present there most of the time on that body; his role was clearly advisory and educational--to bring knowledge to the workers. They conducted lectures, and gave advice. The workers insisted that they retain control over their own organization. They alone made the crucial decisions. While many intellectuals wanted more influence over the workers' move-

---

[28] The main source for information concerning this group can be found in M.S. Ol'minskii's (Aleksandrov's) article, "Gruppa narodovol'tsev, 1891-1894 gg.," Byloe, no. 11, 1906, pp. 1-27.

ment, the leadership of the student intelligentsia agreed with Brusnev that, "the intelligentsia was often alien to the ideology of the working class, and its leadership was both casual and unreliable."[29] Thus, throughout the short life span of the Central Workers' Circle, it retained its independence of the intellectuals. The existence of both parallel organizations, the Central Workers' Circle and the Central Students' Circle, was accidental in the similar dates that they were created and in their similar structures.

The Social and Cultural Activities of the Central Workers' Circle

The Central Workers' Circle organized, and then supervised several groups or organs to benefit its workers. A few of these facilities such as libraries had existed in workers' circles since they emerged in the 1880's. A few were new groups for any workers' organization. Two organs, the treasury and the library, were fundamental to the Central Workers' Circle so that it could achieve its goals. Never previously had any groups been

---

[29] Brusnev, "Pervye revoliutsionnie shagi," p. 69.

organized on a city-wide scale by Russian workers for the benefit of their fellow workers. These organs had a combined economic, cultural, and social purpose. They proved critical to the organization and its success. A great many of the circle's meetings were devoted to the smooth functioning of these organs at a time of inadequate funding. Varying amounts of information are known about these organs. For some a great deal of material exists. For others, little is known. Often very sketchy material adds to the difficulty of assessing their effectiveness. Therefore their effectiveness must be evaluated in those terms.

Most likely the most important organ of the Central Workers' Circle was the Central Labor Fund, its treasury. Each workers' circle down to the lowest level had its own treasury. Most of these treasuries were small, and were raised completely through members' donations. The amounts that were contributed depended on each person's salary. If a person earned less than thirty rubles a month, he or she contributed two kopeks for each ruble of salary. If the individual earned over thirty rubles a month, he or she contributed three kopeks for each ruble.[30] A candidate for membership also had to make a contribution. Yet his donation was approximately one-half of the full members' rates. It was interesting that the amount contributed was proportional to an individual's income. Therefore if a worker earned twenty-five rubles a month, his contribution to his circle's treasury was fifty kopeks a month. If he earned sixty rubles a month, which few Russian workers did, then his contribution was 1.8 rubles each month. The <u>rukovoditel</u> (organizer or leader) of the circle was usually placed in charge of the treasury which was an indication of the treasury's importance for the group. The funds in these treasuries were used mostly to purchase literature.

As the Central Workers' Circle organized during the winter of 1890, it decided to set up a Central Labor Fund to handle the expanded functions of the local circles and the new city-wide organization. Each local circle and <u>raion</u> (region) and factory circle contributed an undetermined sum to the newly created Central Labor Fund. Each month it donated part of its

---

[30] Lapsina and Zhuikov, "Novoe," p. 80.

financial resources to that fund. Each member of the Central Workers' Circle contributed fifty kopeks a month to the Central Labor Fund.[31] Besides members' and circles' donations, the Central Treasury received money from other sources as well. For example, the circle held lotteries or dances from which profits went to the treasury. Sympathetic individuals, such as several members of the liberal intelligentsia, made donations from time to time. Nevertheless, most of the donations were made by the workers themselves.[32] Sometimes members collected money from sympathetic co-workers in evening and in factory schools, as well as on the factory floor itself. The sums raised through all these methods became considerable, especially when one considers the marginal income most Russian workers earned. By 1891, the Central Labor Fund had 1400 rubles in it.[33] Until his arrest in 1891, Egor Afanasev (Klimanov) was in charge of the fund with the official title of Treasurer. Afterwards,

---

[31] Sviatlovskii, "Na zare," p. 141.
[32] Ol'minskii, "Gruppa narodovol'tsev," p. 7.
[33] Sviatlovskii, "Na zare," p. 145.

V.A. Shelgunov became Treasurer, a position he held until mass arrests virtually destroyed the Circle in 1894.

The formation of the Central Labor Fund had significant implications for the Russian labor movement. Essentially, it combined a large percentage of funds from all of the disparate circles in St. Petersburg. All of the circles had to agree in the goals of having a treasury. This gave the Central Workers' Circle and its integral parts a cohesiveness it probably would not have had otherwise. It cemented relations among the localized circles throughout the city. Having a lot of their money involved, each circle had control over the priorities the Central Labor Fund would have. For example, a decision on whether funding would go only to members, or whether it could go to nonmembers as well, had significance beyond the action itself. Because the Central Workers' Circle was placed in direct charge of the Fund, its authority became enhanced. As a result it believed it represented a large percentage of the "workers' intelligentsia" in St. Petersburg. In this way, the Central Workers' Circle became an embryonic trade union for the highly skilled workers. In fact, it became an educational training ground for leaders from Russian labor a decade later when trade unions became legalized. The members of the Central Workers' Circle decided the money from the Central Labor Fund should be devoted both to the group's activities, and to the labor movement as a whole in St. Petersburg. In fact, the largest single portion went into a strike fund to aid striking, arrested, or exiled workers and their families.[34] That action showed that the members of the Central Workers' Circle developed a bond with, at least other skilled workers. The rest of the funds went to the purchase of books and journals for educational work in the circles, and to cover daily expenses that the group incurred. The Central Workers' Circle was committed to retaining control of the treasury. At all levels only workers were placed in charge of funds. They resisted attempts by students to gain control of the treasuries. At least four times, in 1890 and 1891, the Central Students' Circle through its representative on the Central Workers Circle urged that the treasury be incorporated into the treasury of the

---

[34] Korolchuk and Sokolova, Khronika, p. 75. The information is based on unpublished sources from the Leningrad archives. While there are no exact records of how the Labor Fund disbursed its money, R.G. Lapsina in his recent article "Novoe o deiatel'nosti," p. 80, mentioned that half of the Treasury's sums went into a strike fund.

Central Students' Circle. The workers insisted their treasury retain its separate structure and leadership.[35] Nevertheless, members of the Central Students' Circle "borrowed" the considerable sum of 600 rubles for the publication of the Protocols of the Paris Congress of the Socialist Internationale held in 1889. That sum was never returned to the workers.[36] No source mentioned the reaction of the workers to this large "borrowing" of funds. Given the workers' control over their treasury, they had to approve such a large loan to the intelligentsia. The Central Labor Fund became a central feature of the Central Workers' Circle. It provided the funding for most of the group's activities. Its aid to striking or arrested workers and their families allowed the reputation of the Circle to spread far beyond the small confines of the members' circles. It allowed the Central Workers' Circle to develop a sense of cohesiveness and purpose that it might not have otherwise developed. The Central Labor Fund was the mortar that enabled the structure to stand.

---

[35] Takhtarev, *Rabochee dvizhenie*, p. 14.

[36] Ol'minskii, "Gruppa narodovol'tsev," p. 14.

A major focus of the Central Workers' Circle was educational. It wanted to improve its own and its affiliated circles' educational development. All of these workers' circles began as discussion groups. The workers' intelligentsia yearned for further education. Members of the students' intelligentsia commented on the remarkable striving for self-education among the skilled workers. At every available moment they went to the city's libraries and reading rooms, attended public lectures, and subscribed to the city's better quality newspapers. One intellectual, S.I. Mitskevich, who maintained frequent contacts with workers, even declared that the workers became as educationally developed as the student intelligentsia, even in fields such as Russian literary criticism, political economy, and literature.[37] Perhaps that statement was an exaggeration emerging out of the author's enthusiasm over the workers he had contact with; but it was certainly accurate that the workers' intelligentsia made tremendous progress from near illiteracy within their native villages.

---

[37] Nevskii, Ocherki, p. 280.

Several members of the Central Students' Circle aided the Central Workers' Circle in introducing a comprehensive educational system that included all levels of circles from what had been a haphazard program of education. This printed list was found in Brusnev's apartment at the time of his arrest in 1892. It gives an excellent indication of the type and the variety of subjects covered in the lectures during circle meetings. The procedure stated:

1. Reading, writing, and arithmetic.

2. Chemistry, physics, botany, zoology, physiology, anatomy, hygiene; briefly: geology, cosmography, astronomy. Various theories of the origin of the earth and the universe.

3. Darwin's theory. The theory of the origin and the evolution of organisms and the origin of man.

4. The history of culture. The period of savagery and of barbarism. The life of man in each of these periods (his food, occupations, family, customs, laws, beliefs, property, the full communism of that time and social life and evolution of all this). The development and evolution of authority, religion, morality, family, and property. The dependence of all aspects of human life on economic conditions.

    The period of civilization. The same but more detailed study of this period with the addition of the political history of ancient and modern peoples--and this includes the entire evolution of all aspects of the life of the Russian people, and especially of Russian history. The history of science, philosophy, discoveries and inventions.

5. Political economy. The history of the evolution of forms of organization of labor (slavery, feudalism, capitalism, the inevitable evolution of the latter to collectism). The history of political economy.

6. The condition and history of peasants in Russia and the West. The peasant commune, artels, allotments, food supply, and taxes. Banks-peasant (and landlords). Resettlement, the Old Believers and sectarians.

7. The condition of the working class in Russia and the West. The history of the labor movement in connection with the theories of various reformers. Palliatives for the labor problem (consumer and building societies, etc.), factory legislation.

8. The history of social movements in Europe, and its fullest, most detailed history in Russia, including Narodnaia Volia. The present-day condition and importance of all the classes in Russia (gentry, clergy, bourgeoisie, peasantry, and workers; bureaucracy, army, government).

9. Economic policy and its history in the West and in Russia. The essence of Socialism.

10. The full and detailed program--minimum of demands for the present time, precisely and explicitly grounded.[38]

As source material for their lectures, intellectuals used several basic texts, scientific articles and collections. A partial list of these was also dis-

---

[38] Ol'minskii, "Materialy po delu," Ot gruppy Blagoeva, p. 85-86.

covered in Brusnev's apartment.[39] To teach astronomy the texts used were: A. Flamarion's *Popular Astronomy*, Gil'emen's (Gilman's) *Astronomy*, and M. Betkher's (Boetcher's) *Beginning Course in Cosmography*. For physics and chemistry, the intellectuals used I.I. Gerasimov's *Survey Course of Physics* and Iu. Bernstein's *Chemistry*. To explain the recent and highly controversial theories of Darwin, intellectuals resorted to various articles such as Simonovich's "Theories of Natural Selection," Osboni's "Theories of Darwin," Ferrera's "Darwinism," and K.A. Timiriazev's "Theories of Darwin." These articles or books were difficult. They were geared to either a *gymnasium* or university level. While it was quite true that the students had to clearly explain and simplify this material, these texts indicated the level of this stage of worker's education was high. The listing of texts and articles found in Brusnev's apartment further indicated that the primary focus for these lectures was educational rather than political propaganda. The educational program and the reading materials indicated the ambitiousness of the project.

---

[39] *Ibid.*, pp. 86-87.

The program further suggests the breadth of the educational plan and the gradual manner in which the workers were introduced to socialism. Only the latter part of the program focused on labor and revolutionary history. Only the last subject in the program specifically mentioned socialism. Given the huge scope of this program and the educational level of many workers' circles, it was most likely that few intellectuals were able to get as far as points seven through nine. In fact, most circles did not get beyond point three. Thus, the teaching of socialism was an idealization few intellectuals realized in their circles. The goal of the intellectuals was to give the workers the most broad based education as possible, and what was possible most likely was quite limited.

To provide for any extensive lecture and educational programs, the circles needed libraries for the necessary texts and articles. Almost always there was a direct link between the existence of a library and a treasury. One needed the funds provided by a treasury to purchase the necessary books. Therefore, the second largest amount of money from treasuries, ranging from the Central Labor Fund down to the lowest circle's treasuries, went to the acquisition of reading matter for the libraries. Nevertheless, despite economizing measures and a careful selection of books, there was never enough money for sufficient purchases.[40] The workers used diverse methods to build up their library. They browsed through the second-hand bookstores in St. Petersburg for books and journals. Yet even second-hand books were expensive. A collection of the works of Chernyshevskii cost thirty rubles, while Belinskii's works went for as much as seventy-five rubles.[41] Sometimes travellers from abroad brought in books in their baggage or in their pockets. Yet book smuggling was always risky for both the carrier and the recipient. Frequently, the individuals donated what books they could. In an unusual example, I.I. Timofeev, a machinist, donated his huge collection of nearly one thousand volumes to the Central Workers' Circle, even though it was kept in his apartment.[42] Through such methods, given its very limited financial resources, the Central Workers' Circle created a very extensive library for its time.

To avoid implicating the workers in any unnecessary problems with the police, the illegal literature

---

[40] Ol'minskii, "Gruppa narodovol'tsev," p. 20.

[41] Sviatlovskii, "Na zare," p. 150.

[42] Norinskii, "Moi vospominaniia," Ot gruppy Blagoeva, p. 10.

was kept at the flat of Brusnev, a member of the Central Students' Circle. The illegal section was a repository for any material--books, brochures, and manuscripts--that were banned in Russia and that might interest St. Petersburg's workers. The legal library, located in Bogdanov's and Timofeev's flats, had a fair selection covering a number of different fields. There were numerous Russian and West European literary classics and histories, especially histories of the labor movement such as A.K. Mikhailov's *Proletariat vo Frantskii, 1789-1852* (*Proletariat in France*), or V.V. Bervi-Flerovskii's *Polozhenie rabochego klassa v Rossii* (*Position of the Working Class in Russia*).[43] Other books were devoted to the natural and physical sciences covering fields such as astronomy, geology, physics, chemistry, and biology. These scientific books were in greatest demand.[44] Other books were about political theory and economy such as works by Ferdinand Lassalle and Karl Marx's *Das Kapital*. Many of these works had been published in the 1870's, often by the Chaikovskii group, at a time when Russia experienced a much less

---

[43] Sviatlovskii, "Na zare," p. 149.

[44] Ol'minskii, "O vospominaniiakh N.D. Bogdanova," *Ot gruppy Blagoeva*, p. 40.

severe censorship. In the second-hand book shops, the workers purchased old journals such as Sovremennik (Contemporary), Otechestvennie Zapiski (Notes to the Fatherland), Russkoe Slovo (Russian Word), and Delo (Affairs). They contained articles by leading Russian Populist writers and critics such as Nikolai Chernyshevskii, Nikolai Dobroliubov, Dmitrii Pisarev, N.V. Shelgunov, and Nikolai Uspenskii.[45] Furthermore, the legal collection contained several reports describing Russian factory conditions written in the 1880's such as E.M. Dementev's, Erisman's, and Pogozhaev's. Finally the legal collection contained copies of the politically more liberal newspapers such as Russkie Vedomosti. The legal collection had several functions. For one thing it served as the primary source for circle lectures and discussions. Secondly, often these books were passed from worker to worker in St. Petersburg's factories. That distribution gave good publicity for the Central Workers' Circle among the other skilled workers. Some of them, as a result, joined one or another of its circles. Thus, the library served as a recruitment tool as well as a good tool for public

---

[45] Nevskii, Ocherki, p. 274.

relations. Finally, of course, the books raised the educational level of Russian workers. Ostensible legality of these books did not provide immunity from seizure. In November 1891, Bogdanov was arrested with his roommate. During the subsequent search of his apartment, police found the library, and seized the whole collection.[46] The factory and raion circle libraries, in particular, Timofeev's undetected collection, had to fill the void, but managed to do so. Because Timofeev was never arrested, his huge library became the core collection for the Central Workers' Circle.

Besides the legal collection, the Central Workers' Circle possessed an extensive illegal collection. When the police raided Brusnev's apartment, they found that entire collection which had been stored there. The following is a listing of what they discovered:

- --printed appeal-"From the Gruppa Narodovol'tsev to youth (1 March 1892)."
- --printed sheet-the Gruppa Narodovol'tsev program, March 1892.
- --program of the Social Democratic group, "Emancipation of Labor," Geneva, 1884.

---

[46] Ol'minskii, "O vospominaniiakh," Ot gruppy Blagoeva, p. 44.

210

--brochures, eight pages, "Questions for clarification and work of the program of the Social Revolutionary Party of Russia, 1888."

--printed brochures, 90 pages, "Russian workers in the revolutionary movement."

--printed brochure, 37 pages, "Russian survey," author: Georgii Plekhanov.

--a note that begins with the words, "to read, to write, and to count. . ."

--a half sheet of note paper with the words, "develop scientific statistics and collections. . ."

--appeal "to Russian youth," from the Central Committee of the Union of the Youth, party of Narodnaia Volia, (1 Feb. 1884).

--printed matter, "Program to the Workers," from the members of the party of Narodnaia Volia.

--speech of Petr Abramovich Telalov.

--Plekhanov's book, Nashi raznoglasiia, (Our Differences).

--printed brochures both by Proudhon: Anarchy, part two, and Confessions of a revolutionary.

--brochure, G.V. Plekhanov, "Socialism and Political Struggle."

--brochures: "Science and life," "Tasks of Socialism," and "Role and the forms of Socialist propaganda."

--brochure in German by F. Lassalle, "Program of Workers."

--brochure by V. Korolenko, "Miracles."

--brochures: "1 May 1891, with appendix," "address to N.V. Shelgunov," both printed by the Gruppa Narodovol'tsev, 1892, St. Petersburg.

--manuscript, 127 pages, entitled, Series.

--manuscript, 26 pages, entitled, *Fate of Capitalism in Russia*.

--letter signed by "Vash Petrov."

--two copies of "Russian workers in revolutionary movement."

--one copy, "Collection of Social Democracy."

--brochure, seven pages, P. Akselrod, "Letter to Russian workers," "Tasks of the workers' intelligentsia in Russia."

--book, G.V. Plekhanov, *Ferdinand Lassalle, his life and work*.

--one copy: *Yearbook of the World wide holiday for workers*.

--three copies, "Workers' Movement and Social Democracy."

--one copy, *The Communist Manifesto*.

--two copies, "What does Social Democracy want?"

--two copies, Tikhomirov's "Autocracy: to defend or to grieve about?"

--one copy, "Our poor philosophy."

--31 copies, "Russian wide survey."

--A. Chaffee, *Die Bekämpfung der Sozial-demokratie* (*The Fight of Social Democracy*).

--"The Religion of Socialism."

--The *Efhuz* (sic) of Socialism."

--"Socialism in England."

--Exercise book beginning with the words, "Scientific and utopian socialism," translated from a brochure of F. Engels.

--14 sheets signed P. Akselrod.

--"Introduction, necessities of consumer needs."

--written on two sheets of notepaper a manifesto beginning with the words, "Welcome by the International Union of Socialists. . ." and ending with "program of preparatory work of the Committee."[47]

Virtually all of these materials were written by socialists on subjects which were supposed to interest St. Petersburg workers. Most were propaganda pieces designed for political agitation by the teachers in the workers' circles. For that reason, there were few long books; instead short brochures predominated. Yet the ideology was not fixed. Obviously many of these brochures were written by Social Democrats reflecting their political perspective. Nevertheless, many important recent Populist brochures were contained in the collection. Had relations between Social Democrats and Populists been unsatisfactory, it would have been highly unlikely that a Marxist such as Brusnev would have kept this material, along with brochures by the anarchists, F. Lassalle and Proudhon.

Many of the Russian materials were printed on a hectograph that was not a satisfactory process for several reasons. First, only a relatively few copies

---

[47] Ol'minskii, "Materialy po delu," Ot gruppy Blagoeva, pp. 84-85.

could be made by that method, perhaps 45 to 60. The letters were dim and hard to read. Often, there were smudges, bare patches, and poor separation between lines.[48] Nevertheless, the Central Students' Circle was able to make the hectographs themselves. They did not have to depend on material from abroad that might not make it across the border. Nor did they have to be completely dependent on the Gruppa Narodovol'tsev's printing press, the only one belonging to a revolutionary organization in the city. Nevertheless, the process was very complicated and exacting. It was difficult to find the necessary chemicals. As it was, everything had to be printed secretly, yet the process made a great deal of noise.[49] For that reason, workers and their teachers supplemented the collection with materials printed by emigre Russians in Switzerland. Despite all the difficulties involved, the illegal section was considered a necessary part of the library. It caused a greater cohesion and interdependence between the Central Students' Circle and the Central Workers' Circle than otherwise would have

---

[48] Vladimir Bonch-Bruevich. Na zare revoliutsionnoi proletarskoi bor'by (vospominaniiam), Moscow, 1932, p. 18.

[49] Mironov, Iz vospominanii rabochego, p. 28.

occurred. It provided the intellectuals with agitational materials needed to propagandize among workers who might be receptive.

The Central Workers' Circle established several consumer cooperatives for workers at factories where they were particularly active. The purpose of these cooperatives was to provide the factory workers with cheap food, tobacco, tea, coffee, along with a wide assortment of other items. They were to circumvent the high priced shops where workers traditionally shopped. Their intention was good. They would aid the poorly paid workers. The cooperatives made good publicity for the Central Workers' Circle and could be utilized as a recruitment tool. It would instill a self-help ethic among the city's workers. Rapidly five cooperatives were established at the Putilov, Baltic, and the Obukhov factories. The organizer for them was Vladimir Fomin.

Nevertheless, despite the good intentions, the consumer cooperatives did not accomplish their intended purpose. Right from the start of the operation, the cooperatives had several problems. The food stuffs, which were obtained in grain stores and wholesale shops, were of poor quality and selection. The cooperatives rarely had in stock at any particular moment more than a dozen different items.[50] The members of the cooperatives contributed some money from their wages for the purchase of supplies and for the upkeep of the cooperatives. However, the total sum collected was never sufficient to allow for a large stock in each cooperative. Because the organizers could not get government approval for the operation, the cooperatives were housed in members' apartments, people who had little room for a shop. Finally, the leadership of these cooperatives was very poor. None proved experienced in purchasing supplies, in making deliveries, and in keeping account books. The whole operation was very inefficient. Instead of providing the workers with cheap food, the managers often had to charge prices higher than in the usual shops the workers got their food in. In fact, Viktor Bartenev, a student at the Technological Institute and a tutor in several workers' circles, charged that one manager of a cooperative intentionally overcharged his customers.[51] However,

---

[50]Kazakevich, Sotsial-demokraticheskie organizatsii, p. 145. Based on unpublished documents found in the Leningrad Party Archive.

[51]V. Bartenev, "Iz vospominanii peterburzhtsa vtoroi polovini 80-kh godov," Minuvshie gody, 1908, no. 10, p. 193.

Bartenev never provided any evidence supporting his charges. The government never supported their operations and kept a constant suspicious eye on them. Many workers who recognized the failure of the effort said that it was better to use their hard earned money for some good uses, such as the circles' treasuries. However, the decision was made for them by the government. In June 1892, police arrests destroyed the consumer cooperatives.[52]

To attract new members to the workers' circles, the Central Workers' Circle repeatedly discussed organizing workers' clubs.[53] They would provide an alternative to the beer bars and the <u>traktirs</u> located throughout the city where workers got drunk and fought. In workers' clubs, interested people could meet after work and read easy books and brochures, dance and sing, and perhaps discuss various things which bothered them. Yet the hope for having workers' clubs was never fulfilled. The Central Workers' Circle decided they would not get government permission for the venture. It would be very difficult to illegally organize workers' clubs where any participants, including

---

[52] Bonch-Bruevich, <u>Na zare</u>, p. 16.

[53] Brusnev, "Vozniknovenie," p. 25.

innocent workers, could become liable for arrest. Finding suitable sites for illegal clubs would also be very difficult because frequent large gatherings would attract considerable attention. Nevertheless, the Central Workers' Circle organized two or three evening gatherings for workers, for members and nonmembers of circles alike. The workers and their families who attended, danced, sang, and held discussions on scientific and political themes. The organizers for these evening gatherings were Gavril Mefodiev and his wife. While several people were invited, few actually attended any of the evenings.[54] After those few initial gatherings, no more were ever held. For various reasons, the "grey masses" for whom these clubs were designed were not interested in any alternatives to their bars and their carousing.

Finally, the Central Students' Circle attempted to establish a newspaper which would be distributed among interested workers. The Central Workers' Circle discussed the idea, and agreed to cooperate with them. V.S. Golubev, a member of the Central Students' Circle and their liaison, for a time, with the Central

---

[54] Ibid.

Workers' Circle, was placed in charge.[55] In February 1891, the first issue of <u>Proletarii</u> came out. The whole process of printing and distribution occurred clandestinely. The paper contained articles on the workers' movement in St. Petersburg, especially news about unrest, conditions, and strikes in the various plants and factories. Correspondence among the different circles was collected in it. Yet the project met with grave difficulties. The paper was poorly printed because it was handwritten. It was supposed to be printed once a week, but came out irregularly. Even though members of the Central Workers' Circle and the Central Students' Circle considered the project a success because many workers read it; the paper had a short life span. Its editor, V.S. Golubev, and several correspondents were arrested in April 1891.[56] No further issues were printed, as the arrests forced members of both circles to reorganize.

    The various ventures organized by the Central Workers' Circle met with varying degrees of success. The Central Labor Fund and the library proved successful. The effectiveness of the Central Workers' Circle

---

[55] <u>Ibid.</u>, p. 30.
[56] Korolchuk and Sokolova, <u>Khronika</u>, p. 91.

depended on them. Both enhanced the reputation of the Central Workers' Circle and allowed it to spread far beyond its small membership. Workers and their families appreciated even the tiny financial support the treasury gave them. Both the treasury and the library made other workers, who were not members, respect the organization. It showed that the group represented more than just the interests of its few members. Both ventures gave the group some validity in its claim of being the representative of the workers' intelligentsia. Yet only the library and the treasury met with any success. The other ventures, such as the consumer cooperatives, the workers' clubs, and the newspaper met with failure. The organization did not have the necessary facilities and funds to support such ambitious projects. The consumer associations provided the opposite of the cheap food and provisions that it was supposed to. The workers' clubs were meant to appeal to the "grey mass" who simply did not want them. Therefore, that idea was an illustration of the huge gulf between the workers' intelligentsia and the huge mass of the Russian working class. The newspaper was, again, an overly ambitious project which needed more funding and preparatory work. Therefore, the record of the Central Workers' Circle in these areas was a mixed one.

CHAPTER V

THE POLITICAL ACTIVITIES OF THE CENTRAL WORKERS' CIRCLE

Once the Central Workers' Circle was formed and became consolidated by 1890, it quickly embarked on the path of political activity which simultaneously accompanied the group's social and cultural activities. These political activities, along with the entire circle itself, were divided into two phases: an earlier phase and a later one. The earlier phase began in 1890 as soon as the organization formed, and then lasted until the middle of 1892 when arrests nearly destroyed the entire organization. These political activities were intense, sustained, and marked by repeated attempts, often successful, to reach out to the members' fellow workers. In May 1891, for the first time, Russian labor appeared publicly in a political demonstration in conjunction with their fellow workers in Western Europe and the United States.

After a new period of reorganization and reconsolidation, a second and quite different phase of the Central Workers' Circle commenced in late 1892. That phase lasted until April 1894 when arrests destroyed the Central Workers' Circle, this time permanently. Unlike the earlier period, the group's overt activities were fewer and much less successful. Public demonstrations were relatively rare. Instead, the Central Workers' Circle focused on narrower educational and cultural activities. The treasury again expanded into a large and active fund. Instead of reaching out among its co-workers in factories and plants throughout the city, the group retreated into activities designed to benefit only its members, that particular segment from the workers' intelligentsia. A major reason for this change in tactics was that the group's new leadership feared that overt activities only led to quick arrests. The new leadership played only a small role in the previous Central Workers' Circle and also had a much more narrow view of the group's purposes. As a result, the new Central Workers' Circle lost a great deal of credibility among their fellow workers. By the time of the group's demise, it represented only the tiny group of workers who took part in the workers' circles. Thus by the time the group was destroyed, it had already lost its claimed voice as the spokesman for the growing number of skilled and educated workers in St. Petersburg (the members and potential members of the workers' intelligentsia). That fact clearly weakened the group for the ensuing struggle for control over the small workers' intelligentsia and also the much more significant struggle for the rest of the workers in St. Petersburg. With huge consequences in 1894, that struggle was won by the student intelligentsia.

The Strikes at the Thornton Factory and at the Port, 1891

In late January 1891, two spontaneous and independent strikes broke out at the Port and at the Thornton Textile Factory. At the Port about 400 workers were building a new pride for the Baltic fleet, the battleship Gangut. In the midst of construction, the New Admiralty plant administration led by Admiral Verkhovskii claimed proudly that their workers were better paid and more privileged than other comparable workers.[1] While it was true the workers were part of the elite of the workers, he delivered them a double blow. Verkhovskii not only ordered that the workers' salaries be immediately reduced, but also that the fines for any factory violations be raised. When the

---

[1] A.M. Pankratova, ed., Rabochee dvizhenie v Rossii v xix veke, v. III (Moscow, 1952), p. 52.

workers learned that news they suddenly stopped construction on the ship. Admiral Verkhovskii and the city police exhorted the workers to resume their operations to no avail. The workers declared that the strike was on.

Unfortunately, few details have been available on the origins of the sudden strike at the large Thornton Textile Plant. As a result of the worldwide economic depression which struck Russia in 1890-91, wages were lowered at the Thornton plant. Several hundred workers reacted by going out on strike. While having no role in either strike's origins, members of the Central Workers' Circle saw their opportunity. For a long time, they wanted to publicize their group to bring the nearly unknown organization to greater attention. Here were two strikes conducted by several hundred workers at two of the city's largest factories. The strikers were an army without officers. They lacked leaders. If they captured the leadership of the strikes, the Central Workers' Circle had their grand moment to become a visible organization amongst their fellow workers. Discussion raged at meetings of the Central Circle. Not all of it was favorable. At least one member believed that the strikers would not listen to them, because the strikers were less educated. Their efforts would get nowhere. "I do not think we will find a good response by the striking workers. I do not think of them as good material. But, if we can exploit it, we will if possible."[2] Therefore, the Central Workers' Circle agreed to aid the two strikes.

For strike assistance members of the workers' intelligentsia and the student intelligentsia combined their time and resources. The strike galvanized the two groups. All over St. Petersburg student circle meetings collected money to aid the strikers and their families. Money even came from far away. For example, ten rubles was sent from student groups in Kazan.[3] Altogether between 500 and 600 rubles were collected, which was a large sum for those days, but barely a ruble per striker. Almost simultaneously the student circles, led by the Central Students' Circle, along with the workers' groups, similarly led by the Central Workers' Circle, decided to write and then distribute leaflets among the workers at the two striking factories as well as nearby ones. The workers agreed that the

---

[2] V.S. Golubev, "Vospominaniia," in Pankratova, ed., Rabochee dvizhenie, p. 128.

[3] Ibid., p. 127.

intelligentsia would draft the leaflets, but the workers alone would control the content. The Central Workers' Circle made it quite clear to the intellectuals that they were in charge of the effort.[4] V.S. Golubev wrote the leaflet for the Thornton plant, while another student, L.B. Krasin, wrote the one for the Port strike. As speed was of the essence, the leaflet was hastily and crudely written. Its level was very basic. Political analysis along with detailed background was omitted. Instead this handwritten brochure discussed the needs of the workers at their particular factory. The leaflets included complaints by the workers concerning their miserable factory conditions. They stressed the justice of workers' protests against newly lowered wages and the higher fines. They urged that the strikers not succumb to the factory administration. They urged a continuation of the strike for as long as possible. Yet the proclamations warned that these strikes were ineffective without organization. The leaflets stressed that the strikers must organize, either in their own strike committee, or else, by implication, through the leadership of the

---

[4] Ol'minskii, "O vospominaniiakh," Ot gruppy Blagoeva, p. 42.

Central Workers' Circle. In fact, Bogdanov, the secretary of the group, flatly declared that the workers should organize under the banner of the group.[5] The group saw its opportunity to seize control of the strike.

The next day, the striking workers gathered in their factory yards. They intended to continue the two strikes. Members of the Central Workers' Circle had contacts in one plant. P.E. Evgrafov worked in the New Admiralty Plant, the particular one at the Port that was on strike. Members of his circle were also employed there. However, they had no on the scene contacts at the Thornton Factory. Initially one of the members of the Central Workers' Circle entered the Thornton Plant and gave the workers some money which the group had collected. Once the workers favorably responded, then he distributed the leaflets stamped with the "Provisional Workers' Committee" on it.[6] Evgrafov and his group distributed similar leaflets at the Port. There the response by the workers was even more favorable. Yet the speed with which the leaflets were printed

---

[5] Ibid. No actual leaflets have been preserved, even in the archives. All the sources paraphrase the leaflets.

[6] Golubev, "Stranichka," Byloe, p. 112.

ultimately hurt this first public action by the Central Workers' Circle because the group was able to print only relatively few leaflets.[7] Despite the scarcity of leaflets, some were distributed in other nearby factories urging those workers to support their fellow workers who were on strike. The leaflets told them that their needs and conditions were similar to those who were on strike, and that the strikes were important for all workers. Yet Golubev conceded that this idea of solidarity, "was new and unusual."[8]

At the same time, the Central Student Circle drafted an "appeal to society," in other words, to the small affluent liberal intelligentsia and middle class in St. Petersburg. Shrewdly, it sent some copies of the appeal to the city's liberal press, especially Russkie Vedomosti. The appeal asked that group of potential sympathizers to aid, especially financially, the strikers and their families. It appealed to their compassionate side, in an almost patronizing tone, regarding the workers. It "invited them to show their moral and material support to the

---

[7] Pankratova, Rabochee dvizhenie," p. 52.
[8] Golubev, "Vospominaniia," in Pankratova, Rabochee dvizhenie, p. 128.

poor workers."[9] The student intelligentsia were quite successful. Donations flowed in to aid the striking workers who were engaged in an almost futile struggle against their factory owners and the central and city governments. Following a famine and plague in 1890-91 and the subsequent tardy and insufficient government relief program, the government of Tsar Alexander III had reached the nadir of its popularity. As far as most urban intellectuals were concerned, the strike was one more example of tsarist injustice against the bulk of Russia's people. The proclamations even caused the Western press to take notice. For virtually the first time, Western workers read in their local press about strikes by Russian workers. Almost always the publicity was highly favorable.[10]

Despite these actions by the students and the workers, both strikes ultimately failed. After three or four more days the strikes ended with no results except for the exiling of thirty of its leaders from St. Petersburg. Economic conditions were poor. Russia

---

[9] Pankratova, *Rabochee dvizhenie*, p. 50.

[10] Brusnev, "Vospominaniia," in Pankratova, *Rabochee dvizhenie*, p. 110. Brusnev, an eyewitness to the strikes, was the student advisor on the Central Workers' Circle and had stated that he received clippings from Western newspapers from Russian friends who were living abroad.

was in the throes of a near depression. Even the higher ranks of Russian workers could not remain without a paycheck for long. There were too many unemployed workers who could and did fill their places. No matter what the grievances were, it simply was not the proper economic time to strike. As far as the workers of both plants were concerned, conditions remained the same regarding wages and fines. Yet the two strikes along with the participation of the Central Workers' Circle and the student intelligentsia had a wider significance. The grievances of Russian workers reached the attention of Russian society. The Central Workers' Circle remained no longer an unknown tiny group. Everyone knew that it had tried its utmost to aid its fellow workers. The workers at more than these two plants did not forget the Central Workers' Circle the next time the group appeared in public. It built up a reservoir of good will.

The Shelgunov Funeral Procession, April 1891

In February 1891, the Populist writer, N.V. Shelgunov, became seriously ill.[11] For years, his works, especially his article, "Survey of Russian Workers," had been very popular among Russia's more educated workers. Members of the Central Workers' Circle only learned of the seriousness of Shelgunov's illness at the very end, when he lay close to death. The group held a meeting to discuss their possible options. Gavril Mefodiev insisted that the group send a delegation to Shelgunov's house. Most of the workers who were present agreed. Nevertheless, the student advisors attending the meeting opposed that unprece-

---

[11] Nikolai Vasilevich Shel'gunov (1820-1891) was a leading Populist author who was not only interested in the peasants, but also in urban workers. He had a strong faith in the future development of a democratic Russia based on peasant communes in the villages and workers' cooperatives in the cities. His writings, especially in Sovremennik (Contemporary) made him very popular among students by the 1860's. Then he wrote a scathing manifesto "To the Young Generation" in which he denounced the backward state of Russia and its government. It urged the youth to conduct mass demonstrations against the government. After the attempt on Tsar Alexander II in 1866, which he did not support, the government exiled Shel'gunov to Vologda province in the far north. After several years, he was allowed to return to St. Petersburg.

dented action.[12] Never before in Russia had an organized delegation of workers ever appeared at any noted writer's home. The students pointed out that a delegation would draw too much attention. That would lead to numerous police arrests of workers' leaders. The necessity to preserve security was more important than the desire to see Shelgunov. After a lengthy discussion, the workers insisted and declared that they would send a delegation to Shelgunov's house with a formal address of condolence, with or without the assistance of those students. Yet they had to make their plans quickly known to Shelgunov, and get the permission of his family. Through Semen Petrovich, a student, they met a writer, E.T. Vartenevoi, who was a good friend of the Shelgunovs.[13] She got their consent for a condolence delegation from the workers. Shelgunov was genuinely surprised to learn that workers had read any of his writings, and that an organized delegation of workers wanted to see him before he passed away. He was very touched by this unprecedented gesture.

---

[12]Brusnev, "Vozniknovenie," p. 109.

[13]Vlasov, Tkach Fedor Afanas'ev, p. 17.

Once the Central Workers' Circle got permission, they quickly discussed the wording for an address to Shelgunov, and the composition of the delegation. They wanted the delegation to be made up of leading members of the Central Workers' Circle, who represented the best educated and most highly skilled workers in St. Petersburg. Nevertheless, they were concerned that the group should be fairly small because all who composed the delegation became highly vulnerable to arrest. By now, the intellectuals agreed to support the workers' action, and even declared they would help to edit the address. The workers made it very clear that while they welcomed their assistance, the writing and the content of the speech was their affair. The delegation contained four of the leaders of the Central Workers' Circle: the brothers F.A. Afanasev and E.A. Afanasev (Klimanov), N.D. Bogdanov, and G. Mefodiev. E. Afanasev (Klimanov) held the critically important position of treasurer. N.D. Bogdanov was the group's secretary. Mefodiev was one of the founders of the Central Workers' Circle. Yet the acknowledged leader was F.A. Afanasev, the <u>starik</u> (elder) of the group at the ripe old age of forty. "We regarded him as the most intelligent and most important comrade."[14] To greet this venerable old publicist, they wanted the group's leader to be the eldest and most "dignified appearing." Accompanying the group were two members of the Central Students' Circle, V.V. Bartenev and V.S. Golubev. The latter was the group's representative on the Central Workers' Circle. The address was finished. Then sixty-six members of workers' circles, all representatives of the workers' intelligentsia signed the address. They would go the next day.

In late March 1891, the delegation of workers and students arrived at Shelgunov's house. Unexpectedly, several leading intellectuals, including the noted Populist author N.K. Mikhailovskii, were there. The workers acted very respectfully. While they knew Shelgunov was dying, they inquired about his health. Then they told Shelgunov that they were well acquainted with his works. Shelgunov told the workers that he was both surprised and very pleased that was the case. Then the workers read their address to Shelgunov. Its tone was highly respectful; they were honoring a great man who meant so much to them. It began with the words,

---

[14] Ibid., p. 18.

"Dear teacher, Nikolai Vasilevich."[15] Then they told Shelgunov that they learned so much from his writings. As far as this group of workers was concerned, Shelgunov was the first Populist writer to address himself specifically to the concerns of Russian urban workers. "You were the first to recognize the pitiful state of workers in Russia. You have always strived to explain to us our conditions. . ."[16] The speech reflected a sense of bitterness concerning their poor conditions. They blamed those conditions on the government and the whole system of capitalism. It was ironic that this Marxist influenced address was delivered to a leading Populist, representing an ideology which was a rival to Marxism. Perhaps exaggerating Shelgunov's role, the address credited Shelgunov with giving the workers their direction and goals. "You showed us the path to freedom, and as a result, we will try to achieve your goals."[17]

The speech produced a strong impression on Shelgunov. Tears even flowed from his eyes. While he had

---

[15]Nikitin, Pervye rabochie soiuzy, p. 88.
[16]Ibid.
[17]Golubev, "Stranichka." p. 120.

written about the Russian workers, he had never personally made their acquaintance before that day. He was genuinely surprised that there were politically conscious workers in Russia. Once again the Central Workers' Circle brought itself to the attention of the liberal society. Now all of them know that, at least, some of the city's workers were organized in a regular group. Subsequently, other workers' circles and individual workers read the address which spread all over St. Petersburg. The prestige and the reputation of the group rose considerably. Even the city's newspapers noted this public action by the Central Workers' Circle. After the speech, the group could only stay a little while longer. Shelgunov was very sick and weak. They told Shelgunov about some of their activities, and that they believed the workers' groups had become a strong movement. Shelgunov and the group discussed some of Russia's new writers. Finally, it was time to go. As they parted, the workers knew it was probably the last time they would see the man alive.

When the deputation returned they held another meeting of the Central Workers' Circle. They decided to send a large delegation of workers to his funeral whenever that would be held. Yet they agreed the decision should be kept secret because the government would be very alarmed over that prospect. As a result, it would probably utilize different measures to keep them away. They decided to say nothing about their future plans.[18] The government was already concerned over any expected large funeral procession on the occasion of Shelgunov's death. That procession could easily turn into a huge anti-government demonstration. The city administration, prompted by the central government, attempted to send the dying man out of St. Petersburg. Before this plan could be implemented, on Friday, April 24, 1891, Shelgunov finally died. News of his death traveled quickly throughout the city. The workers had to organize quickly because the funeral was scheduled for the coming Sunday. The next day at work members of the circles urged sympathetic fellow workers to attend the funeral. Several other members of the group went to an Estonian engraving firm on Sadovaia Street whose management was sympathetic to the workers. There they had a ribbon inscribed with the words, "Dear Teacher and leader of the workers, N.V. Shelgunov, who showed us the way to freedom and brotherhood, from the St.

---

[18] Ol'minskii, "Gruppa narodovol'tsev," p. 10.

Petersburg workers."[19] The ribbon was placed on a red metal wreath. The necessary money to pay for both the ribbon and the wreath was raised at several factories. Many metal workers contributed one ruble each.[20] The next morning, just before the funeral, ten representatives of the Central Workers' Circle carried the wreath and the ribbon over to Shelgunov's house. Later they carried the wreath on the funeral march. At the last minute, at the government's insistence, the funeral was postponed until the next day, Monday, April 27, 1891 (NS). Fewer people could attend during a workday.

On Monday morning crowds gathered at Shelgunov's house. "The street was filled with excited people, mostly students and high schoolers."[21] After a while an estimated seven hundred to one thousand people congregated on the streets surrounding his house. Of that number about 10% were workers. They came despite the fact that it was a working day. Upon government insistence factories implemented higher than normal

---

[19] Norinskii, "Moi vospominaniia," Ot gruppy Blagoeva, p. 12.

[20] Karelina, "Na zare," p. 14.

[21] Iu. Martov, Zapiski sotsial-demokrata, Vol. I (Berlin, 1922), p. 57.

fines for absences from work that day.[22] The workers had their own banner. However, few if any women workers were able to attend. Unlike male workers, they were unable to take off from work because their salaries were much lower. Therefore, women activists absolutely could not afford to take the day off. Furthermore, textile factories where women predominated enforced the government's regulations much more strictly than the machine factories where the male members predominated. As Vera Karelina, a leading woman activist, stated: "For us to leave the factory was different (from the males), we would be found out if we were absent, and would lose our jobs."[23] The workers attended solely on their own insistence because once again their intellectual contacts opposed their participation in an open demonstration saying that it would lead to arrests. The Central Workers' Circle did take a great risk by attending. It would be the first public rally in St. Petersburg by workers since the demonstration in front of Kazan Cathedral in

---

[22]Pankratova, ed., Rabochee dvizhenie, v. III, p. 118.
[23]Karelina, "Na zare," p. 15.

1876.[24] As the intellectuals had warned, any and all participants in the funeral procession became liable to arrest. Yet the workers made it very clear that they were no different from anyone else.

The atmosphere at Shelgunov's house that morning was very tense. Crowds of different groups milled around carrying banners and shouting slogans. Large numbers of uniformed police along with plainclothes agents of the tsarist secret police were also there. While the government retreated from forcefully preventing a public procession, they flatly stated that no banners would be allowed. The police became very

---

[24] Following the failure of the "to the people" movement in the summer of 1876, a group of desperate revolutionaries in conjunction with a group of St. Petersburg workers, organized a demonstration to protect the imprisonment of hundreds of young Populist agitators. Georgii Plekhanov, often considered the father of Russian Marxism, helped organize and delivered the speech at the rally on December 6, 1876, in front of the large Kazan Cathedral. A crowd of several hundred students and workers listened to Plekhanov's impassioned harangue, and also unfurled a red banner. Quickly, the police dispersed the crowd in the course of which several participants were injured or arrested. Plekhanov and most of the crowd escaped. The following sources mention that the Procession was the first public rally by St. Petersburg workers: R. Pipes, Social Democracy, pp. 31-32; Brusnev, "Pervye revoliutsionnyne, shagi," p. 74; and Korolchuk, Khronika, p. 158.

agitated at seeing the numerous banners, which carried anti-government slogans. The police agitation stimulated the crowd. Their protesting mood grew. The organizers of the procession, mostly respected scholars and intellectuals, became very concerned that violence would break out. Despite the lack of time, they had carefully organized the procession to include marshals to keep the march orderly and well disciplined. In vain, N.K. Mikhailovskii urged the militant and predominantly youthful crowd to obey police orders.[25] Fortunately, the police finally relented and allowed the banners. In recognition of their new importance, the delegation from the Central Workers' Circle led the procession. Cries of "workers, forward" rang out. An estimated 70 to 100 workers, who carried the thick wreath with its green banner, opened the march. They moved from Shelgunov's house on a path which would eventually lead to the Volkov Cemetery. There Shel-Gunov was to be buried.

Despite all the precautions of the marshals, trouble between the police and the demonstrators soon erupted. The coffin was in a hearse. Yet several

---

[25] Vlasov, Tkach Fedor Afanas'ev, p. 20.

people at the march wanted to carry the coffin by hand as a public display of affection for Shelgunov. The police regarded that as a provocative act and would not allow it. Both sides, the police and the demonstrators, grabbed at the coffin. A struggle ensued. Several policemen roughly tore the hands from the grooves of the coffin. The coffin bent toward the side. To the horror of the demonstrators, the body of Shelgunov nearly fell to the road.[26] The demonstrators realized they had gone too far in allowing Shelgunov's body to become a political pawn between them and the police. They placed the coffin back on the hearse, and replaced all the wreaths which had fallen off in the struggle. The tension which had briefly erupted into violence dropped somewhat to the noticeable relief of the organizers of the demonstration. Once again, the workers at the front of the demonstration shouted, "Forward."

The procession path went along Voskresenskii Prospekt where it would continue along Znamenskii Street, until they reached the cemetery. Here again the more militant demonstrators seized the initiatve

---

[26]Morshanskaia, Afanas'ev, p. 26.

from the organizers. Provocatively they turned the
procession toward the crowded Liteinyi Street, where
a group of carriages stopped to observe despite
police protests. The government unrealistically
wanted the city populace to carry on with their normal
day's operations as if this unprecedented event was not
occurring. That was impossible. From Liteinyi, the
demonstration went down the main street of St. Petersburg, the Nevskii Prospekt. When they got to the
Obvodnyi Canal, new groups of workers were attracted
and joined the march.[27] Steadily the march grew.
From the Nevskii, the march went down Nikolaevskii
Street until it got to the Volkov Cemetery. Then the
procession approached the gravesite were a service was
planned. By now well over 1,000 people were present.
A priest from the area conducted the service. Some of
the younger people, not approving this religious part
of the procession, took out bread and sausages, and
ate them in an almost picnic fashion ignoring the
funeral. After the requiem service, the coffin was
lowered. At that point, a good friend of Shelgunov's,
a writer, Vologdin-Zasodimskii, delivered a eulogy of

---

[27] Ol'minskii, "Gruppa narodovol'tsev," p. 13.

the newly departed writer.[28] A student then read some poetry. Several other people spoke in memory of Shelgunov. The last speech was delivered by a worker. In between speeches, many students went around the crowd collecting money for the Red Cross to aid famine and plague victims. Finally, the service and demonstration ended. People hurried away in small groups arm in arm. The police let the groups pass without any trouble. Only a small group remained by the gravesite where they stayed until the next morning.

When the large demonstration had ended then the repercussions began. As the student intellectuals had predicted, participation in the demonstration cost both the workers and the intellectuals dearly. Within two weeks, the arrests began. The two leaders of the demonstration, the literary figures, Gleb Uspenskii and N.K. Mikhailovskii were forced to leave St. Peters-

---

[28] Norinskii, "O vospominaniiakh," Ot gruppy Blagoeva, p. 13.

burg.[29] Then, many of the students, who had been involved in circle work were arrested and also exiled. The most important student activist arrested was Golubev, who was the Central Student's Circle's representative on the Central Workers' Circle. Golubev was betrayed by a worker who was a police agent, Semen Petrovskii. The police banished Golubev from St. Petersburg. No longer was Golubev a part of the St. Petersburg oppositional movement.[30] His absence, as

[29] Ol'minskii, "O vospominaniiakh N. D. Bogdanova," Ot gruppy Blagoeva, p. 43. Gleb Uspenskii (1843-1902), in his works, discussed the break-up of the old rural Russia following the emancipation of the serfs in 1861. His works illustrated the Populist idealization of the patriarchical village and their alleged rejection of capitalism. Nikolai Konstantinovich Mikhailovskii (1842-1904) was another leading publicist and theoretician for the Populist movement. He contributed articles or edited several journals or newspapers such as Otechestvennye Zapiski, Servernyi Vestnik, Russkaia Mysl', Russkie Vedomosti, and finally Russkoe Bogatsvo. He told the intellectuals that they had a responsibility and a duty to serve the people, and to struggle against the tsarist government. His relations with the Marxists turned sour. In the 1890's, he attacked them for betraying the heritage of the 1860's and 1870's, and for furthering capitalism.

[30] In exile, Golubev became first a Social Revolutionary, and later joined the liberal Constitutional Democrats. Golubev settled in Saratov, and edited the local zemstvo publication until his death in 1910. Even though Golubev was one of the leaders and founders of the Central Student' Circle, Soviet authors minimize his role because of his turn from revolutionary politics.

one of the brightest and most cautious student leaders, would hurt the organization. The Central Students' Circle then designated M.I. Brusnev as their representative on the Central Workers' Circle. Several workers were then arrested. The most important were Central Workers' Circle members Gavril Mefodiev, his brother Ivan, and also I.V. Krutov, who had led an affiliated circle. Gavril Mefodiev was exiled to Reval, the Baltic port, where he resumed his activity with workers there. Then L.B. Krasin, a student at the Technological Institute and a member of the Central Students' Circle, was expelled from the Institute, and subsequently exiled to Nizhni Novgorod, where he continued his political work. Despite these major arrests which hurt the organizations, the demonstration did have some positive significance. For nearly the first time (with the exception of the Kazan Cathedral demonstration), Russian workers openly displayed their strength. Russian society learned about the demonstration and the participation of numerous workers in it. The publicity aided the Central Workers' Circle amongst its fellow workers. The small circles increased in both size and numbers. The power and authority of the Central Workers' Circle grew among the workers' intelligentsia in St. Petersburg. As a result, it could thrust its dictates on the affiliated circles more easily. The Central Workers' Circle had come out on its own.

The May Day Holiday, 1891; the Background and the Events

The climax of the overt activities by the Central Workers' Circle occurred on May 1891 when Russian workers, on their own initiative, participated in that international holiday for workers. Russian workers showed that if they were not yet equal in political consciousness to their European counterparts, at least they were not too many years behind. The Shelgunov Procession and the previous winter strikes were mere dress rehearsals to this event. With May Day, Russian labor leadership entered its own because their two previous occasions had been initiated by others; the intellectuals at the Shelgunov Procession and the rank and file factory workers at the strikes.

The origins of this holiday, celebrated today in most industrialized nations except for the United States, paradoxically lay in the United States. In December 1888, the newly formed American Federation of Labor (A.F.L.) held its annual convention in St. Louis,

Missouri. Some delegates at the convention proposed a resolution for an international holiday for workers to be celebrated next spring, "as it best suits the conditions of their different countries."[31] The resolution overwhelmingly passed along with the urge that other countries adopt it as soon as they could. During the following year, the Second International, a loosely knit predominantly Western European association of Marxist socialist parties, held its first Congress in Paris.[32] At the Congress, several delegates raised the A.F.L. resolution. Only a few delegates opposed the resolution. Most delegates believed that factory workers deserved their own holiday, and if that holiday was held on the same day, it would be an expression of working class solidarity. Despite all the factional arguments within that organization, one of the main purposes for the Second International was working class solidarity. They passed a resolution which stated: "We prescribe a great international demonstra-

---

[31] S.N. Valk, "Materialy k istorii pervogo maia v Rossii," *Krasnaia letopis'*, no. 4, 1922, p. 254.

[32] The best source on the Second International: its strengths and weaknesses, and its agreements and divisions is James Joll, *The Second International, 1889-1914*, revised edition (London, 1975).

tion now in such a form for all countries and in all cities. In one prearranged day the workers should display their public power and demand restrictions on the working day to eight hours and also the fulfillment of all the other decisions of the International Congress in Paris."[33] The Congress urged that all of its member parties organize demonstrations and celebrations for May 1890, and that on each subsequent May all workers refuse to go to their jobs, but instead celebrate the holiday.

Delegates from Russia proper and Russian Poland attended, representing the Russian Empire at the Paris Congress. However, only four people, all emigres, represented Russia: Petr Lavrov, Georgii Plekhanov, and two unnamed individuals, one living in London and the other in New York. Neither Lavrov (1823-1900), a noted Populist who was very sympathetic to the urban working class, nor Plekhanov (1856-1918), the founder of the Emancipation of Labor organization in 1883, had lived in Russia for years. They were unaware of the recent upsurge in workers' circles culminating in the formation of the Central Workers' Circle earlier in 1890 or many other developments in Russia's labor move-

---

[33] Valk, "Materialy," p. 256.

ments. Reflecting its more advanced industrial development and its larger working class, Poland's delegation was more representative of Poland's labor. Not only did it contain emigres, but it also contained activists from <u>Proletarjat</u>, a revolutionary Marxist organization founded in 1879 in Poland. The Polish delegates told the Congress that their workers would participate in May Day in 1890. Reflecting both the general weaker condition of the Russian labor movement all Plekhanov promised was, "We will <u>try</u> to follow our Polish socialists."[34] (underlining is mine) He could promise nothing more.

---

[34] Ibid., p. 255. Just as in Russia, the emancipation of the serfs in the 1860's opened a new chapter for the "Vistula Lands," the name given to Russian Poland. It underwent an industrial revolution, one much greater than that in Russia proper. High Russian tariffs protected the emerging Polish coal, steel, and iron industries. The largest Polish industries were textiles, coal, iron, steel, and sugar beets. By 1890, the "Vistula Lands," containing only 7% of the population of the whole Russian Empire, had a quarter of the Empire's total industrial production. A large group of well educated workers and craftsmen developed in Poland. By 1900 Poland had nearly 450,000 workers and artisans. As legal trade unions and strikes were forbidden, conspiratorial trade unions and socialist organizations formed. In April 1883 several thousand workers participated in a huge textile strike in Warsaw. Government troops and police crushed the strike. It would take nearly a decade for Polish labor to recover. On the occasion of May Day 1892, a fresh wave of strikes swept Warsaw and other cities. Workers demanded an eight hour day and a 15% rise in wages. The government was adamant in rejecting the demands and severely repressed the strikes. One of the strike centers, Łódź, had a large Jewish population. Utilizing the pervasive anti-semitism of many Poles, the police organized anti-Jewish riots and used these riots as a pretext for sending troops against the striking workers. As a result of the bloody clashes, there were numerous casualties--46 deaths, and 200 injuries. Arrests followed which crippled the strike organizers. Nevertheless, in Paris, France, that same year a small group of Polish intellectuals and workers formed a unified socialist party, the Polish Socialist Party (PPS). For further information on this subject see: Piotr S. Wandycz, The Lands of Partitioned Poland, 1795-1918 (Seattle, 1974), pp. 193-213 and pp. 277-281; and M.K. Dziewanowski, The Communist Party of Poland, an Outline of History, second edition (Cambridge, 1976), pp. 1-21.

As planned, workers in major cities throughout Western Europe and in the United States entered the streets marching with red banners, singing revolutionary songs, and announcing political demands. In Warsaw and Łódź in Poland thousand of workers participated. Most of them were from small factories or were self-employed artisans. Government measures and the threat of disciplinary penalties prevented most workers from large factories from celebrating the holiday. The government took reprisal measures against those workers who participated. Many of the more visible leaders were arrested. Because many Jewish craftsmen participated, large scale <u>pogroms</u> ensued against Jews in Vilnius, Kaunas and other towns in Eastern Poland and in Lithuania. In St. Petersburg, a leaflet was distributed to hundreds of factory workers at major plants in the city. The appeal entitled "To the People, 1 May," stated:

> The Russian government poorly oversees the Russian people, enslaves them with their taxes, fines, and insufficient laws to protect the workers. Further it limits their land allotments, and enacts other despotic actions. All of this is accomplished in order that our people can not leave serfdom. But there will come a time when the Russian people will awake to their greatest strength, and will shake the power of the government. Within ten years, a Russian proletariat, both rural and urban, will have their own 1 May. These

actions will have to be prudently organized. We will also have to wait for a time when our organization will have enough people to begin serious activity.

This first proclamation of the "Russian workers' anti-government detachment" was written and printed under very difficult conditions in only one night. The membership of the group is currently around 800 people. So to a <u>rendez vous</u> (<u>sic</u>) soon, brothers.

<u>Rabochii</u>.[35]

Yet this proclamation, which was actually distributed, raises numerous questions. Except for the proclamation, there are no other records of a "Russian workers' anti-government detachment." Surely any organization of allegedly 800 people would have generated a lot more publicity than just this one proclamation. No one knows who organized the group or who composed it. We are fairly certain it was not representatives from the Central Workers' Circle because not one member ever mentioned the organization in his memoirs. Except for their existence, the leaflets displayed only weaknesses. They were crudely written by hand, and hastily produced in one night as the authors conceded. They declared that the organization would have to wait until it had enough people to begin

---

[35] <u>Ibid</u>., p. 260.

serious activity. The leaflets referred to activities by the workers within ten years; certainly that is not the near future. Apparently the existence of 800 people in the group was a gross exaggeration because the Central Workers' Circle organized and participated in several events with far fewer people than 800 members. One can easily infer that 800 people would have accomplished far more than just a leaflet. The only record, in fact, for this document, is one copy found in the secret police headquarters after the Revolution of 1917.[36] Besides that May Day leaflet there was no other evidence that St. Petersburg workers marked the May Day holiday. There were no parades, demonstrations, or work stoppages that day. The celebration of the holiday in St. Petersburg would have to wait for another year.

---

[36] Valk, who has written the most thorough history of the May Day holiday ("Materialy k istorii pervogo maia v Rossii," *Krasnaia letopis'*, 1922, #4) stated there is no original to the leaflet. In fact, he could not even verify its authenticity, but did state the document's very crudeness in language and production give the reader some confidence in its validity. The governor of St. Petersburg province Gresser was sufficiently alarmed by the document to urge that a search be conducted to find its author. The governor's fears further demonstrated at least its potential appeal, if not, any actual effect on St. Petersburg's workers.

Discussion among workers and students for the first celebration of May Day in Russia proper began right after the Shelgunov demonstration. The members of the Central Workers' Circle were excited and optimistic following their participation at the funeral procession. Rather than just resting on their laurels, most members of the group wanted their organization to join workers in the West in the, by now, well known holiday. Their reasons were two-fold. For one thing, a successful celebration would further raise the prestige of the group following its previous successes over the past four months, and would continue the momentum that had already begun. A rise in prestige and in publicity would lead to an expansion of its circles and in the group's membership. Holding a celebration would further the authority of the Central Workers' Circle as the spokesman for St. Petersburg's working class. Secondly, the celebration would show the leaders of the labor movement in the West that Russia's workers were acquainted with the Second International and their decision in 1889 which designated May Day. Implicitly, the celebration by Russian workers would show their Western European colleagues that Russian workers were no longer (as in 1890) far behind the rest of Europe. Despite these obvious advantages, discussion within meetings of the Central Workers' Circle became quite heated and lengthy.[37] Several workers pointed out that their previous actions, participation in the winter strikes and in the Shelgunov demonstration, had produced a great deal of attention on the group from the police. A large, public, and defiant demonstration on the occasion of May Day would surely lead to the destruction of the Central Workers' Circle. For the exhilaration of one momentous day, should the organization commit probable suicide? Besides the argument that a demonstration would lead to mass arrests, several members feared that the demonstration would be a fiasco. For various reasons, most workers would not attend. Despite the Central Workers' Circle's growth of membership, and despite the precedents of the successful Shelgunov demonstration, the organization was still very small, fragile, and isolated from the bulk of the working class, including the workers' intelligentsia. This argument that few people would attend a May Day only illustrated the degree of the group's isolation and small size. Nevertheless, the Central Workers' Circle decided to hold a May Day celebration on the first Sunday of May.

---

[37] Brusnev, "Vozniknovenie," p. 25.

Holding it on a Sunday, a rest day for most workers, would allow an optimal attendance. Then the group decided it would be a workers' event. Few intellectuals would be invited to attend. Workers alone would organize the event. Representatives of the Central Workers' Circle would write and deliver any speeches. The group retained sole charge of all aspects of the event. This fact illustrated the group's desire to retain full independence from the student intelligentsia with a reaffirmation of Vasilii Shelgunov's declaration: "The liberation of the working class is the affair of the working class alone."[38] The author believes that the workers' very insistence on their independence, at least, shows that the workers wanted to be independent from any outside control. While their very stress on independence from the intellectuals can lead the observer to dispute the success of that independence, the author believes that no impartial observer can contest the workers' intent.

At first the group wanted to hold the May Day events in Ekateringofskii Park, located near the large Putilov factory. That idea was quickly abandoned

---

[38] Shel'gunov, "Vospominaniia," *Ot gruppy Blagoeva*, p. 55.

because the park was too public an area. While the members of the group certainly knew they faced a great risk of arrest by just holding the event, they did not want to maximize those prospects. After further discussion, the Central Workers' Circle delegated one member of the Circle, Egor Afanasev (Klimanov) along with the current intellectual representative on the Circle, Mikhail Brusnev, to find an appropriate site.[39] After a lengthy search, the two men settled on a spot on Krestovskii Island, a sparsely populated island north of Vasilyevskii Island and northwest of Peterburgskii Island. The selected spot was perfect. To maximize the event's seclusion, they chose a grassy area surrounded on almost all sides by trees which could be reached easily only by boat because it was along a river. Therefore, unless the police specifically knew in advance that particular spot, they would be highly unlikely to stumble onto it.

Once the Central Workers' Circle approved the place, the group then issued several directives to explain the format of the event. They decided that the attending workers should arrive on foot or by boat

---

[39] Brusnev, "Vozniknovenie," p. 27.

in small group of no more than thirteen people. Again the reason was security. People would likely notice large numbers of workers going to a certain spot, and then they might alert the police. Furthermore, to allow people enough time to get to the site from all over the city, the events would not start before noon. Publicity was spread by word of mouth to sympathizers of the Central Workers' Circle at meetings of local circles and at factories. Thus, by the time the selected day arrived, everything was organized. Now the Central Workers' Circle had simply to wait and see if anyone showed up.

That designated Sunday, May 17, 1891 (OS), was warm and clear. The organizers could not have asked for a nicer day for a holiday in the woods. Early in the morning people started arriving. Patrols were posted along the footpaths to watch for police and plainclothesmen. By noon an estimated sixty to two hundred people had gathered.[40] There were several women, including labor activists such as Vera Karelina, who attended. Nevertheless, women were a distinct minority there. One woman, the wife of a metal worker, Andrei Fisher, even complained over the lack of attention given to women. Consequently, she left soon after the start of the formal program.[41] Most people who attended the May Day rally were highly skilled workers from large metal works factories such as Putilov, Obukhov, and Baltic. Few of the lesser skilled workers attended. The Central Workers' Circle created a holiday for the workers they represented, the workers' intelligentsia. It did not represent the much more

---

[40] The sources vary considerably as to the number of workers who attended the holiday. N. Bogdanov, one of the workers who delivered a speech at the gathering, estimated in his memoirs ("O vospominaniiakh N.D. Bogdanova," Ot gruppy Blagoeva k soiuzu bor'by.) there were at least 200 workers there. Yet most sources mention that the numbers who attended were much smaller, between 60 and 100: K. Norinskii, "Moi vospominaniia," V.V. Sviatlovskii, "Na zare," I.I. Vlasov, Tkach Fedor Afanas'ev, and Brusnev, "Vozniknovenie." Given the numbers of sources that mentioned the lower estimate, given the lack of formal publicity for fear of police attention and given the relatively small site, the smaller estimate of the crowd size is most likely to be the accurate figure.

[41] Morshanskaia, Tkach Fedor Afanas'ev, p. 27.

typical members of S. Petersburg's labor. However, it was not an occasion for the student intelligentsia. Only three attended, Brusnev, the intellectual representative who also helped select the site; V.V. Sviatlovskii, who aided the planning of the celebration; and W.F. Cywiński (Tsivinskii), a Polish student at the Technical Institute who was very popular with the workers. All three intellectuals were dressed like workers. The Central Workers' Circle made it very clear the holiday was for workers. Intellectuals were not invited; consequently only a few came. From beginning to end, intellectuals remained in the background.[42]

By noon, everyone had arrived. The program began. A worker, not identified, was elected by the crowd as Chairman. The whole day was spent in animated discussions by groups of workers, broken from time to time by formal speeches by predesignated workers. After each speech, the crowd returned to their discussions in a holiday fashion, eating fried pork, drinking, as though everyone was at a picnic. A major purpose for the day was social, to allow workers to gather together in large groups in the healthy outdoors and eat and drink. Politics was only one aspect for the gathering,

---

[42] Sviatlovskii, "Na zare," p. 145.

though an important one. The organizers were very pleased with the day's event. The doubts by some of the members evaporated before the happy crowds and warm sun. There was no evidence of police surveillance.

The highlight of the day's activities was the major speeches delivered by four of the leaders of the Central Workers' Circle: N.D. Bogdanov, F. Afanasev, V. Proshin, and E. Afanasev. All of the speeches were written by the above-mentioned workers. Vladimir Proshin, a rubber worker, and member of the Central Workers' Circle, wrote his speech in advance. Once he completed it, he gave it to a few intellectuals to edit. The only corrections they made were insignificant grammatical points.[43] The whole content of the speech was maintained exactly as Proshin had written. The other speeches, except for E. Afanasev's, were written without any intellectual assistance. E. Afanasev (Klimanov) felt confident enough to deliver his speech extemporaneously from notes. As delivered, several observers noted that the speeches were very successful and well written.[44]

---

[43] Brusnev, "Vozniknovenie," p. 28.
[44] Vlasov, Tkach Fedor Afanas'ev, p.23.

Egor Afanasev, the treasurer and one of the founders of the Central Workers' Circle, delivered the first speech.[45] He described the poor conditions Russian workers had both in their jobs and at home. Militantly, he told Russian workers to oppose the tsarist government in order to achieve political and economic advances. N.D. Bogdanov, the secretary of the Central Workers' Circle, gave the next speech. He discussed the common needs of the movement. Russian workers had to organize, and through a single group, they could achieve improved living standards, a just social system, a constitution, an elected assembly, freedom of speech, and a reform of the army. Bogdanov linked these various political, economic, and social aims. Despite educational assistance from the intelligentsia, the workers had to accomplish these goals on their own. They had to remain independent of the intelligentsia. Thus Bogdanov reasserted a common theme of the workers' intelligentsia that they control their own affairs, and that the student intelligentsia cannot control their movement. The concept that the workers' movement had to be directed by, controlled by,

---

[45] All of the speeches are printed in Appendix B of this dissertation.

and operated for the benefit of the workers was reiterated throughout all the speeches. As Fedor Afanasev stated in his speech, "Our workers must also become aware that labor is the mover of all progress, the creator of all science, art, and inventions. . . then no army will be able to prevent its self-emancipation."[46]

Vladimir Proshin's speech compared the situation of Russian workers with their Western European counterparts. Clearly, according to Proshin, Russian workers lived in much worse conditions than those of Western European ones. He then outlined the need for Russian workers to organize to improve their living and working conditions.

Fedor Afanasev's speech was perhaps the most inflammatory and bitter. Just as in the other speeches, Afanasev compared Russian workers to their Western European counterparts, specifically the Germans. Like the others, Afanasev urged the Russian workers organize into trade unions to get the same rights as the other workers achieved. Then Afanasev's tone became very bitter and he lashed out at the unfeeling educated Russian population. "It is a pity, comrades, that no

---

[46] Valk, "Materialy," pp. 266-67.

one gives us (workers) any help as had been given the (western workers) of earlier times, except for a small group of people (the student intelligentsia) to whom we shall always owe a debt of gratitude."[47] Afanasev emphasized the lonely nature of the struggle in Russia and that few people, very few people, cared about the workers. He declared then that Russian workers must achieve their own gains. Afanasev closed his speech with great derision, almost hatred against the bulk of the youth in Russia. "Present day youth does not hear the people's cry and does not see its suffering; it does not even bother to think about the people. This youth is nothing but a parasitic element in society."[48] Afanasev's speech underlined the need to achieve political rights in Russia, and to accomplish that it was necessary to replace the current system.

Certain themes had a thread throughout all the speeches. Russian workers were much worse off than their Western European counterparts. Yet earlier in the nineteenth century those western workers had similar conditions to the Russian workers of the 1880's.

---

[47] M.S. Ol'minskii, "Rechi rabochikh na pervomaiskom sobranii 1891 g.," Ot gruppy Blagoeva, p. 126.

[48] Valk, "Materialy," p. 267.

To counter that, they organized trade unions. Russian leaders from the workers' intelligentsia espoused the concept of trade unionism, a network controlled by the workers, without any interference from the intelligentsia. They all asserted the independence of the workers, an idea that would work against the leaders of the intelligentsia within a few short years. The speeches stressed the self-development of Russian workers. The workers themselves must organize their fellow workers. Despite the political rhetoric against the tsarist government, the speakers reiterated that the workers had to improve themselves economically. Thus the workers showed an amazingly clear note of social and political consciousness. May Day 1891 was indicative of the rapid progress Russian workers had made over the past ten years.

After the speeches, the large gathering once again divided into smaller groups where they discussed the speeches. The workers felt jubilant over the day's events. As soon as the speeches ended, the crowd shouted out the concluding line from the <u>Communist Manifesto</u>: "Workers of all countries, unite." In another, but much smaller display of pride, a worker, A.E. Karelin and his intellectual friend, V.V. Sviatlovskii, immortalized the day by carving their initials, the date and the year on a tree trunk.[49] By now the day was drawing to an end. Plainclothes agents of the police got wind of the demonstration, and began to surround the woods. As the main events were over, anyway, and not desiring any arrests, the participants decided to leave. The crowd left quickly in small groups either by boat or by foot, attempting to avoid the attention of the police. Despite those precautions, there were several arrests that night: Vl. Fomin, I.V. Egorov, Yakovlev, Mefodiev, Kirillov, Saveliev, and P. Kaizo.

Earlier that night there was a large gathering at Egor Afanasev's (Klimanov's) apartment, a second planned May Day event. Many workers wanted to participate in the day's events, but were unable. For that reason, the organizers decided to hold an evening meeting. Between sixty and seventy people, nearly the same number as at the events in the woods, packed Afanasev's apartment. Virtually all the organizers were there. Significant numbers of women were present for the first time. They were wives of labor leaders and leaders of women workers' circles who were affiliated with the

---

[49] Sviatlovskii, "Na zare," p. 139.

Central Workers' Circle.[50] Egor Afanasev delivered again his speech of that afternoon. Then Ivan Egorov, a worker unable to be present earlier in the woods, gave a rousing speech. He urged that workers go beyond forming trade unions, and instead, form their own political party, independent of any other group. He said that active workers might not currently be a large group, but they made up in enthusiasm what they lacked in quantity. The group cheered Egorov's extemporaneous speech most of all.[51] After some more eating, drinking, and talking, the group dispersed happily to their homes determined that the evening gathering should become a May Day tradition, as important as the day's events.

For several months, for security reasons, the speeches' texts were kept secret. Only in the fall of 1891, did the members of the Central Workers' Circle decide to give the text of the speeches to a teacher at a Sunday school.[52] Then that unnamed teacher gave the handwritten text to the Gruppa Narodovol'tsev, headed by M.S. Olminskii (Aleksandrov). Despite the Central Workers' Circle's ties to the heavily Marxist oriented

---

[50] Fisher, V Rossii i v Anglii, p. 13.
[51] Ibid., p. 14.
[52] Ol'minskii, "Gruppa narodovol'tsev," p. 7.

Central Students' Circle, the workers entrusted their speeches to a Populist organization. That action illustrated the workers' great respect for the doctrine of Populism. Nevertheless, a year later, emigre Marxists in Geneva, Switzerland published the speeches.[53] In their edition, sections of the speeches were deleted, especially the sections referring to the independence of the workers from the intellectuals. Olminskii himself discussed this gulf between workers and intellectuals, and the patronizing tone of the intellectuals. Olminskii wrote that, "the intellectuals did not want to believe that there existed in Russia, workers talented enough to deliver such speeches, and who could write such speeches."[54] This lack of confidence by the workers in the intellectuals appeared over and over again, and led, subsequently, to arguments between the two groups.

---

[53] Faced with isolation, the Emancipation of Labor Group set out to give a new direction to the Russian revolutionary movement. It proposed to distribute in Russia Marxist literature--translations of Marx and Engels as well as the group's analyses of Russian social and economic life. Therefore, by 1884 the group began a small publishing house in Geneva, Switzerland.

[54] Vlasov, *Tkach Fedor Afanas'ev*, p. 27.

The May Day events made a good impression on all the participating workers. On their own initiative and hard work, they successfully celebrated May Day for the first time in Russia. Also for the first time, women activists participated with the males. In a much smaller fashion, they acted like their Western European counterparts. Consequently, Western socialist leaders could no longer declare that Russian workers were backward. After all, these Russian workers had a full day's activities in the face of much greater adversity than workers in Western Europe currently faced. Because the Central Workers' Circle organized and conducted May Day, the group reaped most of the benefits. The author contends that their authority and respect grew among the other workers in St. Petersburg. The ties among the different groups of circles became stronger. The Central Workers' Circle became a much more cohesive group. The Central Workers' Circle had seized the initiative and they hoped to lead the course of the workers' movement. Enthusiastic over their successes, the Central Workers' Circle started preparations for an expansion of their group to other cities in Russia.

Expansion of the Central Workers' Circle to Other Cities

After the May Day activities, the members and their affiliated intellectual activists were jubilant over the past six months. Circles that had been only loosely affiliated became closely tied into one organization, the Central Workers' Circle. That group increasingly represented the hopes and goals for, at least, the workers' intelligentsia. The intellectuals had more respect than ever before for the workers and their organizational abilities. For a couple of reasons, the groups decided to establish contacts with workers in other industrial cities in Russia, and establish new circles where none had previously existed. For one thing, the Central Workers' Circle's successes convinced its members that the workers in other cities would be responsive to their organization. News of the Shelgunov demonstration and May Day had spread far beyond St. Petersburg. The Central Workers' Circle became convinced that it had become the potential nucleus for a nationwide workers' organization, an embryonic workers' party. Secondly, the Central Workers' Circle believed it had no choice. Several of its members were arrested and exiled after the May Day events. Those people, such as Gavril Mefodiev, either had to cease their prior activities, or else resume them in their new city. Therefore, from the summer of 1891 until the spring of 1892, representatives of the Central Workers' Circle expanded their activities to include Moscow, Tula, Riga, Kostroma, and Nizhni Novgorod. Those activities only ended when virtually all the leaders in those cities were arrested, and either thrown into prison or else exiled to Siberia or the far north.

The first labor activist to leave St. Petersburg was Fedor Afanasev, one of the founders of the Central Workers' Circle. Things were getting too hot for him in St. Petersburg. As a result of this prominence on both the Shelgunov demonstration and on May Day, the police began a close surveillance on Afanasev. To escape probable arrest, Afanasev left St. Petersburg for Moscow during the summer of 1891. In the last decade of the nineteenth century, the labor movement was much smaller and less developed in Moscow than in St. Petersburg. S.I. Mitskevich, a Muscovite intellectual active in labor circles, said that, "the few ties that existed were almost exclusively of a cultural character. The workers were given good books to read and discussed them over cups of hot tea."[55] The new doctrine of Marxism had taken little hold among either the intellectuals or among the workers. The intellectuals never abandoned their Populist attitudes, while the workers were fairly apolitical. Mitskevich stated that "even in the most developed workers' circles, the teachings of Marx were not especially popular."[56] The intellectuals maintained that the workers were supplementary raw material in the revolutionary movement, a group to assist them in politicizing the peasantry, rather than a group to be politicized. Fedor Afanasev's mission was to form quasi-Marxist labor circles in Moscow that would become tied to the Central Workers' Circle in St. Petersburg. For a while, Afanasev found his efforts were a failure. He got a job as a weaver at the Filonov Factory. No workers listened to his views. Relations got so bad with his fellow workers that Afanasev was forced to leave the factory.[57] After several months, Afanasev was out of work, and he had established no contacts.

---

[55] Nevskii, Ocherki, p. 280.

[56] Ibid.

[57] Morshanskaia, Tkach Fedor Afanas'ev, p. 34.

By this time, Mikhail Brusnev arrived in Moscow to assist the lonely Afanasev. In June 1891, Brusnev graduated from the Technological Institute. Instead of remaining in St. Petersburg, Brusnev said that he wanted to continue his political activity outside the capital. As a result, the position of intellectual representative was transferred with the workers' consent to M.S. Olminskii (Aleksandrov) that June. Even though the position was transferred from a Marxist Brusnev to a Populist Olminskii, it made little difference in the conduct of policies for the Central Workers' Circle. Olminskii regarded the position solely as a formal one, advisory if that.[58] After visiting his parents in his place of birth and subsequent short visits to Moscow, Tula, Nizhni Novgorod, and Kiev, Brusnev decided to settle in Moscow where he would help Afanasev. Afanasev told Brusnev of his poor results in establishing contacts. To establish some real contacts with workers, Brusnev pretended to be a worker, and entered the Brest-Moscow Railway Plant as an engineer during the fall of 1891. By the start of the new year, 1892, Afanasev was able to get a new

---

[58] Ol'minskii, "O vospominaniiakh," Ot gruppy Blagoeva, p. 44.

job as a weaver in the Prokhorovskii Factory. At this plant Afanasev found the workers much more receptive to his views. Soon Afanasev and Brusnev started a small organization encompassing a few circles at their plants. Then Brusnev went back to St. Petersburg for a short visit to tell his friends on the Central Workers' Circle and the Central Students' Circle of their new good fortune in Moscow. He started ties between Moscow and St. Petersburg. Yet the Brusnev-Afanasev organization remained very fragile, and it was merely only one of several tiny groups of circles.

While Afanasev was out of work, he went briefly to Tula, an armaments center about 150 miles south of Moscow. Because of its small population and greater geographical isolation, Tula obviously had less labor activity than Moscow. Nevertheless, several labor activists exiled from St. Petersburg, such as Gavril Mefodiev, V.V. Buyanov, Nikita Rudelev, and Ivan Krutov, were forced to live there. These very bright and hard working skilled workers formed a potential nucleus for a local organization. Afanasev stayed with them for several days. He learned that they had been quite busy. All the workers formed circles in their respective factories. Just as in Moscow, the intellectuals in Tula were Populists. There had been

little cooperation between the workers and students
because the intellectuals still focused on the peasantry, but excluded the workers as an oppositional
force.[59] Afanasev and his fellow labor leaders consolidated a network of six circles based on the St.
Petersburg Central Workers' Circle. The four leaders
formed a Central Workers' Circle in Tula. It agreed
to establish ties with St. Petersburg. Soon it
organized a library and also collected money from
numerous workers to aid their less fortunate co-workers.
After that, Afanasev returned to Moscow. Yet the Central Workers' Circle in Tula was very weak, had no
intellectual assistance, and then finally had to compete with the Populists. To add to those problems,
the police discovered the existence of the organization,
and arrested Buyanov. Buyanov was exiled to Kostroma,
a city 300 miles northeast of Moscow. Rapidly Buyanov
started circle work there. The Central Workers' Circle
realized the importance of consolidating its contacts
with other cities. As an indication of the significance of that decision to broaden itself through
expansion, the organization named its secretary N.D.

---

[59]Brusnev, "Vozniknovenie," p. 28.

Bogdanov to handle affairs outside St. Petersburg. Furthermore, the Central Workers' Circle sent some money to Moscow and to Tula.

After the Shelgunov demonstration, L.B. Krasin was exiled to Nizhni Novgorod, about 300 miles east of Moscow. He also wanted to continue his St. Petersburg work among the workers there. Nevertheless, he was able to establish contacts only with intellectuals.[60] As in most Russian cities, workers and intellectuals lived in separate worlds, and had virtually no contact with each other. Krasin formed in intellectual circle, composed of several young students such as M.A. Silvin and P.N. Skvortsov; the former later became active in the Union of Struggle in St. Petersburg, an embryonic Social Democratic Party, while the latter became a well known Marxist theoretician. Yet this gifted group was unable to establish contacts with workers. Finally, they were forced to ask St. Petersburg for aid. They asked them for some real live workers. The Central Workers' Circle agreed to the request and sent them a few workers from both Moscow and St. Petersburg. Once that occurred in early

---

[60] M.I. Brusnev, "Pervye revoliutsionnye shagi L.B. Krasina," in M.N. Liadov and S.M. Pozner (eds.) Leonid Borisovich Krasin (Moscow-Leningrad, 1928), p. 70.

1892, those workers and intellectuals planned to form an organization. Yet the group had few local roots.

In Moscow by late 1891 there were three mixed worker-intellectual organizations. Each competed with the others for the affiliation of the highly skilled workers. Of the three groups only the Afanasev-Brusnev one was predominantly Marxist. The other two were Populist. The debate between the Marxists and the Populists concerned the workers. The workers listened twice as the intellectuals from both ideological camps presented their arguments to them. The workers made their decision based on the different points of view and the workers' own interests. The Moscow Afanasev-Brusnev group was a mixed workers' and students' group. However, it contained few Moscow workers in the group. Most workers, such as Afanasev, had moved to Moscow recently. Afanasev worked with the leader of the more moderate circle, Kashinskii. Afanasev recognized the need for collaboration, if not formal unification, between the two groups. Therefore, Afanasev arranged a meeting between Kashinskii, Brusnev, and himself. They had long discussions over a common plan of action, and also over Populism. The discussions proved very difficult. Brusnev conceded that it was very difficult to get Kashinskii to turn to a more Marxist perspective.

The three spent a lot of energy in that struggle.[61] After several meetings, they succeeded in affiliating the two groups. Both sides compromised their ideological programs in the interest of unity. Yet contacts with the third group proved much more difficult. Mikhail Egupov, the leader, had been a former student at the Novo-Aleksandovsk Institute. There he began his activities propagandizing in first Moscow and then in Tula. He formed a circle in Moscow that became very adept at collecting money and books. Egupov's circle developed a dual structure. Amongst intellectuals, his organization advocated political and social revolution through the tactic of political terror. Those intellectuals then relayed this program, on a much simpler level, among the city's workers.[62] Brusnev and Afanasev collided directly with Egupov and his group. The two accused them of being mere "terrorists." Unlike with Kashinskii's group, they did not want to discuss any type of collaboration. Yet Kashinskii pressed Brusnev and Afanasev to be less stubborn. He pointed out that, with the two groups at

---

[61] Brusnev, "Vospominaniia," in Pankratova, Rabochee dvizhenie, p. 113.

[62] Ol'minskii, "Materialy po delu M. Brusneva," Ot gruppy Blagoeva, p. 79.

each other's throats, little organizing could be accomplished. Their real enemy was not Egupov, but the government. The workers had little respect for these dogmatic, abstract debates. Furthermore, Egupov's group was the stronger organization. Egupov himself traveled on December 3, 1891, to Lublin and Warsaw by train where he stayed for two weeks. Outside Russia proper, Social Democratic organizations recognized his strength. In Poland, Egupov began relations with the Social Democratic organization, <u>Proletarjat</u>. They gave Egupov money and books.[63] Brusnev conceded that his group needed Egupov's group, no matter how much they disliked Egupov's personality and politics. Despite that, Kashinskii had warm relations with the whole Egupov group. At last, through the mediation of Kashinskii, Brusnev agreed that the two groups would propose better relations with Egupov's group. Pragmatism won out over ideology, but Brusnev never ended his distrust of Egupov. Even when Egupov later agreed to many of Brusnev's ideas, in his memoirs, Brusnev said Egupov had acted insincerely.[64]

---

[63] Ibid., pp. 79-80.
[64] Brusnev, "Vozniknovenie," p. 36.

Gradually, almost reluctantly, the opposing Muscovite groups moved toward not just collaboration, but unification. Once again Kashinskii acted as the agent. Even though he was the leader of the stronger organization, in the interests of unity, Egupov was more conciliatory. At first they discussed combining their actions. They exchanged literature and tried to utilize their meager funds together. Now Kashinskii thought the moment was ripe to discuss a full merger. Once again Brusnev and Afanasev raised several objections about merging with a Populist group that espoused the use of political terrorism. They seemed to ignore the fact that Egupov's group had moderated its position significantly on that question. Once again, Kashinskii's pragmatic arguments over the benefits of a merger won out. Brusnev and Afanasev yielded.[65] In January 1892, Egupov, Kashkinskii, Brusnev, and Afanasev merged their three circles into one organization. The four leaders composed a central committee of themselves, the "Provisional Organizational Committee." They also formed a common treasury.

At about the same time, a former student from the Petrovskii Academy in St. Petersburg, Aleksandr

---

[65]Vlasov, Tkach Fedor Afanas'ev, p. 30.

Mikhailovich, moved to Moscow. He carried with him recommendations from the Central Workers' Circle to both Brusnev and Egupov.[66] These recommendations urged that Egupov go to the Baltic region and also Poland to strengthen his contacts with the groups there, and also to help the Riga group form a more closely knit centralized organization. The Central Workers' Circle wanted to expand the group and its authority to other cities. In the near future, it planned to become an all-Russian labor organization, six years before one actually formed. Egupov had good contacts in Poland and in the Baltic region. He was the obvious person to try to get the Central Workers' Circle recognized as an all-Russian party of workers. Outside of St. Petersburg, Moscow had the strongest organization; yet unlike St. Petersburg the Moscow organization relied much more on intellectuals such as Egupov and Brusnev. In fact, Afanasev was the only worker on the decision making Central Committee. Now that the three Moscow groups were formally united, they were in a position to help the St. Petersburg Central Circle expand its network.

---

[66] Ol'minskii, "Materialy," <u>Ot gruppy Blagoeva</u>, p. 80.

On February 16, 1892, Egupov arrived in Riga. There he met with Mikhailovich, who had arrived in Riga several days in advance to prepare the activists for Egupov's visit. Mikhailovich and Egupov met several activists in Riga, both workers and students. For the first time ties were established between Moscow, St. Petersburg, and Riga. From Riga, Egupov went to Vilnius and Warsaw. There he collected money and literature. Through his travels he did some dangerous and clandestine intelligence activity. He learned the railway routes and schedules to determine how money and literature could more easily be imported from the West, via Poland.[67] At the end of February, Egupov returned to Moscow carrying both money and literature, in particular materials from the emigre Emancipation of Labor group. For example, he brought with him several issues of the journal <u>Sotsial-demokrat</u>. Egupov became the group's courier with the West. Despite personal dislike, Egupov had become invaluable.

On Easter eve, 1892, at Brusnev's flat, a large and very important meeting was held. The Central Committee decided to tighten their new fragile organization. They would formulate a joint program of goals

---

[67] <u>Ibid</u>., p. 82.

and tactics. Attending this critical meeting were all the members of Egupov's circle, all in Kashinksii's group, all of the Afanasev-Brusnev group along with N. Rudelev from Tula. Kashinskii, who represented a middle ground between Brusnev and Egupov, wrote the program. The program attempted to blend contradictory Populist and Marxist views. For example, one point stated that "political freedom could only be established through the use of terrorism." Another point said, "The proletariat served as the highest bearer of the idea of socialism."[68] A little further on, the program stated that the group had to work closely with factory workers by education and by agitation. Their ultimate goal was the creation of a worker's party. Kashinskii read the program; then the debate began. Afanasev and Brusnev denounced the Populist sections, especially the one defending terrorism. Nevertheless, Kashinskii utilized his skill of conciliation. He pointed out to the two that his program was a careful compromise designed to appeal to all Moscow's groups. A vote was finally taken. Only Brusnev and Afanasev voted against it. Because of the lack of a consensus, no final

---

[68] Nikitin, Pervye rabochee soiuzy, pp. 92-93.

decision was made. Apparently major decisions required unanimous consent.

The group still lacked a program. However, most of the people attending the meeting favored Kahinskii's draft. Kashinskii's program would have passed by majority vote. As a result, the meeting decided to send representatives to other cities to get their opinions. Brusnev said in his memoirs: "In our room was raised the question of widening our organization into other cities and about the organization of workers' circles in those places where we don't have existing ties with the workers."[69] If they accepted, then Kashinskii's program would be submitted to the Central Workers' Circle in St. Petersburg as a proposed draft for an all-Russian workers' organization. It seemed an appropriate compromise. If the other organizations agreed to this major decision, then the Marxists in Moscow would relent. The debate between Populism and Marxism could be settled nationwide. Therefore, Kashinskii would take his draft to Kiev where he knew one of the activists, a worker, Melnikov. Egupov would go first to Tula, and then to his contacts in the Baltic, to Riga, and Revel. Brusnev went to St. Petersburg to

---

[69] Nevskii, *Ocherki*, p. 308.

his former associates on the Central Workers' Circle of these plans, and to show them the proposed draft.[70] The members hoped a decision could be reached soon.

By now the Moscow group had established some ties with other cities. Illegal materials were being sent back and forth between Tula and Moscow. Rudelev represented the Tula group in the Moscow meeting. Brusnev and L.B. Krasin, now located in Nizhni Novgorod, had been acquainted with each other from their St. Petersburg days. Brusnev and Krasin had kept each other informed about the activities of the other in their respective cities. On the surface, plans were progressing well for the Moscow group. It and the Central Workers' Circle of St. Petersburg had become the nucleus for a potential all-Russian organization. The Moscow groups had merged. Yet in reality the Moscow organization was very weak. The feuds between the Populists and the Marxists had continued, as that critical meeting had showed. The wide fissures in the organization had only been papered over because of the brilliant diplomatic work of Kashinskii. The organization could be rent asunder any time again. Despite this weak unification, the organization still had few

---

[70] Brusnev, "Vospominaniia," p. 116.

ties with the Muscovite workers. There were no listed Moscow workers at that meeting. Brusnev conceded this point. He said: "We grew in breadth, but not in depth. In Moscow we counted all of two or three solely workers' circles."[71] Furthermore, in many of those cities which would form the "all-Russian organization," the groups composed only exiled students from St. Petersburg. To add to their problems, the group's activities had not gone unnoticed. The plan which could have led to a unified labor organization never came off.

For a while the police kept watching Egupov. They recognized the danger that he posed. Consequently the police noted whom he saw and where he went. They discovered that the network of circles stretched to other cities such as Tula, Riga, Nizhni Novgorod, Kostroma, and Kharkov. As Egupov walked to the railway station that April 26, 1892, he had no idea that he was walking into a trap. The secret police were at the station waiting for him. At the same time, they had orders for the arrest of Brusnev, Kashinskii, and Afanasev, the entire leadership of the Moscow organization. Thus, while he held his ticket for Tula in his hands, Egupov

---

[71] Nevskii, *Ocherki*, p. 309.

was arrested at the station. Brusnev was arrested at his apartment with his suitcase full of literature as he prepared to leave soon for St. Petersburg. The police missed Kashinskii at both his flat and at the station, but a few days later they rounded him up in Kiev. At that point, Afanasev managed to elude the police, went underground, and escaped to St. Petersburg. When Afanasev arrived in St. Petersburg, he became a blacksmith at the Baltic factory. Even though Afanasev was an illegal, he did not remain cautious for very long. "He entered the thick of organizing work right away," and organized workers' circles in his factory.[72] His activity brought him to the attention of a secret agent. Some of his friends noticed his apparent overconfidence and urged him to go into seclusion. Afanasev disregarded their advice, and continued his work. At long last, on September 12, 1892, the police arrested him in St. Petersburg. From St. Petersburg, Afanasev was transferred back to Moscow, where he waited for the activities that spring. In Moscow, Afanasev was subjected to solitary confinement for 9½ months until June 30, 1893. Despite extensive interrogation of Afanasev, the police had

---

[72] Morshanskaia, Tkach Fedor Afanas'ev, p. 36.

little hard evidence. Ultimately, they gave him a fairly light sentence, exile in his native village, Yazvishchi, for one year.[73]

In the meantime, Egupov did not stand up well to police interrogation. They showed him collections of illegal materials directly traced to Egupov. At the same time they promised him a light sentence if he cooperated. Egupov proved extremely cooperative. Not only did he name all the members of the Moscow organization, but he also named virtually all his contacts with other cities. Immediately, the police issued warrants for the arrest of the people Egupov had named, who composed the leadership of the circles in several cities. Many arrests followed: in Nizhni Novgorod, L.B. Krasin, on May 6, 1892, and A.M. Mikhailovich on May 19, 1892; in Tula, both N.I. Rudelev and G.A. Mefodiev in June and in August 1892; in Kharkov, four students or ex-students, the leaders of the organization, were arrested in May and June 1892. Rapidly by the end of 1892, the organizations in these four cities were destroyed. The organization, so carefully nur-

---

[73] Afanas'ev neither returned to St. Petersburg nor to active organizing again. According to some sources, he became a Bolshevik. Afanas'ev fell victim to the 1905 Revolution. Some Cossacks killed him.

tured by the group in Moscow, lay in ruins. Nevskii accurately attributed the group's collapse to their wide diversity.[74] Their different backgrounds, political views and attitudes all caused factional infighting. Internal disputes blinded them from taking security precautions. They became overconfident. The Brusnev group acted obliviously as though the police could never find them. They took great risks traveling on trains carrying large sums of money and materials.

The court's sentences were severe. Afanasev and Egupov were the only activists to receive light sentences. As a result of his testimony, Egupov got five years' exile in a place of his choice under supervision. He went back to his birthplace. The police considered Brusnev to be the leader. As a result, he got the worst sentence for his activities in St. Petersburg and Moscow, four years' prison and then ten years' exile in Eastern Siberia. Kashinskii got five years' exile to Western Siberia. Krasin got three years' exile in Vologoda province located in the far north. N. Rudelev and G. Mefodiev got six months' jail. The other terms ranged from six months' to three years' exile. Most never returned to political work, including Brusnev. He

---

[74]Nevskii, <u>Ocherki</u>, p. 311.

managed to return to European Russian only in 1904. The center of attention now turned to St. Petersburg.

May Day, 1892

The arrests in Moscow and in other cities did not directly lead to arrests within the St. Petersburg Central Workers' Circle. However those arrests led to a weakening and a greater fear within St. Petersburg. In 1891, the workers had celebrated May Day with few fears of police surveillance. In 1892 the fear of police discovery permeated all attempts to celebrate the holiday. Consequently the event was not as freely celebrated as in the previous year. Their fears were far from groundless. The police was aware of all gatherings and their leadership. That summer arrests devastated the Central Workers' Circle. It would be months before the workers recovered.

A possible foreboding for these events occurred at the Second International Congress at Brussels, Belgium in 1891. Unlike the first Congress, Russia had no delegates attending, even emigres. However, Russian Poland sent six activists, perhaps indicative of the much more advanced state of the movement in Poland.

The Brussels Congress again reaffimed the May Day holiday. The resolution said:

> The international People's holiday 1 May is dedicated simultaneously to the principles of an eight hour working day, better work regulations, and an international (worldwide) strengthening of the proletariat in its attempt to establish peace among the world's people.
>
> The Congress, in order to preserve May Day's true economic character, demands an eight hour working day and a strengthening of the class struggle. It establishes: a single demonstration for workers of all countries. This demonstration is fixed for 1 May. It recommends stop working then, where this is feasible.[75]

The last sentence, "where this is feasible," pertained directly to the Russian Empire. Not only police surveillance but also conditions within the labor movement dictated the type of celebrations. The largest events occurred in the borderlands of the Empire--in Poland and in Lithuania. For example, Jewish workers gathered in Vilnius. There they listened to four speeches delivered by workers including a woman.[76] The woman, Fania Reznik, urged more militant action in workshops and factories: "In order to overcome fragmenta-

---

[75] Valk, "Materialy," p. 265.

[76] Pervoe maia 1892 goda: Chetyre rechi evreishikh rabochikh (Geneva, 1893).

tion and to achieve unity we must organize frequent meetings of workers. All workers must strive to found kassas (treasuries) and to try and make them expand. We must organize strikes. For strikes as well we must have kassas." Yet Russian workers in St. Petersburg and elsewhere did not have the same opportunities. Despite these attempts at meetings not one proved completely successful. In contrast to the previous year, no speeches were published.

Once again, the Central Workers' Circle took the leading role organizing May Day activities, specifically, Petr Evgrafov, one of the founders of the Central Workers' Circle, and Fedor Pashin, who led a circle at the Baltic factory.[77] Despite the arrests that April, they urged that the Central Workers' Circle organize a May Day celebration as their colleagues in Poland already had. They pointed out the benefits in a celebration. A successful May Day event could further unify the circles in St. Petersburg, and also enhance the prestige of the Central Workers' Circle. In fact, over the past year except for its role in aiding groups outside St. Petersburg, the group had conducted few public activities. The leaders believed they had to do

---

[77] Valk, "Materialy," p. 266.

something once again to rally the city's workers behind it. Other members in the circle pointed out that police supervision was much tighter this year than it was last year. After further discussion, the group decided to celebrate it not on May 1 but instead on May 24 (OS), long after the holiday was celebrated elsewhere. Once again the group settled on the sparsely populated Krestovskii Island, this time along the shore near the summer house of Prince Beloselskii-Belozerskii, who was expected to be away. Plans were formulated in advance. The routes to the site were given in advance to all anticipated participants.[78] Publicity spread throughout several factories where the highly skilled organizers were employed.

That day, May 24, 1892, was sunny and clear. To avoid attention people traveled to the site in small groups by foot or by boat. An estimated 100 to 200 workers gathered at a precise prearranged time on the shore. Unlike the previous year, this time many women attended. People happily arrived thinking they had successfully eluded the police. Members of the Central Workers' Circle distributed proclamations, a few books, and several caricatures of the unpopular Tsar Alexan-

---

[78] Karelina, "Na zare," p. 16.

der III. Once again this was a workers' event. It was planned, directed, and attended virtually only by workers. In fact, only two intellectuals attended.[79] One was a Pole, W.F. Cywiński (Tsivinskii), the current intellectual representative on the Circle. The other was V.V. Sviatlovskii, who had been active with workers since the founding of the Central Workers' Circle in 1890 and who also aided them in May 1891. Both disguised themselves in peasant clothes. Refreshments of bread, sausage, and beer were distributed to the crowd. One participant at the event, the only woman member on the Central Circle, described what happened then:

> Then just before we were to deliver our speeches, Prince Beloselskii-Belozerskii appeared. We were on his property. He told us to get off his land. We would have defied the Prince, but a worker, Maklakov, arrived and told us that the police were coming right now. Those who arrived on boat, left on their boats rapidly. By the time the police arrived, we were in the middle of the river. There were not enough police to try and stop us. They looked at us. In response, Sviatlovskii waved his cap and said 'Goodbye.'[80]

The crowd got safely away. Nevertheless, despite the defiant words of Sviatlovskii, the holiday was

---

[79] Sviatlovskii, "Na zare," p. 159.

[80] Karelina, "Na zare," p. 17.

aborted. No speeches were ever delivered, or even remained for later publication. The long planned event became a nonevent.

Meanwhile, a great wave of industrial strikes rocked Poland in the wake of May Day celebrations there. These strikes centered on Łódź where antistrikers and police soon degenerated the unrest into a vicious anti-Jewish pogrom.[81] The Central Workers'

---

[81] Jews, concentrated in Poland, Lithuania, and the other western borderlands of the Russian Empire, also became part of the industrial drive in the late nineteenth century. Jews were particularly prominent in jewelry, footwear, tailoring and other highly skilled crafts. For years many of the most skilled Jewish workers and craftsmen had organized themselves in mutual assistance societies or kassas. For example, by 1890, most Jewish workers in the jewelry and footwear trades in Vilnius had joined a kassa. The mass labor unrest in May 1892 affected Jewish workers as well. In Vilnius, workers demanded that the owners of the city's workshops conform to the 100 year old law enacted by Catherine II which required that the work day should be no more than 12 hours. Just as with the Polish workers, an alarmed central government suppressed the strikes. In the fall of 1897, Jewish workers organized themselves into the General Jewish Workers Union of Lithuania and Poland--the Bund--which became affiliated with the Russian Social Democratic Party. For further information on the Jewish labor movement see Louis Greenberg, The Jews in Russia: The Struggle for Emancipation, 1881-1917 (New Haven, 1951); and T.M. Kopel'zon "Evreiskoe rabochee dvizhenie kontsa 80-kh i nachale 90-kh godov," in S. Dimanshtein, ed., Revoliutsionnoe dvizhenie sredi Evreev (Moscow, 1930), pp. 65-80.

Circle was both impressed by the extent of the strikes, and disgusted by the pogrom. Between 30,000 and 60,000 workers participated in the Polish strikes. In response, the Central Workers' Circle congratulated Polish workers in an open letter, concluding with a declaration emphasizing the weakness of the labor movement in St. Petersburg: "You are terribly persecuted, but you are more fortunate than we. You have already entered upon an open struggle, while we are only getting ready for it. But soon we shall follow in the footsteps of our brothers from the other countries and wage war against the common enemy: the tsar, the lords, the manufacturers, and the priests."[82] Thus the open letter concluded on a note of defiance.

After the aborted holiday on Krestovskii Island, the Central Workers' Circle planned another celebration within a few weeks. They selected a place near the Moscow Gates, a wooded area in the southern section of the city. The approximate date and time were announced to those workers who came to the first event. Yet the second attempt never occurred. Secret agents notified the police. The Central Workers' Circle postponed the event, and changed both the date and the location. The

---

[82] Valk, "Materialy," pp. 282-283.

Circle thought more time was needed to allow for preparations by local circles, and to write a few speeches. This time the Central Workers' Circle was determined to have a successful May Day.

The newly selected site was in the Volkovo-Yamskii woods, an isolated spot eight <u>versts</u> (about five miles) from St. Petersburg near the railroad line to Tsarkoe Sebo. Approximately 100 people gathered in the early afternoon, around 1 p.m. on June 28, 1892 (OS) from various circles in the Narvskii and Nevskii Gates regions, the Vyborg side, and from both Petrogradskii and Vasilyevskii Islands. Again many of the participants were women. The workers carried red banners and sausages, bread and drink. As in the previous year, the speeches delivered by the workers were the highlight. The first speech was given by Egor Afanasev (Klimanov). He allegedly outlined the plight of Russian workers, their exploitation by factory owners and by the government, and the need for workers to struggle to improve their lives.[83] Eight speeches were written for the occasion. The authors of those eight speeches were: G. Lunegov, V. Fomin, P. Kaizo, I. Egorov, E. Tumanov, E. Afanasev, P. Evgrafov, and the wife of Egorov, A.G. Egorova. P. Evgrafov's speech reflected both a bitter, and defiant tone, characteristic of the beleaguered group. He accused Russian society of living from the toil of the workers, and he emphasized the necessity that labor rely on its own forces.

---

[83] Karelina, "Na zare," p. 18. Information concerning the speeches was contradictory. For example, Vera Karelina said that the first speech was given by E. Afanas'ev. On the other hand, another worker Krylov who was present said flatly that Afanas'ev did not even attend the meeting. He got lost, and arrived too late for the gathering. Someone else had to read his speech (Korolchuk and Sokolova, eds. Khronika, pp. 220-221). There has been little definite information about the speeches. The Central Workers' Circle never had the opportunity to print them. Most of the texts were destroyed during police raids. Only two speeches were saved, those of E.F. Tumanov and Petr Evgrafov (Valk, "Materialy," p. 285). Those were kept in police headquarters until after the Russian Revolution. It is not even clear how many of those speeches were actually delivered at the assembly. It is known that not all eight speeches were actually delivered. Of those that were delivered, a few, such as Egor Afanas'ev's (Klimanov's) were delivered by someone else.

> Let us overthrow and crush these parasites!
> There are hundreds of them and millions of
> us, but we are weak because we are uneduca-
> ted and unorganized. Let us then, brothers,
> learn and develop, so that sooner or later we
> shall be able to unite in closed ranks, like
> the Western workers. Let us study so that
> we can everywhere instruct and organize to
> the last drop of blood our uneducated
> brothers, so that we ourselves can teach
> circles instead of the intellectuals who are
> fewer and fewer all the time, so that the
> liberation of labor will be achieved by labor
> itself. Thus, in this manner alone can labor
> free itself.[84]

When the speeches finished, the assembly broke up. By now the leaders were convinced the crowd was infested by police agents. Quickly, and in small groups the workers returned to their homes. There is no record of any evening meetings as in the previous year.

As the leaders suspected the police had watched the assembly. Then police agents gave the authorities a large list of people who participated in the June 28th May Day. Soon there were massive arrests. On July 14, 1892, they seized P. Evgrafov, E. Afanasev, V. Fomin, E. Tumanov, along with many others.[85] After these arrests, more occurred. For example, in September 1892, F. Afanasev was taken. Sviatlovskii and Cywiń-ski, the two intellectuals most involved with the

---

[84]Valk, "Materialy," p. 285.

[85]Sviatlovskii, "Na zare," p. 160.

Central Workers' Circle, eluded arrest, and escaped from St. Petersburg.[86] Sviatlovskii left Russia for five years, but Cywiński was apprehended in 1893. Only two or three members of the Central Workers' Circle such as the Karelins avoided the police dragnet. By September, the Central Workers' Circle, so carefully built up over the previous three years, lay crippled. Most of the leaders from the workers' intelligentsia were either in hiding or in jail or deported. It would take months, but then; virtually a new group of labor activists would again revive the Central Workers' Circle.

---

[86] Ibid.

CHAPTER VI

THE RISE AND FALL OF THE REVIVED CENTRAL WORKERS' CIRCLE, 1892-94

The Rebirth of the Central Workers' Circle, 1892

During the summer of 1892 police arrests buffeted the Central Workers' Circle. All except one or two of the group's members, including its two most powerful activists, the Afanasev brothers, were removed from labor organizing. The group virtually collapsed. For several months circle work virtually ceased. Only very gradually did it recommence. Several activists organized educational circles in their factories. Initially these circles were tiny, usually no more than six people, and were isolated from each other as well as from any student tutors.[1] They had little money to purchase books, journals, and newspapers, or to engage in recruitment among other highly skilled workers. The workers were frightened of any activities that could bring them to the attention of the police and lead to their arrests. Labor activism reached a low point. People were discouraged and did not know how to reconstruct the movement that only one year

---

[1] Norinskii, "Moi vospominaniia," Ot gruppy Blagoeva, pp. 16-17.

before had brought its existence to the attention of the whole city's society and even the national government.

Out of these shattered ruins of a labor movement, very gradually, a new Central Workers' Circle reemerged to coordinate these tiny dispersed circles, and to once again expand. The inspiration for the rebirth of the Central Workers' Circle lay in the hands of a few workers who had not been arrested. During the winter of 1892-93, V.A. Shelgunov, K.M. Norinskii, G.M. Fisher, and I.I. Keizer reestablished the Central Workers' Circle. The contribution of Vasillii Andreevich Shelgunov was critical. He became the group's acknowledged leader. K.M. Takhtarev, a student activist, who knew Shelgunov well, accurately summarized Shelgunov's contribution:

> He was definitely the most outstanding worker I had ever met. Shelgunov devoted all his powers to support, develop, and lead in the proper direction the cause of labor. He gave himself wholeheartedly to the common cause of the labor movement and did not miss the smallest detail of factory life. The unification of the labor representatives of the various regions in St. Petersburg was in

very large measure his achievement and that of his comrades.[2]

Shelgunov's background was typical of other members of the workers' intelligentsia. Shelgunov was born in August 8, 1867, of peasant parents in Slavkovichi village near Pskov. As his father and older brother already worked in St. Petersburg, his mother sent him to join them there. Eventually the whole large family of seven children followed suit. His childhood was very tragic. His mother died when Shelgunov was very young, and his father was an alcoholic who had a nasty temper. At the age of nine Shelgunov became employed in an iron foundry in St. Petersburg. After five months, he became ill with peritonitis. His father sent him to live with his older brother, Ivan Alekseevich, back in the country. At the age of

---

[2] K.M. Takhtarev, Ocherk peterburgskogo rabochego dvizheniia 90-kh godov (London, 1902), p. 11. The fullest yet least accurate account of Shel'gunov's life and contribution is in M.D. Rozanov's biography, Vasilii Andreevich Shel'gunov (Leningrad, 1948). While the work is laudatory toward Shel'gunov, it submerges his activities to an adjunct of the intellectual Social Democratic movement. Furthermore, Rozanov inaccurately depicts Lenin's role as central to the labor movement virtually from the moment he arrived in St. Petersburg in the summer of 1893. A more accurate but very brief account of Shel'gunov's life is found in Ot gruppy Blagoeva, "Vospominaniia V.A. Shel'gunova," pp. 52-59.

13, Shelgunov returned to St. Petersburg where he worked in a bookbindery. During his youth, Shelgunov received a general education: reading, writing, arithmetic, and religion then common to working class children. He worked by day and attended school by night. Just as with other members of the Central Workers' Circle the furtherance of his education became central to Shelgunov. Konstantin Takhtarev, a student tutor to Shelgunov's circle, and an old acquaintance of him, commented in the second edition of his memoirs that the shelves in Shelgunov's flat were filled with books, old journals, and newspapers. "Reading was a passion for Shelgunov. He made use of every opportunity to improve his education."[3] After the assassination of Tsar Alexander II in March 1881, control over literature tightened. Shelgunov was working in a bookbindery, and found out that a proposed book for publication by the shop was withdrawn as a result of government pressure. That incident caused Shelgunov's first confrontation with the authorities. He asked the bindery's censor why the withdrawal of the book occurred, and did not accept the censor's reply.[4] Shelgunov's curiosity was

---

[3] Takhtarev, Rabochee dvizhenie, p. 23.

[4] Shel'gunov, "Vospominaniia," Ot gruppy Blagoeva, p. 53.

aroused. He became interested in forbidden books, read those he could obtain, and questioned why the books were forbidden. That small incident started Shelgunov on the path of labor activities.

In fall 1885, Shelgunov was hired as an iron worker at the New Admiralty Shipbuilding plant. There he furthered his education by taking evening classes in physics, chemistry, geometry, and geography at the factory. His ability to absorb information showed in these subjects. Within a couple of years he passed the examination for all four classes in fields such as language, geometry and cosmography. His father did not approve of his education. He told Shelgunov: "If you read too much, you will destroy yourself."[5] By now Shelgunov had met Egor Afanasev (Klimanov), a man who would have a major influence on him. Afanasev pushed Shelgunov's fascination with political literature, gave him illegal Populist books, and convinced him to enter his worker's circle. Shelgunov was being absorbed into the city's tiny but growing labor movement.

In 1888, the same year that Shelgunov finished his formal education, he was drafted into the army.

---

[5] Ibid., p. 54.

In his free time, he managed to maintain his contacts with Afanasev's circle. He attended its meetings held each Sunday. Then the authorities transferred Shelgunov to Oranienbaum which was 40 versts (about 26 miles) from St. Petersburg. In the army he conducted anti-government propaganda work among the other draftees.[6] Nevertheless, Shelgunov was too far away from St. Petersburg to be included in most of the group's activities. That fact proved fortunate because Shelgunov was unaffected by the massive arrests which hit the Central Workers' Circle in 1892. That fall Shelgunov's military service ended, and he returned to St. Petersburg. Shelgunov already knew about the arrests that summer and about the poor state of the organization. He particularly mourned the absence of his friend, Egor Afanasev (Klimanov). Shelgunov energetically set out to reorganize the Central Workers' Circle. He contacted his old colleagues who had been members or at least had been affiliated with the Central Workers' Circle, in particular, K.M. Norinskii, G.M. Fisher, and I.I. Keizer. None had been officers or leaders of the old Central Workers' Circle, for all of them had been removed through arrests.

---

[6]Rozanov, V.A. Shel'gunov, p. 56.

These four workers became the nucleus for a new Central Workers' Circle. Slowly they revived the old organization. Then the four leaders began the laborious process of getting the scattered, tiny workers' circles in the city affiliated with them.[7] By early 1893, the Central Workers' Circle reemerged. As yet it had no centralized treasury, so critical for the conduct of activities. That took another year. During the winter of 1893, the United Fund of St. Petersburg was set up.[8] Yet this treasury never had the sums the old Central Treasury had. K.M. Takhtarev said that it had a sum of 190 rubles. That sum did not compare with the old treasury which partially explains the more modest activities of the new Central Workers' Circle.[9] In 1894 the treasury was to collapse when arrests again buffeted the organization and its intellectual allies.

The new Central Workers' Circle was smaller than its parent organization. Instead of eight to ten members, this organization had at its height no more than six men and one woman, Vera Karelina. Besides the four already mentioned, Fisher, Keizer, Norinskii

---

[7] Norinskii, "Moi vospominaniia," p. 17.
[8] Fisher, V Rossii i v Anglii, p. 23.
[9] Takhtarev, Rabochee dvizhenie, p. 34.

Shelgunov, Sergei Funtikov and Ivan Babushkin were frequently mentioned as members on the Central Circle. Babushin was the group's main link with a new generation of workers' elite, those in their late teens. Babushkin was born in 1873. Differences in temperament and attitudes soon arose between the two generations of labor activists, who were roughly ten years apart. The younger workers had no emotional attachments to Populism. In particular, those younger workers disapproved of individual heroic actions such as terrorism [10] that many Populists espoused. Nevertheless, for nearly a year generational differences were submerged and only sprouted during the winter of 1893-94, when the Populist-Marxist debates occurred. The Central Workers' Circle had two political leanings. Keizer inclined toward Populism, while Babushkin and Fisher inclined toward Marxism or Social Democracy. The Social Democrats favored mainly a continuation and an expansion of the educational and cultural activities. They believed that the Central Workers' Circle should organize among only the highly skilled workers' intelligentsia. Iulii Martov summarized their attitudes when he stated: "Among the most propagandized

---

[10] Norinskii, "Moi vospominaniia," p. 18.

workers, there was an inclination to regard the further growth of the movement as only the gradual increase of circles in which there would be systematic lectures and activities."[11] On the other hand, the Populists remembered and had been active during the momentous year 1890-91 when there were a string of successes from the Thornton Strike through May Day. They believed the group should resume open agitational activities where the members worked. Eventually this difference over tactics along with the question of whom the group should direct its energies toward split the workers' organization. While several authors label this a political dispute between the ideologies of Populism and Social Democracy, in reality, it was a dispute over tactics.[12]

Once the Central Workers' Circle organized, it proceeded both to consolidate the localized circles, and then expand into new factories. Its goal was to eventually achieve the close network of circles its predecessor had. Shelgunov personally led this expansion drive. He frequently changed jobs in order to

---

[11] Iu. Martov, *Zapiski sotsial-demokrata* (Berlin, 1922), p. 94.

[12] No source, Soviet or non-Soviet, mentions the dispute in any but ideological motivations. Differences over tactics are minimized.

meet new workers. When he arrived in St. Petersburg, he got employed at the New Admiralty, his old place of employment, where he organized workers in the Nevskii Gates region. Police surveillance forced him to change to the Putilov factory. Five months later in the summer of 1893 he transferred to the Baltic factory, where along with Norinskii and Fisher, who were also employed there, he extended the Central Workers' Circle to include circles on Vasilyevskii Island.

In 1893 Fedor Afanasev returned from Moscow. Due to a lack of concrete evidence the police authorities were unable to hold him for long. He joined the others at the Baltic factory as an operator on a drilling machine. However police surveillance of him jeopardized the rest of the group's activities in the factory. The Central Workers' Circle decided that he had to transfer to another factory in another section of the city. After some discussion he complied with the group's decision.[13]

In early 1893, Vera Karelina, then attending a midwife course, joined the Central Workers' Circle. She became the group's first woman member, and brought her woman's circle into the growing network. However,

---

[13]Norinskii, "Moi vospominaniia," p. 18.

her membership did not last for very long because in March 1893, she was arrested, thrown into jail, and soon exiled far from the city to Kharkov province.[14] Her loss was greatly felt. Not only was she a leading woman activist because she was the group's only real contact with women workers, but her whole extensive library was seized with her. Gradually new circles were created in different sections. Eventually around twenty different circles were directed by the Central Workers' Circle.[15] While large, it did not match the numbers or the breadth of the previous Central Workers' Circle.

The intellectual level of the new Central Workers' Circle and its affiliated network remained high. All of the members were members of the workers' intelligentsia. In fact, the bulk of them were highly skilled machinists who worked in factories such as the Putilov or the Baltic. Educational work remained paramount. The circles read and discussed subjects, especially in the natural and physical sciences. The group's primary goal was to expand their information. Political activism had an even lower priority than in the previous

---

[14] Karelina, Na zare," p. 17.

[15] Shel'gunov, "Vospominaniia," Ot gruppy Blagoeva, p. 55.

Central Workers' Circle.[16] The group detected a continuing police surveillance. To minimize the risk of arrests at the end of 1892, Shelgunov rented an apartment solely for meetings. The police were keeping a frequent eye on his apartment, and would be highly suspicious of any meetings there.[17] To preclude eavesdropping by curious neighbors who might be police informants, the members disguised their meetings as social gatherings. While some members discussed the group's current affairs or lectured on a particular subject, other members sang or played an instrument such as an accordian. No members were ever addressed by their real names at meetings. Instead they all used pseudonyms. By such methods the conduct of meetings and their preoccupation with security was almost identical to the previous Central Workers' Circle.

However, there was one other major difference between this Central Workers' Circle and the older one. The older circle had an intellectual "advisor" attached to it. While intellectuals never took a commanding role in the organization, they could and frequently did

---

[16] Norinskii, "Moi vospominaniia," p. 16.

[17] Rozanov, V. A. Shel'gunov, p. 56.

sway members with their arguments. The arrests in 1892 hit the intellectuals even more than the workers. Their numbers declined tremendously. For a long time, there were no contacts between the student intellectuals and the workers. The intelligentsia remained outside the organization and never sent a representative to meetings of the Central Workers' Circle. Increasingly they became factionalized between the Populists and the Marxists or Social Democrats. Furthermore, the group after the 1892, not only retained but also deepened their distrust of the intellectuals. Fisher characterized this attitude quite succinctly:

> We realized in general that we were separated from the intelligentsia by many conditions, the way of life, education, and so on. We conceded that we could work together, but <u>not under their direction</u>. We could in no way conceive that the intelligentsia should tell us at every given instant to do this or that. We would not have tolerated this. We also felt that we were incapable of telling the intelligentsia what to do.[18] (underlining is mine)

More strongly than ever before, the group insisted that the "affairs of workers must be the affairs of the workers themselves."[19] Throughout the whole existence

---

[18] Fisher, <u>V Rossii i v Anglii</u>, p. 23.

[19] Takhtarev, <u>Ocherk</u>, p. 15.

of the group, it retained its independence from the intelligentsia. They had to channel all communication with labor through the Central Workers' Circle. They depended on its good will.

This revived Central Workers' Circle had a similar but a smaller structure, and was similar in its goals to its predecessor. It represented and oversaw the members of the workers' intelligentsia in several factories in different sections of the city. It sought the educational and political advancement of the workers' intelligentsia through further education. Just as in the previous Central Workers' Circle, lectures, discussions, readings were central to the organization. Their goal was eventually to include the whole workers' intelligentsia in their organization, but not to go beyond that to include the rank and file workers. That goal ran into direct conflict with the student intelligentsia, an issue the workers' elite lost. Factionalism between those workers who favored Populism, and the newer generation who favored Social Democracy split the group before the police dealt it the final crushing blow. Yet the revived Central Workers' Circle was smaller in numbers, perhaps half the size of its predecessor. Authority was vested in fewer hands; its clear leader was one man, V.A. Shelgunov. The others--

Norinskii, Fisher, and Keizer--were clearly his subordinates. The sources lacked comment on whether the group was less democratic than its predecessor, but the reader can certainly make some reasonable deductions that it was. Those weaknesses, perhaps partially attributable to less contact with the rank and file workers, were exemplified in the group's activities.

The Activities of the Revived Central Workers' Circle

Timidity characterized the revived Central Workers' Circle's activities. The group lacked the self-confidence of its predecessors. New ideas or techniques rarely occurred. Except for cultural activities such as education, successes were rare. The organization lacked the spark of its predecessors, which had launched several demonstrations and Russia's first May Day celebration. The opportunities were still there, but the group did not capitalize on them. The reasons for this timidity are somewhat speculative. The group lacked both the size and the network including several cities that its predecessor had. Simply, it did not command the allegiance of as many workers' intelligentsia. Secondly, the memory of the arrests in 1892 continually haunted the group. It was preoccupied with security, so preoccupied that it was reluctant to do anything that could jeopardize that security. Finally, the group became embroiled in the political polemics that occurred between the Populists and the Social Democrats.[20] That debate divided and fatally weakened the group before the police administered the coup de grâce in spring 1894.

The debate included a more practical issue than ideology. What would be the future of the workers' movement? Many members of the workers' intelligentsia favored the development of a trade union movement that represented only the skilled and educated workers in the author's opinion, not entirely dissimilar to the early A.F.L. Other members favored a development of a workers' party which included both radical and middle class intelligentsia. The first group understood that merger meant submergence under the student intelligentsia. A victory by the latter group was a direct threat against the workers' intelligentsia. One incident illustrates this perfectly. A Marxist historian, M.N. Liadov, discussed the matter with Eleanor Marx, the daughter of

---

[20] For further information, see the latter part of this section.

Karl Marx, who lived in England. "She agreed that we (the intellectuals) should act against the interests of the workers' aristocracy (intelligentsia). Once that decision was made, we concentrated on more agitational methods with the rank and file workers."[21] When that became the policy by both the student intelligentsia and the workers' intelligentsia, then the workers' intelligentsia split. The more educated, skilled, and predominantly older workers split from the lesser skilled, educated and younger workers. The workers' intelligentsia never recovered from that split. Even many intellectuals regretted this apparent empty victory. One Social Democratic intellectual, later a Soviet historian, K.M. Takhtarev, conceded that the split created "an unpleasant spectacle."[22]

May Day 1893 was even less successful than the previous year. Once again, the Central Workers' Circle chose Krestovskii Island, this time in one of the woods scattered throughout the sparsely populated island. While a few people arrived on foot, most arrived by boat. Yet, once again, the selected site was a poor one. Despite being in the woods, the site proved so

---

[21] M.N. Liadov, Kak zarodilas' M. Rab. (St. Petersburg, 1906), pp. 57-58.

[22] Takhtarev, Ocherk, p. 14.

open a place that the group rapidly decided it would
not stay much longer. Fewer people turned up than in
the two previous years. However, this time, at least
two students, V.V. Starkov and G.M. Krzyzanowski, and
probably more attended.[23] Fearing arrest by the ever-
present police, the group was forced to disperse back
on their boats before they even delivered any of their
speeches. The gathering proved a complete failure, a
mere shadow of the last two years. Nevertheless, the
group said they would meet again to hold another May
Day rally. Yet that assembly would never be held
because the group feared police arrests. The
undelivered speeches were never kept for posterity.
Even the authors remained unknown. Despite these precautions, arrests soon followed the non-event. These
arrests took several of the oldest, most experienced
labor activists in the city: Egor Afanasev (Klimanov),
Petr Evgrafov and Grigorii Lunegov. Both student
intellectuals present at May Day, V. Starkov and G.
Krzyzanowski, were nabbed by the police. Once again
Afanasev was exiled from St. Petersburg. Gradually he
drifted away from anti-government activities.[24]

---

[23] Fisher, V Rossii i v Anglii, p. 22.

[24] V.V. Sviatlovskii, "K istorii pervogo maia, 1890-93 gg.," Byloe, no. 16, 1921, pp. 171-172.

The arrests caused the group to act even more cautiously than before. No more attempts to hold a May Day assembly occurred. The group was more careful than ever before in its recruitment of new members.[25] The group rarely conducted anti-government activities. They concentrated on cultural activities, usually for themselves.

The library became the center of their energies. From scratch, the Central Workers' Circle had to recreate a new library. Both the legal and illegal collections in the old library had been seized by the police when they raided N.D. Bogdanov's and M.I. Brusnev's apartments.[26] The revived circle's library was never as large as the old one. Partly for security reasons, the library's collection was dispersed to the individual, localized circles. The dues purchased books, journals, and newspapers. The relatively well paid metal workers, who composed virtually the entire Central Workers' Circle's membership, supplemented their treasury allocations with some added donations from their own salaries. Just as before, the acquisitions concentrated on noted fiction,

---

[25] Karelina, "Na zare," p. 16.

[26] See pp. 209-212 in this dissertation for the account of the seizures.

history, and scientific texts. Decentralization prevented the group's workers from effectively utilizing their books. Furthermore duplication of books unnecessarily occurred in the circles. Not even a central bibliography of the collection existed. That would have enabled a book in the circle's collection at the Putilov factory to be easily borrowed by a different circle, say at the Baltic factory. However, decentralization prevented many of the books from being seized when the leaders of the Central Workers' Circle were arrested in 1894. Most likely that was why there was no common list with locations.

Several strikes broke out from 1892 through the middle of 1894, the period of the revived Central Workers' Circle. During the summer of 1892, about seven hundred workers struck protesting the poor quality cotton just introduced in their factory, the Mitrofanevskii Paper Mill and Weaving Factory.[27] The workers claimed that the low grade cotton hampered the quality of their work. As a result, they demanded a raise in wages. While most workers were prepared to listen to concessions promised by the management, a few militants took over control of the strike and halted

---

[27] Pankratova, Rabochee dvizhenie, v. III, p. 452.

work for two days. Consequently, twelve workers were
exiled from St. Petersburg. Then, on December 25,
1892, approximately 1,000 workers briefly struck at the
Aleksandrovsk machine plant. Many strikers refused to
allow the nonstrikers to report to work. In response,
the administration dismissed the leaders. Finally in
the winter of 1894, 700 workers struck at the I.A.
Voronin paper plant. That strike lasted four days.
A reduction in the piece rate caused that bitter strike.
The governor general of St. Petersburg sided with the
administration. He demanded that the workers return
immediately. The administration dismissed the leaders
of the strike. Throughout the area where the strikers
lived, the streets were filled with police and police
spies. The government closed the area's bars because
it feared drunken strikers might riot. The factory
eventually reopened. Soon activities returned to normalcy.[28] The government and administration exercised
a carrot-stick approach. A noted factory inspector,
Davidov, acted as a mediator between the workers and
the administration. He relayed the government's promise that wage increases would be given to the most
skilled. They happened to also be the most likely

---

[28] Pankratova, *Rabochee dvizhenie*, v. II, p. 452.

leaders. Then the police selected the nine alleged leaders of the strike. The administration dismissed them, but unlike the three workers in the Voronin strike, the police subsequently arrested them. All were given one month sentences in the city jail. Then all of them were exiled from St. Petersburg.

While the strikes were going on, the Central Workers' Circle played little or no role. They apparently did not instigate the strikes because none of the mentioned leaders in the strikes were members of the Central Workers' Circle. Unlike the strikes during the winter of 1890-91, in this strike the group did not distribute leaflets. In fact, M.S. Olminskii, the intellectual leader of the Populist <u>Gruppa Narodovol'tsev</u> (the <u>People's Will Group</u>) sarcastically quipped that both intellectuals as well as the Central Workers' Circle learned of these strikes from the city's newspapers. On top of that, both groups, along with their leaders such as Olminskii, reacted negatively to the strikers. "They call those strikers, '<u>sindikalisty</u>' (syndicalists or anarchists) and describe them in the most abusive ways as individuals who solely commit violence against the established order."[29] The only

---

[29] M.S. Ol'minskii, from an article printed in <u>Rabochii sbornik</u> on April 1, 1894.

aid intellectuals and the Central Workers' Circle gave was to raise some money for the strikers. One time they collected 200 rubles to go to the strikers at the Voronin plant.[30] That was hardly a significant sum, about 30 kopeks per person. Not only the strikers but other workers noticed this lack of reaction by the Central Workers' Circle. The group lost a splendid opportunity to begin and develop some ties with rank and file workers. Yet their lack of action was not unexpected. Throughout the strikes, the group was timid, and displayed no desire to expand beyond the tiny workers' intelligentsia. As a result, the Central Workers' Circle lost a great deal of credibility among the rank and file workers. It lost a potential role as spokesmen for the whole organized Russian working class. That fact was also noticed by intellectuals just when they commenced their great debates in 1894 between Populism and Social Democracy.

The arrests in 1892 which destroyed the original Central Workers' Circle also devastated the Central Students' Circle, both in St. Petersburg and its affiliated circles scattered in several major cities. Intellectual ties with the workers' intelligentsia

---

[30] Pankratova, Rabochee dvizhenie, v. II, p. 258.

completely ceased for a while.[31] From the beginning intellectuals were in a more exposed position than labor activists. The government regarded them as potentially much more dangerous because intellectuals had conducted numerous plots against the government and in particular the life of the tsar. The government placed intellectuals under closer scrutiny. Intellectuals who engaged in propaganda activity with the workers were even more closely matched. Convicted intellectuals received stiffer prison terms. It took months before the intellectuals reorganized again. When they did organize, they formed at least two major groups: a Social Democratic circle led by Stepan Radchenko and the Gruppa Narodovol'tsev led by M.S. Olminskii (Aleksandrov).

Along with these two major circles, there were several smaller and less significant ones that remained unaffiliated with either of the two larger groups. All attracted students from the two largest institutions of higher education in St. Petersburg: the University and the Technical Institute. The largest collection of Marxists was in the Technical Institute because it contained many economics majors who had read and had

---

[31] Golubev, "Stranichka," p. 114.

grasped the theories of Marx. The University, containing a profuse variety of majors, was the bedrock strength of narodniki or Populists. Only a handful of university students turned to Marxism.[32] They tended to remain isolated from the Populist students. In fact, Institute Marxists, mostly from lower middle class backgrounds, had little contact with University Marxists, who mostly came from affluent homes. They called the University Marxists "salon Marxists" and one Institute Marxist told Gorev, a university student, "what, you, a Marxist!"[33] To add to an economic class separation, and an institutional division, students were divided by their ages. The older students tended to be Populists, while younger students often still in their teens, were much more susceptible to Marxism, a relatively recent ideology entering Russia.

After the collapse of the Central Students' Circle, the only member who remained free was Stepan I. Radchenko. Radchenko was born on January 29, 1869 in Konotop, a small village in Chernigov province in the

---

[32] B.I. Gorev (Goldman), "Marksizm i rabochee dvizhenie v Peterburge chetvert' veka nazad, (Vospominaniia)," Novoe slovo, no. 3, Sept.-Oct. 1921, p. 110.

[33] Ibid.

Ukraine. Of Zaporozhets Cossack descent, his father, a small timber merchant, stressed education for his children. However his father died young in an accident, and his mother was left with eleven children and little money. The elder sons worked so that the younger sons (Stepan was the tenth of eleven children) could receive an education. This harsh background instilled a strong sense of discipline in him along with an affinity for the left. Stepan became an excellent and careful student. After attending preparatory schools in Rostov-on-Don and Kiev, in 1887 Stepan enrolled in the Technical Institute in St. Petersburg.

By 1890, he entered a Marxist circle at the Institute led by R.E. Klasson, an engineering student. Among the members of this circle was N.K. Krupskaia, who later became Lenin's wife. In 1891 he joined the Central Students' Circle. Although Radchenko worked in the thick of circle activities, most of the time he escaped the attention of the police. He was the only member who avoided arrest in 1892. Finally, he was arrested in November 1893, but was jailed for only three months.

After the collapse of the Central Students' Circle in the fall of 1892, Radchenko organized his own,

Marxist, circle.[34] Joining his circle were the following people: Radchenko's wife, an engineer G.M. Krzyzanowski (Krzhizhanovskii), V.V. Starkov, A.P. Nevzorova, Ya. P. Ponomarev, G.B. Krasin, and N.K. Krupskaia. Thus, unlike the Central Students' Circle, Radchenko's circle included at least three women. While its members were young, all in their twenties, the individuals in the group were called stariki or elders. That differentiated them from another Marxist circle in St. Petersburg, called molodye or the youngsters. In the mid-1890's, the members of the Radchenko Circle formed the nucleus for the future Union of Struggle, which by the end of the century evolved into the Russian Social Democratic Party.

Radchenko's views on the autonomy of workers' circles differed from his predecessors. He rejected the principle declared by Shelgunov that "the affairs of the workers are the affairs of the workers themselves."[35] In contrast, Radchenko believed that intellectuals should direct the leadership of the workers' circles. The destruction of the Central Workers' Circle in 1892 convinced him that workers

---

[34] I.I. Radchenko, "Stepan Ivanovich Radchenko," Staryi bol'shevik, no. 2, 1933, p. 180.

[35] Nevskii, Ocherki, p. 303.

could not protect themselves from the police. He never admitted that the police destroyed the Central Students' Circle as well. Workers' circles, in his eyes, engaged in trivial self-serving activities which only benefited themselves, not the rank and file workers. He believed that the control over education and propaganda should be removed from the hands of the workers and transferred to a tiny, secretive group of revolutionaries recruited entirely from the student intelligentsia. Each member of Radchenko's group had to organize and direct at least one workers' circle. That circle knew little or nothing about the activities of the center (or about each other for that matter).[36] Hopefully this isolation would preserve the central body from destruction if the police arrested an intellectual and his circle. Over the whole organization, Radchenko was preeminent. Democratic methods did not exist in this group. Thus, the keystone to the entire Radchenko group was threefold: intellectual control over the workers, secrecy, and isolated cells. This organizational structure would have major consequences for the relationship between the workers' intelligentsia and the students'

---

[36] G.B. Krasin, "Stepan Ivanovich Radchenko," *Staryi bol'shevik*, no. 2, 1933, p. 187.

intelligentsia, a relationship never noted for its trust and goodwill.

Radchenko's group's ties with workers' circles developed slowly. Only by the end of 1892 had Radchenko's circle begun propaganda activities among the members of the revived Central Workers' Circle.[37] Yet they never became leaders of the circles Radchenko intended his group to become. Instead Shelgunov utilized them only as teachers. In even that activity, they were not very effective. Fisher, one of the members of the Central Workers' Circle, described his lessons in Marxism, history, and in the political philosophy of Sh. Dikstein with members of the Radchenko group as "unsatisfactory." In fact, one labor activist, Petr Keizer, stopped attending altogether.[38] Except for these brief descriptions in memoirs, we know little about the Radchenko's group's activities. Nevertheless, one can be sure that certain connections

---

[37] Radchenko, "Radchenko," p. 180.

[38] Fisher, V Rossii i v Anglii, p. 19. The Pole, Simon Dickstein, became a Marxist writer and one of the founders of the Proletarjat group in Warsaw in 1883. His brochure Kto chem zhivet? in the 1880's and 1890's became one of the most popular of all pamphlets among Russian workers, and was constantly reproduced during that period.

such as between the previous Central Workers' Circle and the Central Students' Circle would have been recorded in memoirs. Instead, workers' memoirs such as Fisher's, mentioned a lack of intellectual assistance: "During the summer (1892), there were no meetings with intellectuals. We had to rely solely on our workers' intelligentsia."[39]

In St. Petersburg the principal intellectual group which had ties with the workers' intelligentsia was the Populist Gruppa Narodovol'tsev (Narodnaia Volia group or the People's Will Group). The Soviet biographer of V.A. Shelgunov, M. Rozanov, mentioned that.[40] It was founded during the summer of 1891 by M.S. Olminskii (Aleksandov) and A.A. Fedulov.[41] Since 1883 Olminskii had been active among St. Petersburg's workers. In 1885 he was arrested and then exiled to Eastern Siberia. In 1890 he returned to St. Petersburg and was instrumental in forming the Gruppa Narodovol'tsev shortly later. A.A. Fedulov, a recent graduate of St. Peters-

---

[39] Ibid.

[40] Rozanov, Shel'gunov, p. 64. The main source for that group is M.S. Ol'minskii's "Gruppa narodovol'tsev, 1891-1894 gg.," Byloe, no. 11, 1906, pp. 1-27.

[41] Ol'minskii, "Gruppa narodovol'tsev," p. 14.

burg University, was also instrumental in forming the group.[42] The group distributed illegal brochures to workers at their factories. The group's printing press printed illegal literature of all political tendencies. That literature was then distributed to the Central Workers' Circle. Through connections in large factories, they had more dealings with ordinary workers than the Marxists had. They urged their workers to strike at their factories and demonstrate against the government. The group even urged workers to conduct economic sabotage, such as the destruction of machinery, along with political terrorism.

These activist tactics drove a wedge between the workers' intelligentsia and the members of the <u>Gruppa Narodovol'tsev</u>. Shelgunov opposed the intellectuals who leaned too heavily on revolution. He said intellectual agitators should "give knowledge but not agitate."[43] Then, too, many workers believed their Populist teachers acted very condescendingly toward workers. Shelgunov stated at a workers' meeting: "The intellectuals forget that the workers do read on their own initiative. They do not need the intellec-

---

[42] Martov, <u>Zapiski</u>, p. 83.
[43] Shel'gunov, "Vospominaniia," <u>Ot gruppy Blagoeva</u>, p. 55.

tuals to show them the value of reading."[44] In fact on the whole workers reacted negatively to any intermingling of propaganda with education. On the obverse side many intellectuals expressed boredom with merely teaching workers. They thought reading lessons were too passive. They favored more exciting tactics. The workers' intelligentsia, despite their reverence for the great past of Populism, could not side with Narodnaia Volia tactics.

Until the winter of 1893, relations between the Social Democrats and the Populists were friendly. In fact, they were very close. Frequently Marxists used the Gruppa Narodovol'tsev printing press, which the Populist organization readily loaned them. The works of Marx, Engels, and Plekhanov were first printed in Russia under these Populist auspices. The leader of the Gruppa Narodovol'tsev, Olminskii had been appointed by the Central Students' Circle as its representative on the board of the Central Workers' Circle shortly before the crippling arrests in the summer of 1892. The Central Students' Circle included both Social Democrats and Populists. As we have seen, some workers' circles were affiliated with the Marxists;

---
[44]Stepanov, Sotsial-demokratiia v Rossii, p. 28.

others with the Populists; and several were absolutely unaffiliated with any political ideology. Yet regardless of a circle's affiliation, the Central Workers' Circle doled out money to any affiliated circle that required it. Despite this history of good ties, in late 1893, relations between Populists and Social Democrats deteriorated considerably. Within the pages of the thick, liberal journals, Social Democratic intellectuals such as Petr Struve engaged Populist theoreticians such as Nikolai Mikhailovskii in polemical debates over the capitalist development of Russia. Marxists believed their ideology represented the "future and inevitable path of history," while Populism was a "romantic infantile crusade bucking the tides of history."[45] Believing they represented the inevitable future and Populism the faded past, these Social Democratic intellectuals were determined to discredit the Populists. Equally determined, the Populists were determined to put this upstart ideology in its place. These debates spread from the page of journals to large audiences at both the St. Petersburg University and the Technical Institute. As they spread throughout Russia they became more bitter.

---

[45]Martov, *Zapiski*, p. 105.

Inevitably, cooperation ceased between Populists and Social Democrats in St. Petersburg. Soon the workers' intelligentsia became drawn into the growing controversy.

The workers reacted in several ways to this divisive debate. Many disliked the recent acrimony, accurately believing that the debates would prove unproductive and would only aid the government. Some believed the dispute was typical of the intellectuals' character. They declared that intellectuals do not have to work for a living and consequently they have lots of time to argue. More than one worker declared: "Ah, the intellectuals always argue; one says one thing, the other another thing."[46] Arguments would only harm the future of the workers' movement. The rivalry also perturbed workers, who felt caught right in the middle between the two ideologies. They wanted the debates over, so that intellectuals could resume their educational work. Many workers' leaders frequently criticized intellectuals' tendencies to mix politics and education. While not happy with the debates, other workers did not favor the Populist

---

[46] Shel'gunov, "Rabochie na puti," p. 102.

reliance on political terror. To them, the members of Gruppa Narodovol'tsev were mere agitators. As Fisher said in this analogy: "The Populists provided the match which could detonate the whole powder magazine."[47] The Social Democrats, while not openly acknowledging it, stressed less political teaching, until the "potential revolutionary cadres" (politically conscious workers) could be expanded. Revolution for the Social Democrats was in the future, which was non-threatening for the workers; while the Populists declared that they must make the revolution right now. To these workers, Marxism appeared a more moderate and less threatening ideology.[48] They believed that the Central Workers' Circle should reject all Populist assistance and accept only Marxists to tutor their workers' circles. However, there were too many Popu-

---

[47] Fisher, V Rossii i v Anglii, p. 21.

[48] Several workers--Norinskii, Fisher, and Shel'gunov--commented in their memoirs that their differences with the Populists were over tactics, such as the reliance on terrorism and other dangerous activities, which could unnecessarily result in their arrests. They made it clear that outside of those tactics, they did not disagree with Populist political and social ideas. For further information on the issue of Populism versus Social Democracy see: K. Norinskii, "Moi vospominaniia," pp. 16-18; V. Shel'gunov, "Vospominaniia," pp. 56-57; and Fisher, V Rossii i v Anglii, pp. 20-22.

list circles. To keep the workers' movement unified, in early 1894 the Central Workers' Circle invited representatives of the two ideologies to defend their views as soon as possible before a meeting of the Central Workers' Circle. The workers present could then decide which one they favored.[49]

The first of what would be two meetings occurred in V.A. Shelgunov's room in February 1894. All of the current members of the Central Workers' Circle attended: Shelgunov, Fisher, Norinskii, and Keizer. The first three workers' political affinities tilted toward Marxism; the last person, Keizer, favored Populism. Two Populists from the Gruppa Narodovol'tsev, M.Ia. Sushchinskii and A.A. Fedulov, were invited to defend their view. At the same time two members of the Social Democratic Radchenko group, G.B. Krasin and V.V. Starkov were also invited to present their perspective. The Populists delivered their arguments first. "A.A. Fedulov spoke no less than two hours in the course of which he traced the history of the revolutionary struggles of all types from their beginning to the present. He emphasized that the movement took

---

[49]Nevskii, Ocherki, p. 303.

the form of a struggle the foundations of which had been laid by the Populists, and that only their methods would produce results."[50] The two Populist speakers stressed the necessity for immediate action against the authorities. Workers and students should not continue their quiet educational activities which accomplished little for the near future. Furthermore, they reiterated that only through Populist tactics would all concerned people be certain of success.

The two Marxists took the platform next. They "maintained that it was necessary to conduct propaganda."[51] Propaganda, they believed, meant slow, careful, educational work. The Populists spoke more dramatically. Their speeches moved all the workers who attended, even the confirmed Marxists. All of their hearts lay with the Populists. They thought Fedulov was an excellent orator. Nevertheless, the unemotional mind of the workers remained with the more cautious Marxists whose reliance on education was less dangerous. Discussion raged into the night One worker, Norinskii, had to leave. Finally, in the

---

[50] Norinskii, "Moi vospominaniia," Ot gruppy Blagoeva, p. 17.

[51] Shel'gunov, "Vospominaniia," Ot gruppy Blagoeva, p. 56. p. 56.

wee hours of the morning, the group broke up. All the Central Workers' Circle decided that another meeting was essential. The issue was too important for just the few of them to make. More workers had to attend to make a decision. They would convene a wider meeting with at least one representative from each of the workers' circles. Most workers hoped the intellectuals could settle their differences quickly without too many more divisive arguments.

The decisive second debate over the issue of Populism versus Social Democracy occurred at Easter time in early April 1894. After all the arguments were presented, a vote among the workers would be taken. This time a decision would be made. They would vote for either one ideology or the other. They assumed that the minority would agree to the will of the majority.[52] These workers' representatives would decide to accept either the Populists or the Marxists as teachers of their circles. The meeting took place at Keizer's and Fisher's flat on Vasilyevskii Island. The Gruppa Narodovol'tsev sent its three leading members: M.S. Olminskii, B.L. Zotov, and

---

[52] Ibid., p. 57.

Sushchinskii once again. The Social Democrats sent five men: Radchenko, Starkov, Krasin, K.M. Takhtarev, and a dentist, N.N. Mikhailov. Between fifteen and twenty workers including several women, representing the various circles of the Central Workers' Circle throughout St. Petersburg, attended.

The goal of the meeting was to end the bickering once and for all, and to more closely consolidate the local circles. Once again, each side presented its particular arguments. The workers' intelligentsia present were determined to select the program that was best for them.[53] After the intellectuals' speeches finished a vote was taken. All of the workers there except for Khotiabin and Kuziukin opted for the Social Democrats. The majority voted for the Social Democrats out of fear that Populist agitation only meant their inevitable arrests.[54] The Social Democrats promised them a continuation of their education within their individual circles which remained under the control of the Central Workers' Circle. After opting for Social Democratic tactics, these representatives of the St.

---

[53] Fisher, V Rossii i v Anglii, p. 25.

[54] Shel'gunov, "Vospominaniia," Ot gruppy Blagoeva, p. 56.

Petersburg's workers' intelligentsia decided that henceforth, the Gruppa Narodovol'tsev could offer instruction only under supervision by representatives of the Central Workers' Circle. The Populists, very conciliatory after their loss, agreed to this compromise. For the first time an organized body of Russian workers definitely opted for Social Democracy. In any case, the Central Workers' Circle remained determined to retain control over its movement. They would not allow the Social Democrats to take control. Shelgunov warned his fellow workers that it was essential to "tighten the reins on both the Populists and the Social Democrats."[55]

No one among either intellectuals or workers knew that the police were aware of these meetings along with their decisions. Two police informers attended the crucial second meeting. Afterwards the Social Democratic dentist N.N. Mikhailov and also the Populist worker Kuziutkin told the police who attended, from what group, and what the meeting decided. The workers and the intellectuals from both groups fell into a trap. Vasilii Kuziutkin was the main culprit. Later,

---

[55] Shel'gunov, "Vospominaniia," Ot gruppy Blagoeva, p. 57; and Fisher, V Rossii i v Anglii, p. 25.

Norinskii said that on the basis of Kuziutkin's "roughness, impudence, and lack of culture," he always suspected him.[56] Shortly after the meeting, police raids on April 21, 1894, devastated both the Central Workers' Circle and the <u>Gruppa Narodovol'tsev</u>. From the latter group, the police nabbed Olminskii, Sushchinskii, and Zotov. Everyone knew that searches of their apartments and rooms with arrest warrants would soon follow. On May 3rd, the police arrested K.M. Norinskii, Fisher, Keizer, and twenty-six other members of the Circle. The only member of the Central Workers' Circle to escape arrest was V.A. Shelgunov. To elude police attention, he quickly transferred from the Baltic factory to the Obukhov factory.[57] He escaped police detection for a year and a half. But he finally was arrested in December 1895. The arrested workers were exiled from St. Petersburg. For example, Norinskii was sent to Ekaterinoslav and Fisher to Rybinsk. The Radchenko group was less threatened by arrests. Only V.V. Starkov and P.K. Zaporozhets were

---

[56] Norinskii, "Moi vospominaniia," <u>Ot gruppy Blagoeva</u>, p. 17.

[57] Ol'minskii, "Gruppa narodovol'tsev," pp. 24-26.

again arrested and exiled. The rest of the group went underground. All work by workers and intellectuals ceased for a while.

The arrests of April and May 1894 had two major consequences for the workers' movement. Organized Populist activity among the St. Petersburg workers ended. The Populists never recovered from their defeat in the workers' meeting and then the arrests. An independent Central Workers' Circle never reemerged. When a new Central Workers' Circle started in late 1894, it depended on the Marxist intellectuals, the only people who had not been severely affected by the arrests. Except for Shelgunov, few noted workers' leaders remained free. The new Central Workers' Circle conducted no independent activities, and it never claimed to represent the wishes of the workers' intelligentsia. Throughout, it followed the dictates of the Social Democrats, who became much more concerned with working with the lesser skilled rank and file labor through the newly adopted tactic of agitation. The new Central Workers' Circle lacked the power, the finances, the leadership, and the will of its predecessors. Its story belongs inextricably to the Social

Democratic Union of Struggle led by Lenin and Martov.[58] Thus, a chapter in the history of Russia's labor movement closed.

---

[58] Shel'gunov, "Vospominaniia," pp. 57-58; Takhtarev, Rabochee dvizhenie, pp. 42-44; and Korolchuk, Khronika, pp. 184-185.

CHAPTER VII

CONCLUSIONS: THE ROLE OF THE CENTRAL WORKERS' CIRCLE IN THE RUSSIAN LABOR MOVEMENT

The workers' intelligentsia were a rising new force in Russia. Well read and highly skilled, they were born in the image of the West, especially Germany. Some of them knew western languages and a few even traveled to the West. Their May Day demonstrations were an attempt to affirm in Russia the recent resolutions of the Second International. The workers' intelligentsia were young, usually male, often from broken homes but deeply religious backgrounds, seeking economic and cultural progress for themselves. Their numbers were tiny. No more than 1,000 people in St. Petersburg were part of this workers' intelligentsia by 1890. Yet the social group played a role far more significant than their numbers would ever suggest.

Perhaps a dozen activists out of this tiny workers' intelligentsia decided to organize a formal group, the Central Workers' Circle, in 1889 to expand the economic and cultural horizons of their members. Did the organization accomplish the purposes it was created for? It created a central treasury, a library, clubs, and cooperatives for St. Petersburg's workers, and a newspaper. Despite a lack of resources, both the treasury and library were effective. During labor unrest in 1891, the Central Workers' Circle gave needed money that was greatly appreciated by the strikers. Furthermore the fund purchased books and aided needy members. The treasury was one of the few vehicles the Central Workers' Circle had to expand its influence and authority beyond its tiny membership. The library was not large enough to cover all the educational needs of the workers. Yet, it did have at least 1,000 volumes of books, both fiction and non-fiction, along with journals, leaflets, and newspapers of considerable variety all of which provided a good basis for lectures and discussions. Nevertheless, the other organizations which the Central Workers' Circle created proved ineffective. The workers regarded the consumer cooperatives as useless or even harmful. They ignored the workers' clubs which the Central Workers' Circle hoped would provide an alternative to the bar scene. Potentially, the newspaper, Proletarii, could have achieved great success. However, it was hard to read and hard to find. The Central Workers' Circle's organs were most effective with their treasury and library which tended to aid their own membership; they were least effective in groups which could reach out to the rank and file as well as to unaffiliated members of the workers' intelligentsia. Thus its record was mixed.

The Central Workers' Circle was a labor association which had the potential of becoming an embryonic trade union. One definition of a trade union is "an association of workers to promote and protect the welfare, the interests, and the rights of its members, primarily by collective bargaining."[1] The Central Workers' Circle was founded in a formative period of Russia's industrialization over a decade before Russian labor was given the opportunity to legally form trade unions. Through its treasury it sought to protect the welfare of its members. The library promoted the cultural uplifting of its members. It sought to expand the educational horizons of Russian labor through discussions with liberal and radical members of Russian society. Not only did the group continually attempt to expand the numbers of circles within St. Petersburg; but they also created circles in other cities. Just before crippling arrests in 1892, the Central Workers' Circle was in the process of creating

---

[1] David B. Guralnik, ed., Webster's New College Dictionary, second edition (New York, 1980), p. 786.

a nationwide Central Workers' Circle. Ultimately their goal was to include all members of the workers' intelligentsia inside their organization. The members of the Central Workers' Circle typified the workers' intelligentsia. Their backgrounds, attitudes, and aspirations did not diverge from other members of the workers' intelligentsia. They happened to be the most politically and socially active of that group. Rightly they were the leadership for Russia's workers' elite.

While the workers' intelligentsia formed a distinctive subgroup within Russian labor (on which even contemporaries noted), they were certainly drawn from and remained a part of the masses of Russian people. Almost all members of the Central Workers' Circle were descended from poor peasants in neighboring areas of St. Petersburg. None had comfortable childhoods. All had to work at an early age. Throughout their whole lives, they earned a living by working with their hands. While their incomes were at the top of the pay scale for Russian labor, they were still part of that Russian labor. Nevertheless, they formed a distinctive subgroup. Despite great adversity, they insisted on an education, and never gave up their one unifying trait. The main reason for creating workers' circles and then unifying those circles in a Central Workers'

Circle was to improve their education. A major portion of all circle meetings was devoted to lectures, readings, and discussions. The workers' intelligentsia was isolated; isolated from their student teachers and isolated from the rest of the working class. To them, their teachers were not really concerned for their economic and cultural improvement. All the students wanted was to make the workers a cadre to aid revolutionary activities. That the workers' intelligentsia resented. Yet, in their eyes, the rest of the working class was "a grey mass" who were a group of backward, religious, and often drunken individuals. This isolation gave them great problems and prevented them from achieving their proper role in Russian labor history. Yet their isolation was another major reason for forming circles. They desperately sought companionship. They craved the interaction of each other. For them, the circle meetings became the only bright part of an otherwise dismal boring existence. Their personal lives were generally unsatisfactory. Most members of the Central Workers' Circle left their wives. Those members who maintained a marriage could do so only because their wives joined them. Some even formed circles of their own. The members were essentially married to their circles. Thus, the Central Workers'

Circle was as much a social organization for companionship as anything else.

Relations between the Central Workers' Circle, spokesmen for the workers' intelligentsia, and the students' intelligentsia remained ambivalent throughout this whole period. Relations between an individual workers' leader such as Fedor Afanasev and individual student such as Mikhail Brusnev often became close. One frequently confided in the other. However, as a group, one never trusted the other. While roughly the same age, their backgrounds, attitudes, leisure time, and even dress and speech were all dissimilar. Workers regarded the students as frivolous, immature, naive, and often too sectarian and dogmatic. Students regarded workers as uneducated and uncultured. Both lived in separate worlds. One group aided the other group only when it seemed convenient for them. Despite often lofty claims, both were essentially selfish, thinking of their own interests. Each claimed to know the only true path toward Russia's betterment. The workers sought a better education to improve themselves economically and culturally. The intellectuals utilized tutoring to politicize the workers. The workers resented that. Shelgunov typified that attitude when he declared, "I wish the intelligentsia

make them their leaders. The egotism of the workers' intelligentsia in Russia caused any abdication of any leadership role within the workers' movement. The student intelligentsia was only too happy to fill that role.

As Russia industrialized, the gap between the two elements in urban labor widened rather than narrowed. Wage increases favored members of the workers' intelligentsia. They had more money for books and cultural events. The revived Central Workers' Circle did even less for the rank and file than its predecessor did. The isolation of the workers' intelligentsia only increased. The major reason was their own doing. The workers' intelligentsia repudiated everyone except themselves. They repudiated their origins declaring that the peasants are a backward mass which will play no significant role in history.[3] They repudiated their family, hating their fathers and often leaving their wives. They repudiated the past and the traditions of Russia believing like the most ardent Westerners that Russia had little positive to offer the rest of the world.

---

[3] Fisher, V Rossii i v Anglii, p. 16.

the circles to become a substitute family for its members. The focus of their lives--friendship, time, and activities--was in the circles. Independence, which most members cherished, often meant isolation.

Furthermore, the workers' intelligentsia lacked considerable concern for other workers, the rank and file. Only in 1891-92 in the Thornton and Port strikes, did the Central Workers' Circle aid the rank and file in any significant form. Only for a period of six months from the winter of 1891 through the summer of 1892 when the Central Workers' Circle collapsed were there significant contacts between the workers' intelligentsia and the rank and file. The May Day celebrations were mostly for the edification of the rest of Russia's workers' intelligentsia, for middle class Russian society, and for Western Europe. Few if any rank and file workers were present at each May Day event. The workers' intelligentsia formed a paradox. On one hand they frequently denounced the student intelligentsia for being domineering and elitist. On the other hand, they had disrespect for the rank and file. The rank and file were not "imbeciles." They understood clearly these feelings by the workers' intelligentsia. Thus, they were hardly likely to aid the tiny workers' intelligentsia or to

Gompers, who founded the American Federation of Labor in the United States, August Bebel, who led the Social Democratic Party in Germany, and Keir Hardie, who sat in the 1892 Parliament in Great Britain. All had been members of the workers' intelligentsia in their countries. All eventually assumed leadership roles and were not alone in trade unions and labor parties. Yet that never occurred in Russia. One reason was that there was as great a gulf between the workers' intelligentsia and the rank and file as there was with the student intelligentsia. For one thing, the workers' intelligentsia lacked patience and tolerance for the rank and file. Many members of the workers' intelligentsia never thought the rank and file could ever become their equals. This condescending attitude prevented a link between the two elements of Russia's urban working class. Secondly, most workers were extremely religious, while most members of the workers' intelligentsia were either irreligious or anti-religious. Yet many members' wives were religious. The workers' intelligentsia never understood the importance of religion in most workers' lives. This lack of respect for religion added to the gap between them and the rest of the working class which included their wives. The lack of a real family often allowed would communicate more knowledge and less agitation."[2] Frequently, the student intelligentsia tried to direct the Central Workers' Circle's politics and activities. Throughout the life span of the Central Workers' Circle it was able to resist those attempts by the student intelligentsia. The latter never had more than an advisory role in the Central Workers' Circle. Only after the destruction of the Central Workers' Circle in the spring of 1894, was the student intelligentsia, in the name of Social Democracy, able to take control of the workers' movement. It accomplished that only because the workers' intelligentsia became too weak and divided to resist.

The real tragedy evident in this examination of the workers' intelligentsia was its inability to develop and maintain any rapport with the rest of the working class, the rank and file. The workers' intelligentsia was clearly the best able, most educated part of the working class and most concerned over the formation of trade unions. They could have become leaders of the workers' movement. Several of their Western counterparts had become leaders: Samuel

---

[2] Shel'gunov, "Vospominaniia," Ot gruppy Blagoeva, p. 55.

They insisted that workers control their own affairs, but one can legitimately ask which workers did they mean? Given those attitudes, it was hardly unexpected that little interaction between the workers' intelligentsia and the rest of the working class existed. Their isolation only added to the tone of vulnerability and insecurity which was seen throughout the entire existence of the Central Workers' Circle.

In 1890 Russia was much less developed industrially than either Western Europe or the United States. The latter areas consequently had a much larger workers' intelligentsia than Russia had. They were significant enough in the United States to form the American Federation of Labor in 1881, and they also became a predominant element in the British Labour Party. To those groups the workers' intelligentsia added a voice of moderation. Furthermore, Russia lacked the democratic liberties that existed in the West. Russian dissident groups had to struggle for survival against an authoritarian but clumsy government which sought to deny the group's very existence. Isolation, a tiny size, and governmental opposition forced the inevitable collapse of an organized dominant workers' intelligentsia in Russian history. No Western style Social Democratic Party or trade unions controlled by the workers' intelligentsia, ever developed. The workers' intelligentsia became a casualty in Russian history. That fact was seen in their fate. After their arrest and usual exile, few members of the Central Workers' Circle ever returned to political work.

Yet the workers' intelligentsia as a whole and the Central Workers' Circle in particular played a significant role in Russian history. The Central Workers' Circle was the first labor organization in Russia. It sought to improve its members economically and culturally. In that task the group succeeded considerably. It considered itself a direct part of the labor movement in the West. That was indicated in messages sent to the Second International. It was the first group in Russia to celebrate May Day, a major holiday in the present day Soviet Union. It founded a newspaper, organized and controlled by and for the workers. It was the first newspaper of its kind in Russia. Afterwards, while the workers' intelligentsia never played a dominant role in Russian labor, it did have a significant one. The Revolution of 1905 granted several rights to Russian workers, among which was the legalization of trade unions. In 1906, St. Petersburg had 35,000 workers organized into 44 trade unions.[4] Of those unions, the most developed were the craft unions--printers, engineers, metal workers, and railroad workers--composed of the most skilled and educated. The center of those trade unions were the metal workers, so predominant in the Central Workers' Circle. Just like their counterparts in the West, those unions tended toward moderation. If allied with any group, it was the Menshevik wing of the Russian Social Democratic Party. Few members of the workers' intelligentsia ever became Bolsheviks. Those trade unions, those members of the workers' intelligentsia became casualties in the Bolshevik Revolution of 1917. In that revolution, the coffin was permanently sealed on Russia's workers' intelligentsia. They were the one segment of Russian labor which could have challenged the Bolshevik claim of being the vanguard of the revolution. Yet their isolation from and alienation of both the student intelligentsia and the rank and file workers gave them few allies in their struggle for a workers' controlled trade union movement.

---

[4]L.N. Kleinbort, <u>Professional'nye</u> <u>soiuzy</u> <u>v</u> <u>Rossii</u> (Moscow, 1906), p. 4.

APPENDIX

Address of the St. Petersburg Workers to N.V. Shel'gunov

Dear teacher, Nikolai Vasilevich!

Thanks to you we read your works and love to learn at any cost. You were the first to recognize the pitiful position of the working class in Russia. You always endeavored until now to explain your principles which we knew about for a long time. We have been shackled in the hands of oppressors, the iron chains placed by the government and the capitalists.

You acquainted us with the position of brother-workers in other countries where they had also been exploited. The picture, which you presented, not only aroused interest by workers, but by other classes as well. It was not just for workers that you wrote. Russian workers are forced to work continually just to survive. Therefore, they have no time for reading. Not only do the workers not know how to read, but they do not know what to read. What do they supposedly find in books written for workers? No one teaches us how to break loose from our pitiful conditions which we are now in. For our sufferings all we hear are pronouncements and promises of rewards for the future. The people unfortunately have to see the upper classes and their own class interests. By studying and understanding your writings, just like our fellow workers in Western Europe, we have seen how to fight for our rights and to unite. Through the example of workers in Western Europe, we understand how we Russian workers can expect nothing in real aid from anyone except for ourselves to improve our position and to achieve freedom.

Those workers who understand this situation will struggle without interruption for the improvement of their conditions. In your writings you have shown us the means. In that you have fulfilled your obligation, and have showed us the path for the struggle.

Perhaps neither you nor we workers can attain what we dream of striving for. Perhaps we will all

all victim in the struggle. But that will not keep us from trying to attain our goals.

Workers' Speeches on the first of May, 1891

Speech by F.A. Afanas'ev

Comrades, today for us will indelibly remain in our memories. Today, for the first time, we have gathered from all parts of St. Petersburg for this humble meeting and have heard from our fellow workers some emotional words to struggle against the political and economic enemy with all our strength. Yes, that is the case, comrades! We see the enemy and its small handful of people, and yet we do not know its strength. Some of us do not join in the struggle against this tiny enemy. In desperation and in cowardice they have abandoned our ranks. No, comrades, we absolutely must achieve a victory. We must be armed with our strongest weapons, but these weapons are the knowledge of the historical laws for mankind. Despite oppression and exile to Siberia, these weapons are not taken away from us. We will find victory. To achieve that, we must give knowledge to ourselves, to the peasants in the countryside, and to the arrested in prison. We must make them conscious of our ideas, and organize them in groups.

Yes, comrades, we must read and listen to the statements of the workers in the West, who have made tremendous advancements and have struck fear in their exploiters. It is clear that our struggle is as their struggle was. Let us take even a quick glance at the historic struggle of the Social Democratic Party in Germany, which is the strongest and best organized party in the West. It too emerged from a small group of men concentrated in one productive area like our St. Petersburg. These workers were the first to realize their human rights; they then conveyed their convictions to their fellow workers. For this the government began to persecute them and exile them to the provinces. But even this measure turned to the advantage of the workers. These (exiled) workers found themselves comrades and, banding all together, they formed one undivided union. Why should we Russian workers despair and run away from these fighting comrades who undertake so great a task as the people's liberation? Once we look at all the historical facts, they will boldly give us victory. We must always think about our Russian people. Until then, the people will always carry the heavy burdens on their shoulders. Our workers must have human rights, but above all, they must have the use of all the wealth they produce with their labor. Our workers must also become aware that labor is the mover of all progress, and is the creator of all science, art, and inventions. As soon as the people shall realize this, then no army will be able to prevent its self-emancipation. To carry this realization to the people is the immediate, inalienable right of all developed workers. This was shown to us by the struggle of our intelligentsia in the 1870s and 1880s. Look at this struggle, comrades, from the historical point of view, notice how these friends and fighters of the people carried to the people all their knowledge, and, often at the price of their lives, justified themselves before history and repaid their debt to the people. They responded everywhere to the people's cry and offered a helping hand, but the people did not acknowledge them as friends and viewed them instead, with suspicion. Let us then, comrades, carry out our own modest learning to the people. Will we not succeed in passing it on to the people, and will not the people understand us because we are closer to them than the intelligentsia is? It is only a pity, comrades, that no one gives us any help as had been given to workers in earlier times. Only to a small group of people do we owe a debt of gratitude. Today's youth does not hear the cry of the people, and does not see its suffering. It does not even bother to think about the people. This youth is nothing but a parasitic element of society, and is only capable of consuming the product of social labor. It does not consider repaying the people for this labor.

Speech by N.D. Bogdanov

It is very sad comrades that it is impossible for us to meet on the actual May Day as the workers in the West can. Unfortunately we must meet on another day, a Sunday. Of course, each of us gathered here knows that we are unable to conduct demonstrations similar to those in the West. Each of us here asks about our strength in comparison with the strength of Western workers. Yet we should not give in to desperation due to our small numbers because we still have some strength and energy. Therefore we should not lose heart because these current activities are only the beginning for us.

Just like us, Western workers suffer from the capitalist system. Under capitalism all the products made by workers are given to the manufacturers as profit. For their efforts the workers are given only enough salary to keep them from starving to death. The workers in the West are not satisfied with such a disgraceful situation, which deprives them of the benefits of their work. They have arrived at the conclusion that the only road to intellectual advancement for the people depends on the people alone.

Having arrived at such a conclusion, they do not stop only at words, but they also endeavor to develop and organize themselves and others in a tight knit organization. Their organizations have a treasury, and also have the means to disseminate books and to publish journals and newspapers which will offer their ideas. They support strikes instead of radical means to destroy the evil system. Gradually they improve the position of workers due to their energetic activities. From time to time they have been able to present their strength and their demands to the government and to society. Then the government is forced to give some satisfaction. For example, the governments in the West have been forced to grant a constitution, freedom of press, assembly and the right to form workers' organizations, as well as the right to work for a fair economic system.

One of our ways in which we have to force them to recognize our power and grant our major demands, will be a huge demonstration on May Day. With a successful May Day, we can make the government grant us an eight hour work day. In comparison with last year's activities, our strength has greatly grown. In the future we can only do better.

Our workers greatly suffer from the system. Yet, some of the workers do not recognize that. They keep silent and bear it because they do not have the education to know how to break their silence. We are the most developed workers in St. Petersburg and we must make clear to them the reality of their situation, their horribly poor conditions.

To fulfill our integrity, I declare that we must, with all our strength and ability, develop circles for our workers. Not long ago, with all our sincerest feelings, we presented an address to Shelgunov, and later a wreath at his funeral. We did this to show his influence on the workers' question, and his success in presenting it. Those actions, instead of raising our hopes in the government, only resulted in the workers being punished. Because the workers dared to think about improving their lives, all three of them were exiled to far off cities.

As it is well known to you, always, from the smallest acts of displeasure to largest of demonstrations, we, the workers as well as the intelligentsia receive imprisonment and exile. To those intelligentsia who sincerely try to use their strength and knowledge to aid us in the struggle for a decent standard of living, we give thanks. Despite all the measures of the government, it does not intimidate us at all. Instead, it only arouses great hatred toward it and its social system. The government guards that system with great vigor.

That is why, comrades, we must develop our strength and support each other. We must continue to develop the struggle against the existing system so that we can achieve liberty, equality, and brotherhood.

Speech by V.I. Proshin

Comrades! I want to say some words about today's ceremony for us, an arranged model from our Western brothers.

Brothers! We arrive here at this joyous moment at one of the first celebrations on Russian soil. Our Western brothers have already for a long time made use of these opportunities which we have only just begun to express. We have begun to awaken our great strength from the oppression of the nobility, the priests and the tsars. I say to all Russian workers 'Wake up' and join us in our common progress. Gradually we will learn the full truth. Human genius can not embrace that all at once. In all centuries of human life, workers have wanted to move on the path of true progress and happiness. Of course, comrades, this happiness can not be delivered very easily; it is a very long road

that stands before man. That is the situation that we
see in our brother workers in the West. They have
already achieved power and freedom. While that exists
there, it is only a small part of happiness. Even that
part was obtained at the costly price of human blood.
They struggled for a long time, but had good fortune.
Their will continues to struggle for full freedom,
happiness, equality, and brotherhood. Yet, there,
comrades, we see their demands were recognized by laws
that allowed them to strike, form treasuries, associations, unions, libraries, and other social institutions. But we are unable to achieve that. As all of
you know, all statements that demand rights for the
people are considered subversive. Our cries are
received by the bayonet, by lies, by the birch rod,
Siberia, prison, exile, and by the Cossack whip! But
there, in the West, our brother-workers have been able
to make use of all their political rights. We are
merely serfs and slaves! We must bow obsequiously
before the guns of the city's police. But outside, in
England, France, Germany, Belgium, and all the other
European countries, the workers are free and equal
citizens. We can judge their strength by the last
election to the German Parliament. There, the workers
offered their leaders as candidates, and received
around seven million votes. Under their direction, the
workers had 104 newspapers with 600,000 subscribers.
Their treasury in 1880 had 37,000 marks in it; in 1883
it grew to 95,000; in 1887 to 188,000 marks, and last
year (1890) it had achieved 390,000 marks. See, comrades, how quickly the German workers grew in numbers
and in power. They are represented in their own
organized political party, which struggles against not
only the capitalist exploiters, but also the militaris-
tic government. Yet, comrades, see how they have grown
in strength since 1848 when they first declared:
"Workers of all countries, unite!" Yes, brothers,
these great words belong to the affairs of human
thought. These words disseminated quickly to all parts
of Europe except in our dead Russia. Here, in the
1860s and 1870s only the ranks of our educated youth
were affected. Now these words affect all of us.

People! As we see, this small transference of a
seed, grew, ripened, and let go all its sprouts on all
the Russian lands. It grew, but unfortunately, it had
enemies in the faces of the wealthy, the priests, the
nobility, and the tsar with his military and police.
Workers know their task. Already tens of thousands of

youth have been exiled to Siberia, or to the prisons in Petropavlovsk and Shlisselburg. We must know how to fight. It is not easy for us to stay with this struggle. Each action for us can take us to prison or to exile. Such is the situation for us comrades! It is necessary for us to think about our current position in which we stand against our exploiters and the government.

Comrades! You yourselves see, that we have in all areas of Russia rule by a terrible economic system, affecting both industrial and rural workers. Only quietly do they cry shame.

"This groan will ring an invitation," said Nekrasov, and indeed everywhere, there are shortages and hunger, poverty and sickness which afflict all of us to our death. The leeches are built on our blood, they make us pale, green, and tormented. All of this is for what? So that a small group of factory owners, landlords, and tsarist officials could live in luxury, and intoxicated in corruption. And here, in their name, these swine want to oppress all the people of Russia, all 100 million, forged in shame and slavery, in which we do not have the possibility to raise ourselves up, to cry out.

Comrades, brothers! For us is it possible that the people will learn about their servile position, their full oppression and their lack of dignity? But it is possible and it is necessary. All our lives they tyrannize us and do not give us the possibility to cast a glance at our unfair social existence. All they want is to have a tranquil life at our expense. No, we recognize that we are people just like they are. But as long as we are still under the slavery of the tsar we will live under this disgraceful oppression. Comrades, in the future we must live under rules which will allow us human dignity, to live as people, to think, to speak, to gather together, to discuss our public affairs without hindrance by police spies or uniformed police.

Comrades, it is difficult for us now to enter the struggle with our Western brothers for political and economic rights, but remember that already now, in the present time, 1000 intellectuals are forced to live in Siberia in prison because of us. We remember that it will be difficult to achieve a similar position to our Western brother-workers because it is not easy to to improve ourselves under the raging despotism which is present to us in each step. Comrades, difficult as this will be for us, the liberation of Western workers will serve as an example for us. We will, my friends, fight for equality, not retreating one step until our last death agony. We will fight for political rights, equality, brotherhood and freedom. We will learn to unite ourselves, and comrades, we will organize a strong party. We will, brothers, sow the seeds of this great struggle as long as the sun shines over all the corners of the Russian lands.

Speech by E.A. Afanas'ev

Comrades! Paying attention to our position, we see that all our sufferings are derived from the current economic system.

It follows that in order to improve our position, we must strive to replace the current economic system, which gives the greatest space to the arbitrary rule of predatory exploiters, by the brightest and fairest socialist system.

But in order to achieve such an economic system, it is necessary for us to achieve political rights which currently we do not have. Acquiring these political rights will only be possible when our side is organized and strong enough, and when the government is not determined to deny our demands. We urgently demand from the government the following concessions:

1. The establishment of a constitution, based on an equal and open electoral law. All laws of the country should be approved or vetoed not by the dictates of the tsar, but through discussions in a legislative assembly, where electoral representatives of the people meet. The choices for the legislative assembly must be derived from the people. All citizens of the country, except those convicted of a crime, can be elected deputies in the legislative assembly. The salaries of the deputies for their services must be paid by the state. This is necessary so that deputies can come from the poor population as well.

2. It is necessary that all decisions about the military and the size of the army also be decided by

the legislative assembly. Soldiers must never forget that they came from the people, and that the interests of the soldiers are the same as those of the people. Soldiers should be allowed to maintain close relationships with their families, and therefore, should be stationed near their homes. The size of the army should be reduced by as much as 40,000 troops. Soldiers, who are conscious of their relationship with the people, never go against them. The government should not have the ability to force people by force of arms to carry out orders not confirmed by the legislative assembly.

3. There should be freedom to conduct agitation, freedom of speech and freedom of press that is completely free of censorship so that anyone can express in words or on paper what they believe without punishment. The workers should have the possibility of publishing books, journals, and newspapers.

4. There should be freedom of assembly and the right to organize.

5. There should be freedom of religion.

6. There should be free general education for all people.

7. All types of crime must be fairly investigated, and then tried by a jury.

Do not forget, comrades, these demands, because these are the first and the most important which we can present to the government at the first opportunity. Only then can we have the possibility to improve our conditions by an accounting of our demands.

Once we possess these rights, we can then elect deputies to the legislative assembly who will then confirm these rights, and who will aid a majority of the population. Only then will we have the possibility of reconstructing the economic system in the best and fairest way.

I will not here describe to you this new economic system, but you should read the brochure "Essentials of Socialism" by Shefle or the novel by Bellamy, Looking Backward.

In the future, the economic system must serve all the nationalities who live on the land. The state must purchase all the land which is privately owned, and then distribute that land to its tenants and anyone who wants to work on the land. The allotments of land should be large enough that people can successfully work it. Yet we would prefer this land to be initially organized into <u>artels</u>. Also a bank should be organized to serve the needs of workers and peasants.

With these things, gradually our conditions will improve to a level which we can only now dream about.

In order to have the possibility of achieving a bright future, it is necessary for us to form a strong organization made up of workers. That organization will strive to constantly improve our position, and force the government to give us political rights. Only with such an organization can we have the possibility of altering the political system.

Currently we must develop such an organization of workers, despite all the hindrances and threats by the government. We must make use of all opportunities presented to us.

In order for our activities to have the possibility of success, we must strive harder than ever for an education and to raise our moral level. Then the people will look at us as intelligent, honest, and thoughtful people. Only with their trust will they come closer to us.

Consequently, the success of developing and organizing the workers must depend on our activity and energy. Therefore, comrades, in our duty as honest and educated people, we must prepare ourselves and other suitable people to become experienced propagandists and organizers and struggle for the rights of man and for a bright future.

List of the Membership of the Central Workers' Circle, 1889-1894

Vasilyevskii Island Circles
(Baltic factory)
Ivan Timofeev
Vladimir Fomin
Konstantin Kupriianov
Mikhail Iakovlev
Konstantin Norinskii
Ivan Egorov
Andrei Fisher
Petr Kaizo
Konstantin Beliaev
Ivan Iakovlev
Fedor Kipillov
Fedor Petrov
Sergei Funtikov
Petr Savel'ev
Ivan Krashennikov
Nikolai Khotiabin
Fedor Kuznetsov
Aleksei Tokar
Fedor Maliar

State Paper Mill Factory Circles
G. Lunegov
N. Balabanov
V. Iakovlev
V. Aleksandrov

Nevskii Gate Circles
(Obukhov factory)
Nikolai Klopov
Dmitrii Fomin
Konstantin Chekin
Petr and Pavel Danilov
Aleksei Gorbunov
Sergei Afanas'ev

Lithographers and Printers Circles
Aleksei Karelin
Iakov Ivanov
K. Belov
Petr Keizer

Narvskii Gates Circles
(Putilov factory)
D.D. Rafalovskii
Foma Zhalkovskii
Georgii Vitkovskii
Iosif Tomashevskii
Petr Rodchas
Mechislav Norkevich
Nikolai Vasil'evich
Nikolai Lawkevich
Vikentii Uzello-Uzelevich
Vasilii Buianov
P.K. Pobedimskii
N.D. Danilov
F.G. Ignat'ev
Nikolai Parshukov
Daniil Rafalovich

Obvodnoi Canal
(Varshaw Plant)
N.D. Bogdanov
F.A. Afanas'ev
E.A. Afanas'ev
Anna Gavrilova
Vera Karelina

Vyborg Side Circles
(Rasteriaev factory)
N. Kuchkin
Mikhail Kniazev
Egor Tumanov
A. Boldyreva

Peterburg Side Circles
(Iakovlev and Great Spasskii factories)
Vladimir Forsov
Ivan Keizer
Aleksandr Il'in
V. Kniazev

Shipbuilding Factories
(Berda and New Admiralty factories)
M. Stefanenkov
A. Ivailov
F. Petrov
P. Lopatin
F. Pashin
P. Raskol'nikov
P. Evgrafov

"The Program of the Central Students' Circle"

1. As convinced Social Revolutionaries, we strive for the creation in the immediate future of a vigorous social revolutionary organization. We are deeply convinced that only the complete embodiment of the socialist ideal leads to man fulfilling those radiant ideas of freedom, equality, and brotherhood--the dreams of the great French Revolution.

2. As followers of scientific collectivism, we assert that the socialist ideal can be fulfilled only in the agonizing process of economic development. Our goals in achieving this socialist ideal must be decisively directed.

3. The fulfillment of socialism and politics must be directed by the liberation of the working class. We believe that the maintenance and the forms of these policies are determined by time and place of the directed activities.

4. We turn toward the concrete reality within Russia, in that we see an evil enemy, extreme absolutism, a police state, and an autocracy that concentrates its power against the suffering Russian people.

5. We are deeply committed to the belief that only a system of political liberty can secure to the people an end to that concrete reality. The strength of the working class alone will achieve that political liberty. To strengthen the working class, we must achieve their educational development.

6. Because of the systematic struggle against our people carried out by the government, we must immediately strive to achieve political freedom. That is the first step toward the achievement of a socialist ideal.

7. We are deeply persuaded that given the current alignment of political and police forces of repression in Russia, political freedom in the near future can only be reached through the tactic of political terror. Political terror would have a great effect on a centralized state such as Russia.

8. We strive to create a fighting social revolutionary organization. It must have wide popular support, and conduct propaganda of socialism and political terror.

9. We recognize that the urban proletariat, as an economic category, is the highest repository of socialism. As a result, we apply all efforts for the widest enactment of propaganda and agitation among the factory workers with the goal of immediately creating a workers' party.

10. We further assert that the urban proletariat goes hand in hand with the democratic intelligentsia, which must also struggle for liberation.

11. We recognize that aggressive political terror is the main instrument in the struggle with the autocracy.

This program clearly indicated that the Central Students' Circle was an amalgam of Social Democracy and Populism. First they described themselves as Social Revolutionaries instead of Social Democrats as Marxists would. They harked back to the liberal ideas of liberty, equality, and fraternity that were embodied in the French Revolution. While they did not specifically state that Russia was undergoing a process of capitalism, their "socialist ideals" would only come about as a result of "an agonizing process of economic development," which could only be capitalism. Everyone conceded that capitalist development would be agonizing for Russia. Populists held that the people who would make the revolution for Russia would be the peasantry aided by the intelligentsia. Marxists held that Russia's liberation would come about as a result of an alignment of the urban proletariat and the intelligentsia. As sections three, five, nine, and ten of the program clearly indicated, the Central Students' Circle subscribed to the latter interpretation. Just as the Marxists held to a two-step theory of revolution, the group also subscribed to that view that political liberty must be achieved through the destruction of the autocracy. As section six noted, "that is the first step toward the achievement of a socialist ideal." Furthermore, Social Democrats pointed out how section nine declared the Central Students' Circle would focus its activities among the factory proletariat to get them to form a workers' party. Nevertheless, as section eleven clearly stated, the Central Students' Circle placed the highest hopes in political terror as its most effective method to combat the autocracy. No orthodox Marxist ever subscribed to the use of terror, "as the main instrument in the struggle with the autocracy." Therefore, this organization was not a Social Democratic organization as several Soviet authors contend.

BIBLIOGRAPHY

Books, Brochures, and Manuscripts

Abramov, Ia.U. Nashi voskresnye shkoli. St. Petersburg, 1900.

Ainzaft, S. Stachechnoe dvizhenie devianostykh godov i sotsial-demokratiia. Moscow, 1926.

Ainzaft, S. Istoriia rabochego i professional'nogo dvizheniia derevo-obledochnikov do revoliutsii 1917 goda. Iu. Milonov, red. Moscow, 1918.

Akimov-Makhnovets, V. The Dilemmas of Russian Marxism, 1895-1903. Translated, edited, and introduced by Jonathan Frankel. Cambridge, 1969.

Aksel'rod, P. Istoriia revoliutsionnogo dvizheniia v Rossii. Moscow, 1906.

Aksel'rod, P. Rabochii klass i revoliutsionnoe dvizhenie v Rossii. St. Petersburg, 1907.

Aksel'rod, P. Rabochie i intelligentsiia v nashikh organizatsiiakh. Geneva, 1904.

Alekseev, P.A. Dve rechi. Geneva, 1901.

Amfiteatrov, A. Zhenshchina v obshchestvennykh dvizheniiakh Rossii. Geneva, 1905.

Antipov, A. Obzor pravitel'stvennikh meropriiatiiu po razvitiu v Rossii Metallicheskoi Promishlennosti. St. Petersburg, 1879.

Babushkin, I.V. Vospominaniia Ivana Vasil'evicha Babushkina. 1-oe izd. Moscow, 1925.

Baevskii, D.A. Istoriia rabochei pechati v Rossii. Moscow, 1923.

Bakh, A. Tsar Golod. St. Petersburg, 1895.

Balabanov, M.S. Ocherki po istorii rabochego klassa v Rossii. Tt. 1-2. Kiev, 1923-24.

Barzar, V. Staticheskie svedeniia o stachkakh rabochikh na fabrikakh i zavodakh za desiatiletie, 1893-1904. St. Petersburg, 1905.

Bater, J. St. Petersburg: Industrialization and Change. Montreal, 1976.

Baturin, N. Ocherki istorii sotsial-demokratii v Rossii. Moscow, 1906.

Baturin, N. Ocherki iz istorii rabochego dvizheniia 70-kh i 80-kh godov. 2-oe izd. Moscow, 1925.

Baturin, N. Sochineniia. Moscow-Leningrad, 1930.

Belin, A.I. Professional'noe dvizhenie torgovykh sluzhashchikh v Rossii. Moscow, 1906.

Belyi, A. St. Petersburg. St. Petersburg, 1913.

Bernshtein-Kogan, S. Chislennost', sostav, i polozhenia Peterburgskikh rabochikh. St. Petersburg, 1910.

Bespalov, M. Dvizhenie rabochei molodezhi v Rossii v materialakh i dokumentakh. Moscow-Leningrad, 1926.

Bervi-Flerovskii, V.V. "Polozhenie rabochego klassa v Rossii," in Izbrannye ekonomicheskie proizvedeniia. Tom 1. Moscow, 1958.

Bill, V.T. The Forgotten Class: The Russian Bourgeoisie from the Earliest Beginnings to 1900. New York, 1959.

Billington, J. Mikhailovskii and Russian Populism. Oxford, 1958.

Bisk', I. Ekonomicheskaia i politicheskaia bor'ba rabochego klassa v Rossii. A. Syrat', red. Rostov-on-Don, 1906.

Blagoev, D. Moi vospominaniia. Moscow-Leningrad, 1928.

Bochkarev, V.N. Ocherk istorii revoliutsionnogo dvizheniia v Rossii. Moscow, 1918.

Bonch-Bruevich, V.D. Na zare revoliutsionnoi proletarskoi bor'by. Moscow, 1932.

Botkina, A.P. Pavel Mikhailovich Tret'iakov v zhizni i iskusstve. Moscow, 1960.

Brentano, L. Professional'nye rabochie soiuzy. St. Petersburg, 1904.

Broido, M.I. Ot redakatsii rabochei biblioteki. St. Petersburg, 1900.

Burtsev, V. Za sto let, 1800-96. London, 1897.

Chetyre rechi rabochikh proiznesennye v Peterburge. Geneva, 1892.

Deiateli revoliutsionnogo dvizheniia v Rossii. Moscow, 1931-33.

Deich, L.B. G.V. Plekhanov, materialy dlia biografii. Moscow, 1922.

Dembo, V. Pervaia massovaia organizatsiia rabochikh v Rossii; Iuzhno-rossiiskii soiuz rabochikh 1874-75. Moscow, 1925.

Dementev, Dr. E.M. Fabrika, chto ona daet naseleniiu i chto ona u nego beret. 2-e izd. Moscow, 1897.

Department of Police. Obzor vazhneishikh poznanii proizvodivshikhsia v zhandarmshikh upravleniiakh Imperii po gosudarvstvennym prestupleniiam. St. Petersburg, 1892-1901.

Dikshtein, S. Kto chem zhivet. Geneva, 1901.

Dmitr'ev, K. Iz praktiki professional'nogo dvizheniia v Rossii: organizatsiia soiuza. Odessa, 1907.

Dmitr'ev, K. Professional'noe dvizhenie i soiuzy v Rossii. St. Petersburg, 1909.

Dobson, G. St. Petersburg. London, 1910.

Dombrovskii, F. Rabochie i intelligentsiia. Geneva, 1904.

El'nitskii, A. Istoriia rabochego dvizheniia v Rossii. 3-e izd. Khar'kov, 1925.

Erisman, Dr. F.F. Veshchevoe dovol'stve rabochikh na fabrike Moskovskoi gubernii. Moscow, 1893.

Evgrafovich, N.F. Odin iz pionerov revoliutsionnogo marksizma v Rossii. Moscow-Leningrad, 1923.

Fisher, G.M. V Rossii i v Anglii. Moscow, 1922.

Georgievskii, A. Kratkii istoricheskii ocherk pravitel'stvennykh mer i prednachertanii protiv studencheskikh besporiadkov. St. Petersburg, 1890.

Gerasimov, V. Zhizn' russkogo rabochego polveka tomu nazad. Moscow, 1923.

Gerkner, S. Rabochie soiuzy. St. Petersburg, 1906.

Gershenzon, E. Proletarskie kassy vzaimopomoshchi. Leningrad, 1925.

Getzler, I. Martov: A Political Biography of a Russian Social-Democrat. Cambridge, 1967.

Ginzburg, B.A. and D. Kol'tsov. "Rabochee dvizhenie v 1890-1904 gg.," in Obshchestvennoe dvizhenie v Rossii nachale xx veka. T. 1. St. Petersburg, 1909.

Grinevich, V.P. Professional'noe dvizhenie rabochikh v Rossii. St. Petersburg, 1908.

Gurevich, S. Radikal'naia burzhuaziia i professional'nye soiuzy. St. Petersburg, 1907.

Gvozdev, S. Zapiski fabrichnogo inspektora. Moscow, 1911.

Haimson, L. The Russian Marxists and the Origins of Bolshevism. Boston, 1966.

Istoriia kommunisticheskoi partii Sovetskogo Soiuza. T. 1 (1883-1903). Moscow, 1964.

Itenberg, B. Iuzhnorossiiskii soiuz rabochikh; pervaia proletarskaia partii. Moscow, 1954.

Ivanov, S. Rabochie soiuzy i dr. formy rabochogo dvizheniia. St. Petersburg, 1906.

Ivanov-Razumnik, V. Istoriia russkoi obshchestvennoi mysli. Vol. II. St. Petersburg, 1903.

Iz rabochego dvizheniia na Nevskoi zastave v 70-kh i 80-kh godakh. Geneva, 1900.

Joll, J. The Second International, 1889-1914. London, 1975.

Kamenev, L. Sotsial-Demokraticheskie izdaniia, ukazatel' literatury na russkom iazyke, 1883-1905. Paris, 1913.

Kanatchikov, S. Iz istorii moego byt'ia. Moscow-Leningrad, 1929.

Kanel', V. Rabochii dogovor k voprosu o polozhenii rabochego klassa v Rossii. S. Skirmynta, red. Moscow, 1907.

Karelina, V.M. Leonid Borisovich Krasin. Moscow-Leningrad, 1928.

Karzhanskii, P.S. Moskovskii tkach Petr Alekseev. Moscow, 1954.

Katsenelson, S.G. K voprosu o formirovanii promyshlennogo proletariata v 1870-99 gg. Leningrad, 1947.

Kautskii, K. Professional'nye soiuzy i politika. St. Petersburg, 1906.

Kazakevich, R.A. Sotsial-demokraticheskie organizatsii Peterburga kontsa 80-kh nachala 90-kh godov. Leningrad, 1960.

Kedrov, P. Rabochie soiuzy. Moscow, 1906.

Keizer, I.I. Brattsy-tovarishchi. St. Petersburg, 1893.

Khomov, P.A. Ekonomicheskoe razvitie Rossii v xix-xx vekakh. Moscow, 1950.

Kleinbort, L.N. Ocherki rabochei zhurnalistiki. Petrograd, 1924.

Kleinbort, L.N. Ocherki rabochei intelligentsii. Petrograd, 1923.

Kleinbort, L.N. Professional'nye soiuzy v Rossii. Moscow, 1906.

K-n, A. Kak rabochie soiuzy ustraivaiut. Moscow, 1905.

Kniga pamiatnaia rabochego; sb. st. Petrograd, 1918.

Kniga russkogo rabochego. D. Reichi, red. St. Petersburg, 1905.

Kochakov, B.M. Ocherki istorii Leningrada. T. 2. Leningrad, 1957.

Kolpenskii, V.V. Pervoe maia v Rossii. Petrograd, 1921.

Kol'tsov, D. "Rabochee dvizhenie v 1890-1904 gg.," in Obshchestvennoe dvizhenie v Rossii v nachale xx veka. Vol. I. St. Petersburg, 1909.

Kon', F. Iz istoriia moego byt'ia. Khar'kov, 1924.

Kon', F. Istoriia revoliutsionnogo dvizheniia v Rossii. T. 1. Khar'kov, 1929.

Korolchuk, E.A. and E. Sokolova. Khronika revoliutsionnogo rabochego dvizheniia v Peterburge. T. 1. Leningrad, 1940.

Korolchuk, E.A. "Severnyi soiuz russkikh rabochikh" i revoliutsionnoe rabochee dvizhenie 70-kh godov xix v. v Peterburge. Leningrad, 1946.

Kovalenskii, M.N. Khrestomatiia po istorii klassovoi bor'by v Rossii. 2-oe izd. Moscow, 1923.

Kovalik, S.F. Revoliutsionnoe dvizhenie semidesiatykh godov i protsess 1903-kh. Moscow, 1928.

Kozmin, B.P., red. Rabochee dvizhenie v Rossii. Khar'kov, 1926.

Kozmin, B.P. Rabochee dvizhenie v Rossii do revoliutsii 1905 g. Moscow, 1925.

Kremer, A. Ob agitatsii. Geneva, 1897.

Kropotkin, Prince P.A. Zapiski revoliutsionnera. Leningrad, 1933.

Kuklin, G.A. Severnyi soiuz russkikh rabochikh i Stepan Khalturin. Geneva, 1904.

Kutsentov, D.G. "Naselenie Peterburga. Polozhenie peterburgskikh rabochikh," in Ocherki istorii Leningrada. Kochakov, et al., red. T. 2., pp. 170-230.

Langmann, P. Dramy i rasskazy iz zhizni rabochikh. St. Petersburg, 1906.

Laver'chev, V.Ia. Tsarizm i rabochii vopros v Rossii, 1861-1917 gg. Moscow, 1972.

Lavrinovich, Iu. Rabochie soiuzy. O. Popovoi, red. St. Petersburg, 1905.

Leberg, M. "Marksizm na Putilovtse v 90-kh godakh." Istoriia zavodov. Moscow, 1933.

Lenin, V.I. Collected Works. Vol. 4. Moscow, 1954.

Lepeshinskii, P.N. Na povorote; ot kontsa 80-kh godov k 1905 g. Petrograd, 1922.

Levitskii, V.O. Viktor Obnorskii, osnovatel' 'Severnogo soiuza russkikh rabochikh'. Moscow, 1929.

Liadov, M.N. Kak zarodilas' Moskovskie rabochie. St. Petersburg, 1906.

Liadov, M.N. (Mandel'shtam, M.N.) Istoriia Rossiiskoi sotsialdemokraticheskoi rabochei partii, 1883-1897 gg. St. Petersburg, 1906.

Liadov, M.N. and S.M. Pozner. Leonid Borisovich Krasin. Moscow-Leningrad, 1928.

Lincoln, W.B. In War's Dark Shadow: The Russians Before the Great War. New York, 1983.

Lindov, G. Kratkii ocherk istorii Ross. S-Dem. Rabochei Partii. Petrograd, 1917.

Lindov, G. Rabochie kooperativy i professional'nye soiuzy. Petrograd, 1917.

Losev, I. Professional'nye soiuzy. Moscow, 1907.

Lozinskii, I.E. Itogi i perspektiv rabochego dvizheniia. St. Petersburg, 1909.

Lui, P. Rabochikh i gosudarstvo. St. Petersburg, 1907.

Lunacharskii, A.V. Kak peterburgskie rabochiie k tsariu khodili. Geneva, 1905.

Magaim, E. Professional'nye rabochie soiuzy. Fr. N. Vodovozova, red. St. Petersburg, 1895.

Makhnovets, V.P. Materialy dlia kharakteristiki razvitiia Rossiiskoi sotsial-demokraticheskoi rabochei partii. Geneva, 1904.

Makhnovets, V.P. Ocherk razvitiia sotsial-demokratii v Rossii. 2-oe izd. St. Petersburg, 1906.

Maksakov, V.V. and Nevskii, V.I. Iuzhno-russkie rabochie soiuzy. Moscow, 1924.

Mandel'stam, R.S. Revoliutsionnoe dvizhenie v Rossii xviii-xix veka. Moscow, 1924.

Martov, Iu. Istoriia Rossiiskoi sotsial-demokratii. Petrograd, 1918.

Martov, Iu. Povorotnyi punkt v istorii evreiskogo rabochego dvizheniie. Geneva, 1900.

Martov, Iu. Rabochee delo v Rossii. Geneva, 1899.

Martov, Iu. "Razvitie krupnoi promyshlennosti i rabochee dvizhenie do 1892 g.," Istoriia Rossii v xix veke. St. Petersburg, n.d., T. 6., pp. 114-162.

Martov, Iu. Krasnoe znamia v Rossii; Ocherki istorii russkogo rabochego dvizheniia. Geneva, 1900.

Martov, Iu. Zapiski sotsial-demokrata. Berlin, 1922.

Martynov, A.S.   Rabochie i revoliutsiia.   Geneva, 1902.

Matasova, F.G.   Stachki 1881-1895 gg.   Moscow, 1930.

Materialy ob ekonomicheskom polozhenii i professional'- nykh organizatsiiakh v S. Peterburge rabochikh po metallu.   St. Petersburg, 1909.

McKay, J.   Pioneers for Profit: Foreign Entrepreneurship and Russian Industrialization of Russia. New York and London, 1963.

Mikhnevich, V.   Peterburg: ves' na ladoni.   St. Petersburg, 1874.

Mironov, I.   Iz vospominaniia rabochego.   Moscow, 1906.

Mitel'man, M. et al.   Istoriia Putilovskogo zavoda. Moscow-Leningrad, 1939; 2-oe izd., 1941.

Mitel'man, M.   Pervaia Peterburgskaia maevka, 1891. Leningrad, 1941.

Mitzkevich, S.I.   Na zare rabochego dvizheniia.   Moscow, 1929.

Mitzkevich, S.I.   Revoliutsionnaia Moskva, 1888-1905 gg.   Moscow, 1940.

Morshanskaia, M.   Tkach Fedor Afanas'ev.   Moscow, 1924.

Na l'om maia.   Geneva, 1904.

Nedrov, A.   Rabochii vopros.   St. Petersburg, 1906.

Nemchinov, E.M.   Vospominaniia starogo rabochego. Moscow-Petrograd, 1924.

Nevskii, V.I.   Deiateli revoliutsionnogo dvizheniia v Rossii.   T. 1, chasti 1-2: Sotsial-demokraty, 1880-1904.   Moscow, 1931-33.

Nevskii, V.I.   Ocherki po istorii Rossiiskoi Kommunisticheskoi Partii.   2-oe izd.   Moscow, 1925.

Nevskii, V.I. Pervaia klassovaia sotsialisticheskaia organizatsiia rabochikh v Rossii. Moscow, 1929.

Nikitin, I. Pervye rabochie soiuzy i sotsial-demokraticheskie partii v Rossii. Moscow, 1952.

Nikitin, A. Zadachi Peterburga. St. Petersburg, 1904.

Norinskii, K.M. "Moi vospominaniia," Ot gruppy Blagoeva k 'Soiuzu Bor'by', 1886-1894 gg. Rostov-on-Don, 1921, pp. 7-38.

Norinskii, K.M. "Vospominaniia," in Rabochee dvizheniie v Rossii v xix veke. Moscow, 1952.

Ol'minskii, M.S. "Materialy po delu M. I Brusneva," Ot gruppy Blagoeva k "Soiuzu Bor'by" 1886-1894. Rostov-on-Don, 1921, pp. 79-96.

Ol'minskii, M.S. "O vospominaniiakh N. D. Bogdanova," Ot gruppy Blagoeva k "Soiuzu Bor'by" 1886-1894. Rostov-on-Don, 1921, pp. 39-46.

Ol'minskii, M.S. "Rechi rabochikh na pervo-maiskom sobranii 1891 g." Ot gruppy Blagoeva k "Soiuzu Bor'by" 1886-1894. Rostov-on-Don, 1921, pp. 121-127.

Ol'minskii, M.S. Staryi tovarishch Aleksei Pavlovich Skliarenko (1870-1916). Moscow, 1922.

Orekhov, A.M. Pervye marksisty v Rossii, peterburgskii "Rabochii soiuz," 1887-1893 gg. Moscow, 1979.

Orlov, P.A. and Bydagov, S.G. Ukazatel' fabrik i zavodov Evropeiskoi Rossii. St. Petersburg, 1894.

Orlov, S.I. Zapretnie listki; iz vospominanii rabochego. London, 1900.

Orlovskii, P.K. and Vorovskii, V.V. K istorii Marksizma v Rossii. Moscow, 1919.

Osipovich, N.M. Iuzhno-rossiiskii soiuz rabochikh. Nikolaev, 1924.

Ovsiannikova, S.G. Gruppa Blagoeva. Moscow, 1959.

Ozerov, I.Kh. Iz zhizni truda. Moscow, 1904.

Pankratov, V.S. Vospominaniia, 1880-84. Moscow, 1923.

Pankratova, A.M. "Osobennosti formirovaniia bor'by proletariata Rossii v 60-80kh godakh xix v," in Rabochee dvizhenie v Rossii v xix v. T. 2. chast' 1. Moscow, 1950.

Pankratova, A.M. "Rabochii klass i rabochee dvizhenie v Rossii v 1885-1894," in Rabochee dvizhenie v Rossii v xix v. T. 3. chast' 1, Moscow, 1952.

Pazhitnov, K.A. Iz istorii rabochikh artelei na zapade i v Rossii. Leningrad, 1924.

Pazhitnov, K.A. Polozhenie rabochego klassa v Rossii. St. Petersburg, 1906.

Pazhitnov, E. Rabochee dvizhenie v Rossii. St. Petersburg, 1906.

Pelloutier, F. Istoriia birzh truda. St. Petersburg, 1906.

Pervoe maia v Tsarskoi Rossii 1890-1916 gg. Moscow, 1939.

Pervoe maia 1892 goda. Chetyre rechi evr. rabochikh. Geneva, 1893.

Petrov, M.P. "Moi vospominaniia," Na zare rabochego dvizheniia v Moskve. Moscow, 1932.

Pipes, R. Social Democracy and the St. Petersburg Labor Movement, 1885-1897. Cambridge, 1963.

Plekhanov, G.V. Russkii rabochii v revoliutsionnom dvizhenii. Geneva, 1902.

Pogozhev, A.V. Uchet chislennosti i sostava rabochikh v Rossii. St. Petersburg, 1906.

Pokrovskaia, Dr. M.I. Po podvalam, cherdakam, i uglovym kvartiram Peterburga. St. Petersburg, 1903.

Pokrovskii, V. Statisticheskii ocherk St. Peterburga. St. Petersburg, 1895.

Polevoi, Iu.Z. "Na puti soedineniia s sotsializmom," in Istoriia rabochego klassa Rossii. ed. L.M. Ivanov. Moscow, 1972.

Polevoi, Iu.Z. Zarozhdenie Marksizma v Rossii, 1883-1894 gg. Moscow, 1959.

Portugalov, V. Soiuzy rabochikh v Rossii. Vozniknovenie, organitsatsii i zadachi rabochikh soiuzov v Rossii. Moscow, 1906.

Posse, V.A. Biblioteka rabochego. St. Petersburg, 1906.

Posse, V.A. Rabochie stachki, ocherki v Rossii. St. Petersburg, 1906.

Posse, V.A. Vseobshchie stachki. Geneva, 1903.

Postresov, A.N. Adres peterburgskikh rabochikh frantsuzskim rabochim. St. Petersburg, 1896.

Preobrazhenskii, V.D. Rabochee dvizhenie v Rossii kontsa xix i nachala xx veka. Moscow-Leningrad, 1929.

Press, A. Strakhovanie rabochikh v Rossii. St. Petersburg, 1900.

Pribyleva-Korba, A.P. and Figner, V.N. Narodovolets Aleksandr Dmitrievich Mikhailov. Leningrad, 1925.

Prokof'ev, S.I. Iz perezhitogo. Moscow, 1922.

Prokopovich, S. Biudzhety peterburgskikh rabochikh. St. Petersburg, 1902.

Prokopovich, S. K rabochemu voprosu v Rossii. St. Petersburg, 1905.

Prokopovich, S. Soiuzy rabochikh i ikh zadachi. M. Kuskovoi, red. St. Petersburg, 1905.

Protsess Obukhovskikh rabochikh. Geneva, 1901.

Pukhlov, N. Nachalo rabochego dvizhenie v Polshe, 70-80kh gg. St. Petersburg, 1906.

Rabochii ezhegodnik. St. Petersburg, 1906.

Rabochii sbornik, 1-April 1894 goda. St. Petersburg, 1894.

Raevskii, A. Istoriia pervogo maia v Rossii. Moscow-Leningrad, 1925.

Rappeport, M.L. Tehknologicheskii Institut imeni Leningradskogo Soveta. T. 1. Leningrad, 1928.

Rashin, A.G. Formirovanie promyshlennogo proletariata v Rossii. Moscow, 1940.

Rashin, A.G. Formirovanie rabochego klassa Rossii. Moscow, 1958.

Ravich-Cherkasskii, M. Iuzhno-Russkie rabochie soiuzy. Khar'kov, 1925.

Rikachev, A. Professional'nye soiuzy i ikh znachenie dlia rabochikh. Moscow, 1907.

Rodzhers, T. Istoriia truda. St. Petersþurg, 1899.

Rozanov, M.D. V.A. Shel'gunov. Leningrad, 1948.

Samoilov, D. O rabochikh professional'nikh soiuzakh. Moscow, 1906.

Samoilov, D. Vospominaniia. Moscow, 1922.

Sergievskii, N.L. Partiia russkikh sotsial-demokratov. Moscow, 1929.

Sergievskii, N.L. "Rabochii"--gazeta partii russkikh sotsial-demokratov (Blagoevtsev). Leningrad, 1928.

Shapovalov, A.S. V bor'be za sotsializm; vospominaniia starogo bol'shevika. Moscow, 1934.

Shel'gunov, V.A. "Vospominaniia," Ot gruppy Blagoeva k 'Soiuzu Bor'by', 1886-1894 gg. Rostov-on-Don, 1921, pp. 52-59.

Sheliavin, V.I. Rabochii klass i ego partiia. Petrograd, 1923.

Shenberg, G. Polozhenie truda v promyshlennosti. Moscow, 1896.

Sheprov, S. Na puti i sozdanie partii. Moscow, 1959.

Shesternin, S.P. Perezhitoe. Iz istorii rabochego i revoliutsionnogo dvizhenie, 1880-1900 gg. Moscow, 1940.

Shilov, A.A. and Kozmin, B.P. Deiateli revoliutsionnogo dvizheniia v Rossii, bio-bibliograficheskii slovar'. T. 4. Moscow, 1927-33.

Shippel', M. Professional'nye soiuzy. Moscow, 1905.

Shippel', M. Rabochie soiuzy. Nizhni-Novgorod, 1894.

Shishko, L. S.M. Kravchinskii i kruzhok chaikovtsev. St. Petersburg, 1906.

Shuvalov, I. Rabochee i professional'noe dvizhenie na bumazhnykh fabrikakh, 1750-1914. Moscow, 1926.

Sibiriak, N. Rabochii proletariat v Rossii. Moscow, 1906.

Somov, S. Professional'nye soiuzy i sotsial-demokraticheskaia partiia. E. Kuskovoi, red. St. Petersburg, 1907.

Spiridovich, A.I. Histoire du terrorisme russe, 1886-1917. Paris, 1930.

Spiridovich, A.I. Istoriia bol'shevizma v Rossii. Paris, 1922.

Spiridovich, A.I. Revoliutsionnoe dvizhenie v Rossii v period imperii; partiia sotsial-revoliutsionerov i ee predshestvenniki, 1886-1916. Petrograd, 1918.

Stachka p'esa v z-khd. Iz russkoi fabrichnoi zhizni. Geneva, 1899.

S. Peterburg po perepisi 10 dekabria 1869 goda. St. Petersburg, 1872. Part I.

S. Peterburg po perepisi 15 dekabria 1881 goda. T. 2.
St. Petersburg, 1883.

S. Peterburg po perepisi 15 dekabria 1890 goda. Chast'
2. St. Petersburg, 1892.

S. Peterburg po perepisi 15 dekabria 1900 goda. Part I.
St. Petersburg, 1903.

Steklov, Iu. Russkii tkach P.A. Alekseyev, 1849-91.
Moscow, 1911.

Stepanov, N. Sotsial-demokratiia v Rossii v kontse xix
i nachale xx vekov. Khar'kov, 1931.

Stepniak-Kravchinskii, S.M. Stepan Khalturin. St.
Petersburg, 1908.

Stolpianskii, P.N. Zhizn' i byt peterburgskoi fabriki
za 1704-1914 gg. Leningrad, 1925.

Strel'skii, P. Samoorganizatsiia rabochego klassa.
St. Petersburg, 1906.

Suslova, F.M. Istoriia rabochego klassa. Leningrad,
1963.

Sviatlovskii, V.V. Professional'noe dvizhenie v
Rossii. St. Petersburg, 1907.

Sviatlovskii, V.V. Ukazatel'literatury po professional'nomu rabochemu dvizheniiu. St. Petersburg, 1907.

Sviatlovskii, V.V. Zhilishchnyi vopros v Rossii.
chast' 4. St. Petersburg, 1902.

Takhtarev, K.M. (Peterburzhets). Ocherk peterburgskogo rabochego dvizheniia 90-kh godov. London,
1902; 2-oe izd. Rabochee dvizhenie v Peterburge,
1893-1903. Leningrad, 1924.

Tar, K.M. Ocherk peterburgskogo rabochego dvizhenie
90-kh godov. St. Petersburg, 1906.

Teplov, P.F. Studencheskoe dvizheniie v Rossii.
Geneva, 1899.

Thun, A. Istoriia revoliutsionnykh dvizhenii v Rossii. Geneva, 1903.

Tikhomirov, L. Rabochii i gosudarstvo. St. Petersburg, 1908.

Timofeev, P. Chem zhivet zavodskii rabochii. St. Petersburg, 1906.

Totomiants, V. Formy rabochego dvizheniia. St. Petersburg, 1906.

Totomiants, V. Professional'noe dvizhenie i sotsial-demokratiia. Moscow, 1907.

Tugan-Baranovskii, M.I. Russkaia fabrika. Moscow-Leningrad, 1934.

Uchebyne zavedeniia Ministerstva narodnogo prosveshcheniia. St. Petersburg, 1895.

Valk, S.N., red. Istoriia rabochikh Leningrada. T. 1. Leningrad, 1972.

Valk, S.N. "Rabochee dvizhenie Peterburga v 80-kh i nachale 90-kh godov i pervye sotsial-demokraticheskie gruppy," in Ocherki istorii Leningrada. T. 2. Moscow-Leningrad, 1957.

Vasil'enko, K.S. Istoriia Moskvy. T. 4. Moscow, 1954.

Venturi, F. Roots of Revolution, a History of the Populist and Socialist Movements in Nineteenth Century Russia. Introduction by Isaiah Berlin. Translated by Francis Haskell. New York, 1966.

Vlasov, I.I. Tkach Fedor Afanas'ev, 1859-1905, materialy dlia biografii, "osnova." Ivanovo-Voznesensk, 1925.

Volkhovskii, F.V. Russkii tkach Petr Alekseevich Alekseev. Geneva, 1900.

Von Laue, T. Sergei Witte and the Industrialization of Russia. New York and London, 1963.

Vorovskii, V.V. K istorii Marksizma v Rossii. Sochineniia. T. 1. Moscow, 1933.

Voznesenskii, S. Stachechnaia bor'ba rabochikh v 1870-1917 gg. Petrograd, 1923.

Vseobshchaia Adresnaia kniga S. Peterburga. St. Petersburg, 1867-68.

Wallace, Sir D.M. Russia: On the Eve of War and Revolution. Cyril Black, ed. New York, 1961.

Zaleski, E. Mouvements ouvriers et socialistes de la Russe; chronologie et bibliographie. Vol. 1. Paris, 1956.

Zamiatin, N.N. Ocherk istorii sotsial-demokratii v Rossii. Moscow, 1906.

Zelnick, R.E. Labor and Society in Tsarist Russia, the Factory Workers of St. Petersburg, 1855-70. Stanford, 1971.

Journal Articles

Akimov-Makhnovets, V. "Pervoe maia v Rossii," Byloe, 1906, nos. 10, 11, and 12, pp. 163-192, pp. 78-99, pp. 131-159.

Aleksandrov, D.A. "Vospominaniia," Katorga i ssylka, 1926, no. 4, pp. 129-131.

Aleksandrov, M.S. (Ol'minskii). "Gruppa narodovol'-tsev, 1891-94," Byloe, 1906, no. 11, pp. 1-27.

Alekseev, P.A. "Pis'mo," Krasnyi arkhiv, T. 1, 1931, pp. 170-173.

Alliluev, S.Ia. "Moi vospominaniia o L. B. Krasine," Krasnaia letopis', 1927, no. 1, pp. 5-9.

Anatol'ev, P. "Iz istorii marksistskoi i rabochei pechati Rossii," Istoriia proletariata SSSR, 1931, no. 6, pp. 99-131.

Argunov, A. "Iz proshlogo partii sotsial-revoliutsionerov," Byloe, Oct. 1907, no. 10, pp. 94-112.

Bachin, I.A. "K biografii odnogo iz osnovatelei 'severno-Russkogo rabochego soiuza'," Katorga i ssylka, 1924, no. 6, pp. 48-70.

Bartenev, V. "Iz vospominanii peterburzhtsa vo vtoroi polovine 80-kh godov," Minuvshie gody, 1908, no. 10, pp. 169-197.

Baturin, N. "Eshche o tsvetiako russkogo yakobinstva," Proletarskaia revoliutsiia, 1925, no. 8, pp. 97-109.

Bogdanov, N.D. "Na zare sotsial-demokratii; vospominaniia o peterburgskoi organizatsii, 1885-1892," Osvobozhdenie truda, May 1918, no. 4, pp. 7-10.

Breitfus, A. "Tochisskii i ego kruzhok," Krasnaia letopis', 1923, no. 7, pp. 324-339.

Brusnev, M.I. "Fedor Afanas'evich Afanas'ev," Novaia zhizn', 1905, no. 13, p. 7.

Brusnev, M.I. "Vozniknovenie pervykh sotsial-demokraticheskikh organizatsii," Proletarskaia revoliutsiia, 1923, no. 2, pp. 17-32.

Buiko, A.M. "Put'rabochego, zapiski starogo bol'shevika," Staryi bol'shevik, 1934, no. 6, pp. 7-23.

Burtsev, V. "Severnyi soiuz russkikh rabochikh," Byloe, 1906, no. 1, pp. 174-193.

"Chto chytaet prostoi liud v St. Peterburg," Mir bozhii, Sept. 1898, pp. 16-17.

Deich, L. "Pervye shagi gruppy 'Osvobozhdenie truda'," Gruppa Osvobozhdenie truda, 1924, no. 1, pp. 18-26.

"Delo o prestupnoi propagande v sredi peterburg rabochikh (1881 g)," Byloe, 1907, no. 1, pp. 288-294.

Dushenkin, V.V. "K voprosu ob obstoiatel'stvakh i vremeni gibeli P.V. Tochisskogo," Voprosy istorii KPSS, 1965, no. 5, pp. 106-109.

Erisman, Dr. F.F. "Podval'nye zhilishcha v Peterburge," Arkhiv sudebnoi meditsiny i obshchestvennoi gigieny, 1871, VII, pp. 50-68.

Geshin, E.V. "Shel'gunovskaia demonstratiia," Minuvshie gody, 1908, no. 11, pp. 25-46.

Golubev, V. "Stranichka iz istorii rabochego dvizheniia," Byloe, 1906, no. 12, pp. 105-121.

Gorev, B.I. (Goldman). "Marksizm i rabochee dvizhenie v Peterburge chetvert' veka nazad (vospominaniia)," Novoe slovo, Sept.-Oct. 1921, no. 3, pp. 99-127.

Govorukhin, O.M. "Vospominaniia," Golos minuvshago, no. 16, 1926, pp. 198-220.

Grigoriev, P. "Statisticheskoe issledovanie ekonomicheskogo polozhenie rabochikh na S. Peterburgskikh zavodakh," Vol'noe slovo, 1882, no. 40, pp. 4-6.

Gurvich, V. "Pervye evreiskie rabochie kruzhki," Byloe, 1907, no. 6, pp. 65-77.

Iatsunskii, V.K. "'Rol' Peterburga v promyshlennom razvitii dorevoliutsionnoi Rossii," Voprosy istorii, 1954, no. 9, pp. 95-103.

"Iz byta rabochikh," Mir bozhii, May 1896, pp. 255-258.

"Iz obzora vazhneishikh doznanii po delam o gosudarstvennykh prestupleniiakh za 1894 g," Byloe, 1907, no. 5, pp. 228-252.

"Iz materialov po istorii S. D. dvizheniia v Rossii," Byloe, 1918, pp. 90-113.

Karelina, V. "Na zare rabochego dvizheniia v Peterburge," Krasnaia letopis', 1922, no. 4, pp. 12-20.

Kharitonov, V. "Iz vospominanii uchastnika Gruppy Blagoeva," Proletarskaia revoliutsiia, 1928, no. 8, pp. 152-163.

Kheisin, M.L. "O rabote v Vyborgskom raione," Otkliki, April 1907, pp. 18-27.

Kochergin, K.I. "Do goda na fabrike 'Rabochii'," Krasnaia letopis', 1931, no. 4, pp. 101-119.

Kolpenskii, V. "K istorii rabochego dvizheniia v Peterburge v 1896 body," Krasnaia letopis', 1922, no. 4, pp. 242-249.

Kolpenskii, V. "Rabochee dvizhenie 90-kh gg. i pravitel'stvennoi bor'by s nim," Krasnaia letopis', 1922, no. 2, pp. 197-207.

Korolchuk, E.A. "Iz istorii propagandy sredi rabochikh Peterburga v seredine 70-kh godov," Katorga i ssylka, 1928, no. 1, pp. 14-25.

Korolenko, V.L. "Istoriia moego sovremennika," Golos minuvshago, 1922, no. 1, pp. 69-101.

Krasin, L.B. "Stepan I. Radchenko," Staryi bol'shevik, 1933, no. 2, pp. 186-189.

Krasin, L.B. "Delo davno minuvshikh dnei, 1887-1892," Proletarskaia revoliutsiia, 1923, no. 3, pp. 93-118.

Lapsina, P.G. and Zhuikov, G.S. "Novoe o deiatelnosti grupp Blagoeva, Tochisskogo, i Brusneva," Vopros istorii RKP, 1971, no. 7, pp. 78-80.

Lebedeva, M. (Tochisskaia). "K biografii Tochisskogo," Istoriko-revoliutsionnyi sbornik, Vol. III, 1926, pp. 290-305.

Levin, Sh.M. "Kruzhok chaikovtsev i propaganda sredi Peterburgskikh rabochikh v nachale 1870-kh gg," Katorga i ssylka, 1929, no. 61, pp. 7-27.

Levitskii, V. (Tserderbaum). "Narodnaia Volia i rabochii klass," Katorga i ssylka, 1930, no. 1, pp. 48-66.

Levitskii, V. "Peterburgskii proletariat na vyborach," Nash mir, 1907, no. 1, pp. 45-68.

Lukachevich, A.O. "V narod," Byloe, no. 3, March 1907, pp. 8-20.

Makukhin, V. "M.S. Ol'minskii v S-Peterburgskom universitete v 1883-1885 gg," Krasnaia letopis', 1933, no. 3, pp. 203-208.

"Materialy dlia istorii russkogo rabochego dvizheniia za 1881-1895 gg," Krasnaia letopis', 1922, no. 5, p. 394; 1923, no. 7, pp. 212-227; 1925, no. 1, pp. 249-266; no. 2, pp. 247-253.

Mendelsohn, E. "Worker Opposition in the Russian Jewish Socialist Movement from the 1890's-1903," International Review of Social History, Vol. 10, 1965, pp. 268-282.

Mikhailovskii, N.K. "Literatura i zhizn'," Russkaia mysl', no. 6, 1892, pp. 32-45.

Moiseenko, P.L. "Vospominaniia, 1873-1893 gg," Krasnaia nov', 1924, no. 3, pp. 40-62.

Nevskii, V.I. "K istorii 'Partii russkikh sotsial-demokratov' v 1884-1886 gg," Byloe, 1918, no. 13, pp. 210-223.

Nevskii, V.I. "K voprosu o rabochem dvizhenii v 70-e gody," Istorik-Marksist, 1927, no. 4, pp. 125-178.

Nevskii, V.I. "Narodnaia Volia i rabochie," Istoriia proletariata SSSR, 1930, no. 1, pp. 39-89.

Nevskii, V.I. "Na pereput'e (Brusnevskaia organizatsii)," Istoriia proletariata SSR, 1934, no. 4, pp. 48-58.

Nikolaev, A.S. "Iskliuchenie L. B. Krasina iz S-Peterburgskogo Tekhnologicheskogo Instituta," Krasnaia letopis', 1927, no. 1, pp. 10-27.

Norinskii, K. "Moi vospominaniia," Staryi bol'shevik, 1933, no. 2, pp. 46-51.

Ol'minskii, M.S. "Iz vospominanii revoliutsionera," Rabochii mir, no. 4-5, pp. 63-75.

Ol'minskii, M.S. "'Gruppa narodovol'tsev', 1891-94 gg," Byloe, no. 11, 1906, pp. 1-27.

Pankratov, V.S. "Iz deiatel'nosti sredi rabochikh v 1880-84 gg," Byloe, March 1906, no. 3, pp. 230-251.

Perazich, V. "Eshche o Khar'kovskom rabochikh kruzhke kontsa 80-kh gg," Krasnaia letopis', 1922, no. 4, pp. 21-27.

Persii, M.M. "Avtobiografii rabochikh kak istochnik izucheniia ateizma v rabochem dvizhenii," Voprosy istorii religii i ateizma, 1960, Vol. 8, pp. 101-127.

"Pervoe maia v Tsarskoi Rossii, 1892-1903 gg," Introduced by M. Syromiatnikova, Krasnaia arkhiv, 1937, no. 3, pp. 164-192.

"Peterburgskii 'Soiuz bor'by za osvobozhdenie rabochego klassa'," Krasnyi arkhiv, 1934, no. 1, pp. 75-117.

Petrovskii, G.I. "Vospominaniia o rabote na Buianska zavode v 90-kh godakh," Letopis' revoliutsii, 1923, no. 2, pp. 29-34.

Pokrovskaia, Dr. M.I. "Peterburgskie rabochie i ikh ekonomicheskoe polozhenie," Vestnik evropy, 1899, no. 3, pp. 323-342.

Pokrovskaia, Dr. M.I. "Peterburgskie voskresnye
    sobraniia dlia rabotnitsy," Mir bozhii, March
    1899, pp. 1-14.

Pokrovskaia, Dr. M.I. "Zhilishcha Peterburgskikh
    rabochikh," Vestnik obshchestvennoi gigieny,
    1895, no. 2, pp. 241-259.

Popova, M.R. "Nikolai Pavlovich Shchedrin," Byloe,
    1906, no. 12, pp. 123-130.

Popova, M.R. "Iz moego revoliutsionnogo proshlogo,"
    Byloe, 1907, nos. 5 and 7, pp. 269-305, pp. 241-
    277.

Radchenko, I.I. "Stepan Ivanovich Radchenko," Staryi
    bol'shevik, 1933, no. 2, pp. 178-186.

Radzilovskaia, F. "Podnol'nieia biblioteki pervykh
    marksistkskikh grupp i kruzkov v Tsarskoi Rossii
    80-e nachalo 90kh godov," Krasnyi bibliotekar',
    1939, no. 8, pp. 56-64.

Roslovoi, A.S. "Pervye maevki i politicheskie
    vystupleniia peterburgskikh rabochikh," Voprosy
    istorii, 1956, no. 2, pp. 88-95.

Rubakin, G. "Iz zhizni rabochei intelligentsii," Mir
    bozhii, March 1896, pp. 20-21.

Rubel', A.H. "Zhilishcha bednogo naseleniia g. S-
    Peterburga," Vestnik obshchestvennoi gigieny,
    April 1899, pp. 424-443.

Semenov, K. "Pervye gody Peterburgskoi 'rabochei
    organizatsii'," Minuvshie gody, 1908, no. 12,
    pp. 265-284.

Sergievskii, N.L. "O kruzhke Tochisskogo," Krasnaia
    letopis', 1923, no. 7, pp. 340-344.

Sergievskii, N.L. "Plekhanov i gruppa Blagoeva,"
    Proletarskaia revoliutsiia, 1928, no. 8, pp. 133-
    151.

Sergievskii, N.L. "K voprosu o vozraste Leningradskoi
    organizatsii VKP," Krasnaia letopis', 1930, no. 2,
    pp. 5-25.

Shel'gunov, V.A. "Rabochie na puti k Marksizmu," Staryi bol'shevik, 1933, pp. 98-103.

Shel'gunov, V.A. "Moi vospominaniia o voskresnykh shkolakh," Shkola vzroslikh, 1939, no. 7, pp. 42-44.

Shishkin, V.F. "Propaganda russkimi sotsial-demokratami proletarskoi morali v kontse xix-nachale xx v," Ezhegodnik muzeia istoriia religii i ateizma, VII, 1964, pp. 25-35.

Sibiriak, N. "Rabochee znamia," Rabochee delo, April 1899, no. 1, pp. 142-145.

Skrobot, S.S. "Stachechnaia bor'ba peterburgskikh rabochikh v 1891-95 gg," Istoriia SSSR, 1958, no. 6, pp. 105-114.

Smidovich, I. "Rabochie massy v 90-kh godov," Proletarskaia revoliutsiia, 1925, no. 1, pp. 161-197.

Starynkevich, S. "Vladimirskaia i Nikol'skaia zhenskie voskresnye besplatnie shkoli v Peterburge," Russkaia shkola, 1890, no. 5, p. 167.

Stakovskii, P.S. "S. Peterburgskoe okhrannoe otdelenie v 1895-1901 gg," Byloe, no. 16, pp. 108-136.

Stepniak, S. "The Russian Famine and Revolution," Fortnightly Review, March 1892, pp. 358-368.

Sviatlovskii, V.V. "Na zare Rossiiskoi sotsial-demokratii," Byloe, no. 19, 1922, pp. 139-160.

Sviatlovskii, V.V. "K istorii pervogo maia, 1890-93 gg," Byloe, 1921, no. 16, pp. 167-173.

Valk, S.N. "Materialy k istorii pervogo maia v Rossii," Krasnaia letopis', 1922, no. 4, pp. 250-288.

Vasil'evskii, L. "Pol'skaia s. d. partiia 'Proletariat', 1882-1886," Byloe, 1906, no. 4, pp. 193-207.

Vedenev, I. "V Khar'kovskikh revoliutsionikh kruzhkakh, 1882-1889 gg," Letopis' revoliutsii, 1923, no. 5, pp. 98-108.

Vodovozov, N.V. "Pamiati," *Novoe slovo*, 1897, no. 9, pp. 56-62.

Zelnik, R.E. "Russian Rebels: An Introduction to the Memoirs of Semen Kanatchikov and Matvei Fisher," *The Russian Review*, Vol. 35, no. 3 (July 1976): pp. 249-289; no. 4 (October 1976): pp. 417-447.